APPALACHIAN HERITAGE
C·O·O·K·B·O·O·K

or

—The Steelesburg Sampler—

*A collection of country recipes
from the members and friends
of the*

STEELESBURG
EXTENSION HOMEMAKERS CLUB

Pocahontas Press, Inc.
Blacksburg, Virginia

Appalachian Heritage Cookbook, or The Steelesburg Sampler, by The Steelesburg
    Extension Homemakers Club
Published by Pocahontas Press, Inc., P.O. Drawer F, Blacksburg, VA 24063-1020

Cover design by Ted Guerin, Picturemaker, Vinton, Virginia
Editing by David Bruce Wallace and Mary C. Holliman
Text Design and Typography by Elisabeth Hauser, Boones Mill, Virginia
Printed and bound in the United States of America by Commonwealth Press, Inc.,
    Radford, Virginia

Preface

The Steelesburg Homemakers Club was organized in 1967. The purpose of the club is to enrich home and family life.

Our club is best known for two abilities: cooking and quilt making. We decided to write a book with emphasis on these things. The recipes in this book are tried-and-true favorites of our club members and their friends. Some are family traditions.

The quilt square on the next page is a National Contest Winner designed by Donna Davis, one of our members. Patterns for some of our favorite quilt designs are shown on the beginning page of each section of this cookbook.

You will find helpful "Hints From Our Cooks" not only on pages 40, 82, 172, 177, 216, and 219, but scattered throughout the text at relevant locations. Also, a "Glossary of Cooking Terms," an "Equivalent Measures" chart, and a brief guide entitled "How Much to Buy for 25" appear on page 219.

We hope you thoroughly enjoy this book. Much thought and effort have gone into its making. Proceeds from its sale will go toward scholarships.

We give special thanks to Marilyn Wells, the typist of the first version, and we thank the following poets for permission to quote from their published works:

Clyde Kessler, *Dancing at Big Vein;*
Cecil J. Mullins, *Seining the Air for Sparrows,* and
Preston Newman, *The Land Stacks Up.*

These books can be purchased at any bookstore, or from Pocahontas Press by writing to P.O. Drawer F, Blacksburg, Virginia 24063-1020 or by calling 703-951-0467 or 800-446-0467.

This book is lovingly dedicated
to
Janette K. Newhouse,
Extension Agent,
who has instructed,
advised, and encouraged us
in our endeavor.

—STEELESBURG EXTENSION HOMEMAKERS CLUB
1981

Appetizers

Cornmeal Chips

¹/₂ cup milk	1 cup cornmeal
3 tablespoons vegetable oil	¹/₂ cup flour
¹/₄ teaspoon Worcestershire sauce	³/₄ teaspoon salt
Dash bottled hot pepper sauce	¹/₄ teaspoon soda

Combine first four ingredients, and set aside. Stir remaining ingredients together; add milk mixture and stir until dough forms a ball. Knead on lightly floured surface for 5 minutes. Divide dough in half; place each half on a greased cookie sheet. Roll on each sheet to a 12-inch square. Sprinkle with salt. Cut into 1-inch squares. Bake in 350° preheated oven until golden brown, approximately 15 minutes. Edges will be browner than center. Cool slightly before removing from pan. Store in loosely covered container.

—Wilma Matney

Cucumber Sandwiches

18-ounce package cream cheese	¹/₂ cucumber, chopped fine
3 tablespoons mayonnaise	Small party rye bread
¹/₂ onion, grated	

Cream cheese and mayonnaise. Add onion and cucumber. Chill overnight before using. Spread on small party rye bread or rounds cut from plain bread. Serve on tray garnished with parsley.

For neater party sandwiches, freeze bread first. Cut and spread while frozen.

—Teresa Adkins

C·H·E·E·S·E

Two-Cheese Ball

2 8-ounce packages cream cheese	3 teaspoons Worcestershire sauce
2 cups shredded sharp cheese	2 teaspoons lemon juice
2 tablespoons chopped peanuts	2 tablespoons finely chopped onion
2 tablespoons chopped green pepper	

Combine softened cream cheese with cheddar cheese until well blended. Add remaining ingredients. Mix well. Chill. Shape into a ball. Roll in nuts and dried beef or finely chopped parsley.

—Teresa Adkins

Man's mind stretched by a new idea
never goes back to its original dimensions.

Creamy Parmesan Fondue

1½ cups milk
2 8-ounce packages cream cheese,
   softened

½ teaspoon garlic salt
1 2½-ounce container Parmesan
   cheese (about ¾ cup)

With electric mixer add milk to cream cheese, mixing till well blended. Heat slowly in saucepan; add ½ teaspoon salt and garlic salt. Slowly add Parmesan, stirring until smooth.

Pour into fondue pot; place over fondue burner. Spear dipper with fondue fork; dip in fondue, swirling to coat. (If mixture becomes too thick, stir in a little milk.) Serves 8-10. Suggested dippers: bread sticks, warm cooked turkey, or chicken. —Janette Newhouse

Cheese Puffs

1 cup water
½ cup butter
1 cup flour
¼ teaspoon salt
1 cup shredded Cheddar cheese
   (4 ounces)

2 tablespoons chopped chives
4 eggs
Crabmeat Filling

In medium saucepan bring water and butter to boil, stirring until butter melts. Remove from heat. Add flour and salt, stirring vigorously until mixture forms ball, 1-2 minutes. Add cheese and chives, stirring until cheese melts. Add eggs, one at a time, beating well after each. Drop batter by slightly rounded tablespoons onto greased cookie sheets, allowing 2-inch space between each.

Bake in preheated 400° oven until lightly browned, 18-20 minutes. For firmer cream puffs, pierce side of each with tip of sharp knife. Bake 5 minutes longer.

Cool on wire racks. Cut off tops and fill each with 2 tablespoons Crabmeat Filling. Replace tops. Chill before serving, if desired.

Crabmeat Filling:

6 hard-cooked eggs, finely chopped
1 6½-7½ ounce can crabmeat,
   drained and finely chopped
1 cup finely chopped celery

½ cup mayonnaise
½ teaspoon salt
½ teaspoon dry mustard

Mix all ingredients thoroughly. —Janette Newhouse

If wet or hot dishes and glasses have made
white rings on your table, you can remove the
rings with a half-and-half mixture of salad oil
and salt. Rub it on the spot, let stand for an
hour or two, then rub off.

Pineapple Cheese Ball

2 8-ounce packages cream cheese, softened
½ cup drained crushed pineapple

½ cup chopped green pepper
2 tablespoons chopped onion
⅓ cup chopped pecans

Mix together well. Form into a ball and roll in about ⅔ cup chopped pecans. Refrigerate until firm.
—Opal Honaker

Cheese Ball

2 8-ounce packages cream cheese
1 package shredded cheddar cheese
½ teaspoon lemon juice

1½ tablespoons Worcestershire sauce
¾ cup chopped pecans

Mix together cream cheese, cheddar cheese, lemon juice, Worcestershire sauce. Chill until firm, about 1 hour. Shape into a ball and roll in chopped pecans. Serve with snack crackers.
—Jamie Overbay

Cream Cheese Date-and-Nut Sandwich Filling

2 8-ounce packages cream cheese, softened
¼ teaspoon salt

1 cup chopped nuts
1 8-ounce package chopped dates

Blend cream cheese and salt until soft and creamy. Add nuts and dates; mix well. Makes enough spread for 50 tea sandwiches.
—Evelyn Altizer

Cheese Straws 1

1 cup grated cheese
½ teaspoon salt
1 egg yolk, well beaten

2 tablespoons butter
¼ teaspoon cayenne pepper
1 cup sifted flour

Mix ingredients until blended well. Roll out the dough. Cut into desired lengths or shapes. Bake at 350° degrees until light brown.
—Jennie Tatum

Cream Cheese Sandwich

1 8-ounce package cream cheese, softened
2 tablespoons mayonnaise, or to taste

½ cup chopped pimiento-stuffed olives

Mix and spread on bread slice with or without lettuce.
—Wilma Matney

Cheese Straws II

¾ cup grated cheese
1 cup flour
⅓ teaspoon salt

3 tablespoons water
⅓ cup shortening

Cut shortening in flour. Add cheese and salt, then add water and mix well. Roll out thin on floured board, cut, and bake at 375° degrees for 15 minutes.   —Evelyn Altizer

Cheddar Cheese Puffs

1 egg, separated
1 cup shredded Cheddar cheese
  (4 ounces)

½ teaspoon baking powder
Melba toast rounds

Beat egg yolk and egg white separately. Combine egg yolk, cheese, and baking powder. Fold in egg white. Spread on toast rounds; broil until golden brown and puffy. Makes 2 dozen appetizers.
                                                                —Janette Newhouse

Crisp Rice Cereal Cheesies

8 ounces sharp cheese
2 cups flour

1 cup butter
2 cups crisp rice cereal

Melt butter and cheese in skillet. Pour into flour; then mix in crisp rice cereal. Put on baking sheet by teaspoonfuls. Bake at 350° for 10 minutes.
                                                                —Teresa Adkins

Black-Eyed Susans

1 pound sharp cheese, grated
1 cup margarine
1 teaspoon salt
3 cups flour

½ teaspoon red pepper or paprika
1½ pounds pitted dates
1 pound pecan halves
White sugar

Cream cheese and margarine. Add salt, flour, and pepper; work dough. Roll dough in thin pieces, cutting into 1-inch strips. Stuff each date with a pecan half. Wrap date in dough; roll in sugar. Bake at 300° until slightly brown. Makes about 100.   —Vernelle Herrin

Did you know that furniture scratches can be
covered up easily and inexpensively with nuts?
Simply take a fresh, unsalted pecan or walnut,
break in half, and rub the blemished area with the
broken nut meat. Watch the color return.

APPALACHIAN

Hors d'oeuvre Meat Balls

1½ pounds ground round steak
½ pound sausage
1 cup dressing mix or bread crumbs
2 eggs

2 teaspoons salt
½ cup beer
½ cup onion, chopped
1 teaspoon ground ginger

Mix all ingredients. Roll into small balls. Bake on cookie sheets in 425° oven for 10 minutes. Serve hot.

—Thelma Joyce

Party Beef Turnovers

2 tablespoons butter or margarine
½ pound lean ground beef
¾ cup chopped onion
1 tablespoon fresh dill or 1½ teaspoons dried dill weed (optional)

1 teaspoon salt
¼ teaspoon pepper
Pastry dough for one 9-inch crust
1 egg yolk

In 10-inch skillet over medium high heat, in hot butter or margarine, cook ground beef and onion until meat is browned, separating meat with spoon into fine pieces while cooking; remove from heat. Add dill, salt, and pepper and mix well; set aside.

Preheat oven to 400°. Prepare pie crust. Roll dough ⅛-inch thick. Cut dough into circles with 3½-inch round cookie cutter (empty tuna fish can will do).

In center of each circle place 1 tablespoon of meat mixture. Fold circle in half; with fork, press edge to seal. Place turnover on cookie sheet.

Beat egg yolk with 2 teaspoons water. Brush tops of turnovers with egg yolk mixture. Bake 20 minutes or until golden brown.

Serve turnovers immediately or cool on wire rack and wrap in one layer in foil; refrigerate. Before serving, reheat wrapped turnovers in 400° oven for 10 minutes. Makes about 20 appetizers.

Pastry:

2 cups flour
⅓ cup shortening

About ½ teaspoon salt
4-5 tablespoons cold milk

Mix flour, shortening, and salt until like coarse meal. Add milk to make dough a little wetter than regular pie dough. Roll out thin.

—Marilyn Wells

Try waxing your ashtrays. Ashes won't cling, odors won't linger, and they can be wiped clean with a paper towel or disposable tissue. This saves daily washing.

Tangy Chipped Beef Ball

1 8-ounce package cream cheese,
  softened
1/4 cup dairy sour cream

1 teaspoon prepared horseradish
1/4 cup grated Parmesan cheese
2 1/2 ounces dried beef, finely chopped

In medium bowl, blend cream cheese, sour cream, and horseradish until smooth and creamy. Stir in Parmesan cheese and 1/2 cup dried beef. Chill cheese mixture about 15 minutes for easier handling. Shape cheese mixture into ball. Roll in remaining dried beef. Chill at least 20 minutes. Serve with assorted crackers. Makes a 4-inch ball. —Wilma Matney

Corned Beef Sandwich Filling

1 12-ounce can corned beef,
  chopped fine
1 cup chopped celery
3 tablespoons hot dog relish

1/2 cup mayonnaise
1 tablespoon lemon juice
Salt and pepper to taste

Stir all ingredients until well blended. Chill. Spread on toasted buns; wrap in foil and heat on grill. Makes 2 1/2 cups. —Evelyn Altizer

Party Meat Balls

1 pound ground beef
1 medium onion
2 slices bread
1 tablespoon salt

1/4 teaspoon pepper
1/2 teaspoon thyme
1 tablespoon chopped parsley
1 egg

Mix well, make small balls, and fry in cooking oil until brown.

Sauce:

1 tablespoon flour
2 tablespoons brown sugar
1 tablespoon prepared mustard

2 tablespoons vinegar
1/2 cup catsup
3/4 cup water

Simmer sauce until thickened, add meat balls, and cook on low heat for 45 minutes. —Thelma Joyce

Chicken Liver Wraparounds

1 pound chicken livers, cut in half
1 pound bacon, cut in half

Preheat oven to 375°.

Wrap bacon slice around each liver half; secure with toothpick. Place in shallow baking pan. Bake at 375° until bacon is crisp, about 30 minutes. Serve hot. —Teresa Adkins

Beef Roll Bites

2 3-ounce packages cream cheese, softened
2 tablespoons horseradish

1 2½-ounce package dried beef or dried corned beef

Mix cream cheese and horseradish thoroughly. Separate meat slices and spoon an equal amount of cheese mixture onto each slice, about 1 table-spoon. Spread cheese mixture evenly on beef slices. Roll meat as for jellyroll. Cover and refrigerate at least an hour. Cut into fourths and secure with toothpicks. Makes 3½-4 dozen appetizers. —Janette Newhouse

Hot Chicken Sandwiches

Cooked chicken, sliced or diced
3 tablespoons butter
2 tablespoons flour
½ teaspoon salt
½ teaspoon prepared mustard
2 cups milk

1½ cups shredded American cheese
Toast
Paprika
Tomato slices
Cooked bacon
Chopped green chilies (optional)

Prepare chicken and set aside. Combine butter, flour, salt, and mustard in top of double boiler to make sauce. Add the cheese and cook until melted. Place chicken on toast and pour sauce over. Sprinkle with paprika. Bake at 450° for 10 minutes. Serve with tomato slices and bacon. If desired, garnish with chopped green chilies. Makes 2½ cups sauce. —Teresa Adkins

Cream Cheese and Ham Balls

1 8-ounce package cream cheese
½ medium onion, grated

2 tablespoons mayonnaise
½ pound ham

Soften cream cheese and mix well with the onion and mayonnaise. Roll into bite-sized balls and wrap in thin-sliced ham. Chill well before serving. Makes approximately 4 dozen bite-sized canapes. —Thelma Joyce

WINDOW CLEANER

½ cup sudsy ammonia
1 pint 70% isopropyl rubbing alcohol
1 teaspoon liquid detergent
13 cups distilled water (enough to make a gallon of cleaner)

Mix well and use with sponge or spray.
Wipe dry with white paper towels.

Sausage Appetizers

3 cups biscuit mix
1 pound hot sausage, uncooked

2 cups Cheddar cheese, grated

Combine ingredients. Mix well. Roll in ½-inch balls. Bake at 350° for 12-15 minutes on ungreased cookie sheet, or freeze and bake when needed. Makes 5 dozen.

—Gladys Joyce
Thelma Joyce

Ham and Olive Canapes

1 cup ground cooked ham
½ cup sour cream
2 tablespoons mayonnaise
¼ teaspoon garlic salt
¼ teaspoon onion powder
⅛ teaspoon MSG

2 tablespoons finely chopped pitted ripe olives
20 slices very thinly sliced wheat bread
Margarine, softened (about 5 tablespoons)
1 2-ounce jar chopped pimientos

Combine ham, sour cream, mayonnaise, seasonings, and olives. Spread about 1 teaspoon of margarine on each slice of bread. Trim crust from bread and spread each slice with 1 tablespoon of ham mixture. Cut each slice into eighths. Garnish with pimiento. Makes 160 canapes. You may heat under the broiler until brown and puffy, if you like.

—Janette Newhouse

Bologna Wedges

1 8-ounce package cream cheese, softened

1 tablespoon grated onions or chives
12 slices bologna

Combine cheese and onions or chives; mix well. Spread each slice of bologna with cheese; place slices together (like making a cake), making two stacks of six slices each. Cover stacks with plastic wrap and chill. At serving time cut each stack into 16 wedges and insert a colored toothpick in each wedge.

—Teresa Adkins

Appetizer Balls

1 3-ounce can ham spread
1 tablespoon dry onion soup mix
1 3-ounce package cream cheese

Chopped nuts, parsley, paprika, Parmesan cheese for garnish

Mix ham spread well with onion soup mix and cream cheese. Roll into one-inch balls; chill in refrigerator. Roll in chopped nuts or parsley, or frost with paprika or grated Parmesan cheese. Spear with party toothpicks.

—Margaret Matney

APPALACHIAN

Tuna Sandwich Spread

1 6½- to 7-ounce can tuna,
  finely flaked
½ cup finely chopped celery
1 tablespoon minced green onion

¼ cup mayonnaise
2 teaspoons lemon juice
Celery salt and pepper to taste

Combine tuna, celery, onion, mayonnaise, and lemon juice. Mix well, then season to taste with celery salt and pepper. Makes 1½ cups, or enough for four sandwiches.
—Evelyn Altizer

D · I · P · S

Dill Dip

1 cup mayonnaise
1 cup dairy sour cream
2 teaspoons lemon juice
2 teaspoons chopped onions

1 teaspoon salt
1 teaspoon dry mustard
½ teaspoon dill weed

Mix until well blended. Cover and refrigerate. Serve with assorted fresh vegetables. Makes 2 cups.
—Opal Honaker

Dip for Strawberries

1 8-ounce package cream cheese
1 7-ounce jar marshmallow creme

Combine marshmallow creme and softened cream cheese; mix until well blended. Serve with strawberries.
—Teresa Adkins

Curry Dip

1 tablespoon sugar
1 teaspoon garlic salt
1 teaspoon curry powder
1 teaspoon prepared horseradish

1 tablespoon grated onion
1 tablespoon cider vinegar
½ cup dairy sour cream
½ cup mayonnaise

Mix sugar, seasonings, onion, and vinegar. Add remaining ingredients and mix. Chill and serve with celery and carrot sticks, raw cauliflower slices, radishes, dill bean sticks, pineapple fingers, apple wedges, and tiny clusters of grapes. Yields about 1 cup.
—Evelyn Altizer

It's not how young you are. It's how old you act.

Great Garden Cheese Dip

1 pound small curd cottage cheese
1 3-ounce package cream cheese
1/4 cup minced green onions with tops
1/4 cup minced radishes

2 tablespoons minced parsley
1/4 teaspoon garlic salt
1/4 teaspoon salt
1/4 teaspoon pepper

Beat all ingredients together until blended. Chill several hours. Serve with raw vegetables.   —Teresa Adkins

Onion Dip

1 8-ounce package cream cheese,
   softened
1/3 cup chopped onion

1/3 cup chili sauce
3 tablespoons mayonnaise
1/4 teaspoon Worcestershire sauce

Mix until slightly lumpy. Cover and refrigerate 1½ hours. Cut all types of green vegetables into bite-sized pieces for dipping.
                                    —Vernelle Herrin

Sour Cream Dip for Raw Vegetables

1 cup sour cream
1 cup mayonnaise
1 tablespoon finely chopped onion

1 teaspoon dried dill weed
1 teaspoon seasoned salt
2 teaspoons dried parsley flakes

Combine all ingredients and chill for several hours. Serve with raw vegetables.   —Teresa Adkins

Punch Bowl Tip: Instead of using an ice block for your punch bowl, try this. Prepare a mixture of orange juice and any other fruit juice desired. The mixture should be quite strong. Pour into a mold or plastic container, and add strawberries or other fruit if desired; freeze. Place the frozen juice block in your punch bowl and pour punch over it. The block will prevent punch from becoming watery during a long serving period and will add to the flavor of the punch.

Beverages

Fruit Punch

2 3-ounce packages lemon gelatin
1 3-ounce package orange-pineapple
  gelatin
9 cups hot water
2 46-ounce cans pineapple juice

4 cups sugar and 4 cups water
  boiled together
1 16-ounce bottle lemon juice
2 large bottles ginger ale

Mix gelatin with hot water until dissolved. Add other ingredients except ginger ale. Freeze in plastic containers. About four hours before using, remove from freezer and allow to partially thaw. When ready to use, place partially thawed mixture in punch bowl and stir and mash frozen particles with wooden spoon. Add room-temperature ginger ale just before serving. Serves 50.
—Margaret Matney
Jamie Overbay

Cherry-O Punch

3 .21-ounce packages unsweetened
  cherry powdered drink mix
2 cups sugar
6 quarts water
1 46-ounce can pineapple juice

1 20-ounce can crushed pineapple,
  undrained
1 6-ounce jar maraschino cherries
  (about 16), halved

Mix powdered drink mix, sugar, and water in a large container. Pour in pineapple juice and fruits. Freeze part of the mixture in a 5-cup ring mold. Serve in a punch bowl over frozen ice ring. If refrigerator space or a large enough container is a problem, you can add the 6 quarts of cold water just before serving. Makes 45 6-ounce servings.
—Jennie Tatum

Cranberry Punch

4 cups cranberry juice
4 cups pineapple juice
1½ cups sugar

1 tablespoon almond extract
2 quarts ginger ale

Mix all ingredients except ginger ale. Chill. Add ginger ale just before serving.
—Wilma Matney

Slush Punch

3½ cups sugar
6 cups water
2 3-ounce packages mixed fruit-
   flavored gelatin

1 46-ounce can pineapple juice
1 quart orange juice
⅔ cup lemon juice
2 28-ounce bottles ginger ale, chilled

Combine sugar and water in a large saucepan; bring to a boil and simmer 3 minutes. Stir in gelatin, pineapple juice, orange juice, and lemon juice. Ladle into wide-topped freezer containers, leaving 1-inch headspace. Cover tightly and freeze.

To serve, partially thaw juice mixture at room temperature (about 5 hours). Place in punch powl. Stir with a fork to break up ice chunks. Add ginger ale. Yields 1½ gallons.   —Margaret Matney

Old-Fashioned Lemonade Syrup Base

1½ cups sugar
½ cup boiling water

1 tablespoon fresh grated lemon peel
1½ cups fresh-squeezed lemon juice

Dissolve sugar in boiling water. Add lemon peel and juice. Store in covered container in refrigerator. Makes 2⅔ cups base.

Lemonade by the glass for one 8-ounce serving:

In large glass, combine ¼-⅓ cup lemonade syrup base and ¾ cup cold water; stir well. Add ice cubes.

Lemonade by the pitcher for nine 8-ounce servings:

In large pitcher, combine 2⅔ cups lemonade syrup base and 6 cups cold water; stir well. Add ice cubes.   —Janette Newhouse

Cherry Punch

2 3-ounce packages cherry gelatin
4 cups boiling water
1 cup sugar
1 quart chilled orange juice
1 quart chilled pineapple juice

1 quart chilled ginger ale
2 ripe mashed bananas
1 .21-ounce package unsweetened
   cherry powdered drink mix

Dissolve gelatin in boiling water. Add sugar and mix well. Cool and add juices and ginger ale. Add bananas.

Make a mold using the powdered drink mix and water as directed on package. Freeze.

When ready to serve, add mold to other ingredients. Serves 25-30.
   —Teresa Adkins

Summertime Iced Tea

6 tea bags
4 cups boiling water
1½ cups sugar
1 6-ounce can frozen orange juice
   concentrate, thawed and undiluted

1 6-ounce can frozen lemonade concentrate, thawed and undiluted
10 cups water

Steep teabags in boiling water, about 5 minutes. Discard bags. Add remaining ingredients. Serve over ice. Serves 12.

—Gladys Joyce
Essie Combs

Russian Tea II

1 teaspoon whole cloves
1 stick cinnamon
3 quarts water
Juice of 3 oranges

Juice of 2 lemons
1½ cups sugar
2½ teaspoons tea

Tie spices in a bag and bring to a boil in water. Add tea tied in a bag and allow to steep for 5 minutes. Remove spices and tea. Add fruit juices and sugar. Stir well. Serves 20.

—Margaret Matney

Red Satin Punch

1 2-liter bottle lemon-lime
   carbonated beverage

1 quart apple juice
2 pints cranberry juice

Freeze lemon-lime carbonated beverage in ice trays. When frozen, pour mixed apple and cranberry juices over ice cubes and serve. Serves 35.

—Teresa Adkins

Party Punch

1 .21-ounce unsweetened cherry
   powdered drink mix

1 46-ounce can pineapple juice
¼ cup sugar

Make powdered drink mix as directed on package. Mix with pineapple juice and sugar. Put in 1-gallon plastic jug and place in freezer. Remove from freezer when ice crystals form and serve immediately. May remove from freezer and leave in refrigerator until ready to serve. Serves 20-24.

—Opal Honaker

Instead of using expensive room deodorants in the bathroom and other small areas where needed, place lemon juice in an uncapped bottle and leave it in the room. Odors just seem to disappear in a short time. Bottled lemon juice works just as well as fresh.

Holiday Punch

2 3-ounce packages gelatin
   (any flavor)
2 cups boiling water
2 cups sugar
6 cups cold water

1 cup lemon juice
1 46-ounce can pineapple or
   pineapple-grapefruit juice
2 quarts ginger ale or non-cola type
   lemon-lime beverage

In large bowl, mix first three ingredients. Add next three indredients. Refrigerate until time to serve. Add ginger ale or non-cola type lemon-lime beverage just before serving. Serve in crushed ice.   —Donna Davis

H·O·T

Red Percolator Punch

2 cups pineapple or apple juice
2 cups cranberry juice
3/4 cup brown sugar
1 3/4 cups water

1 1/4 teaspoons whole cloves
1 1/2 sticks cinnamon, broken
Pinch of salt

Put pineapple juice, cranberry juice, and water in bottom of 8-cup percolator. Place remaining ingredients in top basket of percolator. Perk 10 minutes. Makes 8-10 servings. Serve hot.   —Margaret Matney

Instant Russian Tea

1 cup white sugar
1 7-ounce jar instant orange
  breakfast drink
1 teaspoon cloves

1 teaspoon cinnamon
1 .7-ounce envelope instant tea with
  lemon

Mix all together. Store in jar. Use about 2 rounded teaspoons to 1 cup boiling water.   —Opal Honaker

Russian Tea 1

Grated rind of 2 oranges
Grated rind of 2 lemons
1 1/2 cups sugar
2 tablespoons whole cloves
1 gallon tea, medium strength

Juice of 4 oranges
Juice of 4 lemons
1 1/2 cups water
2 sticks cinnamon

Mix tea and set aside. Mix other ingredients and boil 15 minutes. Strain and mix with tea. Serve either iced or hot.   —Gladys Joyce

Hot Punch

2 cups apple juice
1 cup pineapple juice
1½ cups cranberry juice
½ lemon
1 orange

1½ cups sugar
2 sticks cinnamon
1 teaspoon whole cloves
2 teaspoons candied ginger

Combine all juices. Tie spices in bag. Boil with juices 5 minutes. Serve Hot. Makes 10-12 servings.

—Opal Honaker

Hot Cider

1 quart apple cider
1 cup pineapple juice
1 cup orange juice

1 teaspoon whole allspice
1 teaspoon whole cloves
2 2-inch cinnamon sticks

In saucepan, combine ingredients. Simmer 10-15 minutes. Strain. Serve in mugs. If desired, float orange slice in each mug. Makes six 1-cup servings.

—Wilma Matney

Hot Apple Spice

4 cups apple juice
2 cinnamon sticks

2 teaspoons whole cloves
1 teaspoon soy lecithin granules*

Pour apple juice into small saucepan. Add cinnamon sticks, whole cloves, and granules. Cook over medium heat until mixture boils. Cover and simmer for 15-20 minutes. Remove cinnamon sticks and cloves before serving. Yields 4 cups.

*Available at health food stores

—Gladys Joyce

Hot Chocolate Mix for 100

1 pound chocolate drink mix
1 pound confectioners' sugar

1 pound non-dairy coffee creamer
12 quarts powdered milk

Mix dry ingredients in large bowl. Store in jars until ready to use. Put ⅓ or ½ cup mix in a cup and fill with hot water.

—Margaret Matney

Always use standard fractional measuring cups and spoons. One of the newest items on the market is the glass measuring cup that gives the familiar measure as well as the metric measure.

Hot Spiced Cider I

2 46-ounce cans pineapple juice
2 gallons apple cider

20 cloves
10 cinnamon sticks

Put spices in a bag. Mix cider and pineapple juice. Heat juice and cider with spice bag to boiling point. Leave spice in only long enough to flavor slightly. Makes 58 6-ounce servings. —Margaret Matney

Hot Spiced Cider II

2 quarts sweet apple cider
1 teaspoon whole cloves
1 teaspoon whole allspice

2 3-inch cinnamon sticks
$^1/_2$ cup packed light brown sugar
$^1/_4$ teaspoon salt

Bring ingredients to boiling in a large saucepan. Simmer covered for 30 minutes. Remove spices. Serve hot, garnished with slices of unpared apples. Makes about 2 quarts cider. —Gladys Joyce

Hot Cranberry Punch

1 cup apple juice
3 cups cranberry juice
Juice of 1 lemon, strained (2$^1/_2$-
    3 tablespoons)
3 whole cloves
1 1$^1/_2$-inch cinnamon stick

2-4 tablespoons sugar
1 orange, sliced
1 lime, sliced
Whole cloves to stud orange and lime
    slices

Combine juices, spices, and sugar in 2-quart casserole; cover. Place in microwave and cook until punch comes to boil, 9-11 minutes. Carefully strain punch into warmed punch bowl. Serve while hot. Float clove-studded orange and lime slices for garnish on top. Makes one quart or 16 8-ounce cups. —Evelyn Altizer

Sassafras Tea

Dig roots of sassafras tree, wash and dry, or buy in produce department of grocery store. Bring four cups of water to a boil; add two pieces of sassafras about three inches long. Cover and let simmer about 30 minutes. Serve hot with a little sugar. —Thelma Joyce

Breads

— TIPS FOR GOOD BISCUITS —

1. Very soft dough
2. Very little handling
3. Very quick oven
4. Do not allow biscuits to touch each other in pan; they will be lighter and more delicate.

Master Mix

For 12 cups of mix:

8 cups flour
1/3 cup double-acting baking powder
1 tablespoon salt
2 tablespoons sugar

2 cups nonfat dry milk
1²/₃ cups lard (or 2 cups hydrogenated shortening)

For 29 cups of mix:

18 cups flour (5 pounds)
3/4 cup double-acting baking powder
3 tablespoons salt
4 tablespoons sugar

5 cups nonfat dry milk
4 cups lard (or 5 cups hydrogenated shortening)

Spoon flour into measuring cup. Level off at the cup mark but don't shake or pack the flour down. If you do, you'll get too much flour, and the products made from the mix will be dry and heavy.

Measure the baking powder, salt, sugar, and nonfat dry milk and add to the measured flour. Stir or sift these dry ingredients together until well mixed.

Measure the lard or shortening and add to the dry ingredients. Cut in the lard or hydrogenated shortening until the fat is so finely blended you can't tell it from the flour.

Store in a covered jar or can, or in a large plastic bag.

Note: If you use self-rising flour, omit the salt and baking powder. Use master mix as you would commercially prepared product.

Kind Heavenly Father, we thank Thee for this food. Bless it to the nourishment of our bodies and us to Thy service. Forgive us of our sins, we ask in Christ's name. Amen.

Angel Biscuits I

1 package dry yeast
¼ cup warm water (105°)
2½ cups self-rising flour
1 teaspoon baking powder

1 teaspoon salt
2 tablespoons sugar
½ cup shortening
1 cup buttermilk

Dissolve yeast in warm water; set aside. Combine dry ingredients in a mixing bowl. Cut in shortening until mixture resembles coarse crumbs. Add buttermilk; mix well. Add yeast mixture; mix until dough forms a ball. Cover and chill overnight. Turn dough out on floured surface and roll to ½-inch thickness. Cut with biscuit cutter. Place on greased cookie sheet and bake at 400° for 10-12 minutes. Yields 1½ dozen biscuits.

—Evelyn Altizer

Angel Biscuits II

About 5 cups flour
¼ cup sugar
1 tablespoon baking powder
1 tespoon soda
1 teaspoon salt
1 cup shortening

1 package dry yeast
2 tablespoons warm water (105° - 115°)
2 cups buttermilk
½ cup butter, softened

Combine dry ingredients; cut in shortening until mixture is consistency of coarse meal. Dissolve yeast in water; stir yeast mixture and buttermilk into flour mixture, mixing well.

Turn dough out on a lightly floured surface and roll into a rectangle ¼ inch thick. Spread evenly with butter. Fold dough in half, and cut into 2-inch squares. Place on greased baking sheets. Bake biscuits at 400° for 15 minutes. Yields about 2 dozen.

—Jamie Overbay

Angel Biscuits III

5 cups self-rising flour
⅓ cup sugar
1 cup shortening

2 cups buttermilk
1 package yeast
¼ cup warm water

Mix flour and sugar with shortening. Add milk and yeast dissolved in warm water. Knead on floured board. Roll out and cut in biscuits. Bake at 425° until browned. Makes 3 dozen.

—Opal Honaker

Keep staples—such as sugar, flour, rice and spices—in tightly covered containers at room temperature. Staples that are frequently replenished should be rotated so that the oldest is always used first.

Perfect Biscuits

2 cups sifted flour
1 tablespoon baking powder
1 teaspoon salt

⅓ cup shortening
¾ cup buttermilk

Heat oven to 450°. Sift flour into bowl with baking powder and salt. Cut shortening into flour until coarse. With fork stir in milk. Roll out dough on floured board. Cut, and bake on greased cookie sheet for 15 minutes. Don't let biscuits touch; they will be lighter textured.　　　—Evelyn Altizer

Buttermilk Biscuits

2 cups self-rising flour
¼ teaspoon soda

½ cup shortening (lard, if you have it)
¾ cup buttermilk

In large mixing bowl, cut shortening into flour and soda until consistency of coarse meal. Add buttermilk all at once. Stir with fork until mixture leaves sides of bowl and forms a soft, moist dough. Turn onto floured surface and sprinkle dough lightly with flour. Knead gently 10 times until no longer sticky. Roll out ½ inch thick; cut with 2-inch floured cutter. Bake on ungreased cookie sheet at 450° for 8-12 minutes until golden brown.
　　　—Donna Davis

Southern Biscuits

2 cups flour
1 tablespoon baking powder
1 tablespoon salt

6 tablespoons shortening
⅔ cup milk

Heat oven to 450°. Measure flour; mix dry ingredients well in bowl. Cut in shortening with pastry blender until mixture looks like meal. Stir in almost all the milk. If dough does not seem pliable, add enough to make a soft puffy dough easy to roll out. (Too much milk makes dough sticky; not enough makes biscuits dry.) Round up on lightly floured cloth-covered board. Knead lightly about 30 seconds. Handle lightly. Roll dough or pat out (with floured hands) to about ¼ inch thick. Cut close together with floured biscuit cutter. Place close together for biscuits with soft sides, an inch apart for biscuits with crusty sides, on ungreased baking sheet. Place in middle of oven. Bake 10-12 minutes. Makes 20 1¾-inch biscuits.
　　　—Jamie Overbay

Make croutons from stale bread. Cut bread into cubes and toast at 250° until golden; then toss lightly in melted butter.

Whole Wheat Biscuits

2 cups whole wheat flour
4 teaspoons baking powder
1 small egg

$1/2$ teaspoon salt
2 tablespoons shortening
1 cup milk

Sift together flour, salt, and baking powder. Rub in shortening and mix to a light dough with the egg and milk. Roll out on a floured board. Cut into biscuits and bake about 15 minutes in oven at 450°.

—Evelyn Altizer

Parker House-Style Biscuits

2 packages dry yeast
2 tablespoons warm water (105° - 115°)
5 cups self-rising flour

$1/4$ cup sugar
1 cup shortening
2 cups buttermilk
$1/2$-$3/4$ cup melted margarine

Dissolve yeast in water. Sift together flour and sugar in a large bowl; cut in shortening until mixture resembles coarse meal. Add buttermilk and yeast mixture, stirring well. Turn dough out onto a well floured surface. Roll out to $1/4$-inch thickness. Cut with a $2\frac{1}{2}$-inch cutter. Brush biscuits with some of the melted margarine. Fold over so top overlaps slightly; press edges together. Dip biscuits in remaining margarine. Place on a baking sheet. Bake at 400° for 15 minutes or until golden brown. Yields 3 dozen biscuits. Dough can be stored in an airtight container in refrigerator for one week.

—Jamie Overbay

Herb Biscuits

$1/4$ cup margarine
1 clove garlic, minced
2 tablespoons parsley

2 8-ounce cans refrigerated biscuits
$1/4$ cup shredded Parmesan cheese

Melt margarine in baking pan. Add garlic and parsley. Dip each biscuit in mix. Sprinkle evenly with cheese. Bake at 400° until golden brown.

—Margaret Matney

Cheese Biscuits

2 cups flour
4 teaspoons baking powder
1 teaspoon salt

$1/2$ cup shortening
1 cup grated cheese
$2/3$ cup milk

Sift dry ingredients; cut in shortening and grated cheese. Add enough milk to make a soft dough. Roll dough thin and bake on greased pan in 450° oven.

—Vera Tatum

APPALACHIAN

Corn Lightbread

3 cups cornmeal
1 cup flour
¾ cup sugar
1 teaspoon salt

1 teaspoon soda
1 teaspoon baking powder
½ cup shortening, melted
3 cups buttermilk

Combine all ingredients, and mix well. Spoon into a well greased 10-inch tube pan. Let stand 10 minutes. Bake at 350° for 1 hour or until done.

—Jamie Overbay

Spoon Bread I

1 cup cornmeal
3 cups milk, divided
1 teaspoon salt

1 teaspoon baking powder
2 tablespoons vegetable oil
3 eggs, separated

Combine cornmeal and 2 cups milk in a saucepan, stirring until blended; cook over low heat until the consistency of mush. Remove from heat; add salt, baking powder, oil, and remaining 1 cup milk. Beat egg yolks well. Stir into warm mixture. Beat egg whites until stiff peaks form. Fold into cornmeal mixture. Spoon into a greased 2-quart casserole. Bake at 325° for 1 hour. Serve hot with butter. Yields about 6 servings.

—Jamie Overbay

Spoon Bread II

2 cups milk
½ cup cornmeal
½ teaspoon baking powder
½ teaspoon salt

½ teaspoon sugar
2 tablespoons melted butter
3 eggs

Scald milk, add cornmeal, and cook over low heat until thick. Add salt, baking powder, sugar, and butter. Beat egg yolks until lemon colored. Add to cornmeal mixture, mixing well. Beat egg whites until soft peaks form. Fold into cornmeal mixture. Pour into a greased 1½-quart casserole. Bake uncovered at 375° for 25 minutes. Serve from casserole with a spoon.

—Gladys Joyce

Most recipes for French bread call for placing a pan of hot water in the oven while loaves are baking. This makes the loaves crusty. Brushing the loaves with salt water as they bake thickens and hardens the crust.

Sour Cream Cornbread

1 8½-ounce can cream style corn
1 cup sour cream
2 eggs

½ cup vegetable oil
1 cup self-rising cornmeal
2 teaspoons baking powder

Combine corn, sour cream, eggs, and oil; beat well. Combine cornmeal and baking powder; stir into corn mixture. Pour into a greased 10-inch iron skillet. Bake at 400° for 30 minutes, or until done. Yields 8 servings.

—Jamie Overbay

Corn Bread

⅓ cup sifted flour
¾ cup cornmeal
½ teaspoon baking powder
1 tablespoon sugar

½ teaspoon salt
1 beaten egg
⅔ cup milk
2 tablespoons oil

In bowl combine flour, meal, baking powder, sugar, and salt. In another bowl combine egg, milk, and oil. Mix and add to flour mixture. Pour batter into a greased 9-inch skillet. Bake at 400° for 30 minutes. Serves 6.

—Evelyn Altizer

Custard Corn Bread

¾ cup white cornmeal
¼ cup flour
2 tablespons sugar
½ teaspoon salt
1 teaspoon baking powder

1 cup plus 2 tablespoons milk
1 egg
½ cup milk
2 tablespoons butter

Stir together cornmeal, flour, sugar, salt, and baking powder. Beat egg into milk and stir into dry ingredients. Pour into an 8-inch pan in which butter has been melted. Just before closing the oven door, float ½ cup milk over the top of the batter. Bake 30 minutes in a 400° oven.

—Dorothy Tatum

Company Corn Bread

1 cup self-rising cornmeal
1 cup cream-style corn
1 cup sour cream

2 eggs, beaten
½ cup melted shortening or oil

Preheat oven to 400°. Combine all ingredients and mix thoroughly. Pour into a well greased 9"x9"x2" pan. Bake for 45 minutes.

—Teresa Adkins

Deluxe Corn Bread

1 cup yellow or white corn meal
1 cup flour
¼ cup sugar
1 tablespoon baking powder

1 teaspoon salt
2 eggs
¼ cup melted shortening or oil
1 cup milk

Combine corn meal, flour, sugar, baking powder, and salt. Add egg, milk, and shortening. Beat with rotary beater just until smooth, about 1 minute. Pour into a well greased and floured 9"x9"x2" pan. Bake for about 20-25 minutes or until brown.

Note: May spoon batter into hot, well greased corn-stick pan for "Corn Bread Sticks." Bake for about 15 minutes. Makes 14-16 sticks.

—Teresa Adkins

Mexican Corn Bread I

2 cups self-rising cornmeal
⅔ cup vegetable oil
2 eggs
1 cup buttermilk

3 chopped green chili peppers
1 8-ounce can cream-style corn
2 teaspoons baking powder
1 cup Cheddar or Colby cheese, diced

Mix all ingredients except cheese. Pour half of batter, add half of cheese; pour in remainder of batter, add remaining cheese. Bake 45 minutes at 350°.

—Peggy Rasnick

Mexican Corn Bread II

3 cups self-rising cornmeal
1 tablespoon sugar
2 eggs
1 cup grated Cheddar cheese
1 8-ounce can cream-style corn

1 large chopped onion
2 chopped hot peppers
¼ cup vegetable oil
1 cup milk

Mix well. Pour into 2 hot, greased 8-inch skillets. Bake at 400° until golden brown.

—Opal Honaker

Mexican Corn Bread III

1½ cups self-rising meal
⅔ teaspoon salt
3 eggs
1 cup buttermilk

⅔ cup oil
½ cup finely chopped green pepper
1 cup cream-style corn
⅔ cup grated sharp cheese

Mix all ingredients together and pour into greased and floured 9-inch iron skillet. Bake at 375° for 45 minutes. Makes 6 servings.

—Evelyn Altizer

Jalapeno Corn Bread

1 cup corn meal
1/2 teaspoon salt
1/2 teaspoon soda
1 cup cream-style corn
2 eggs, slightly beaten

1 4-ounce can green chili peppers,
  finely chopped
2/3 cup buttermilk
1/3 cup melted shortening
1 cup shredded sharp Cheddar cheese

Combine all ingredients, except shredded cheese, in a bowl. Mix well and pour half the batter into a hot, greased 9-inch baking pan. Sprinkle cheese on top and cover with remaining batter. Bake at 375° for 30-40 minutes. Makes 6-9 servings. —Evelyn Wyatt

Russian Corn Bread

1 1/2 cups self-rising cornmeal
2 eggs, slightly beaten
1/4 cup oil
1/2 cup onion, chopped
1/4 cup cooking cheese, shredded

1 tablespoon sugar
1 1/2 hot pepper, chopped
1/2 cup cream-style corn
1 cup buttermilk

Sift meal and sugar in bowl. Add eggs, oil, and milk. Add remaining ingredients and pour into slightly greased 9-inch square baking dish. Bake at 375° for 35 minutes. Makes 9 servings. —Margaret Matney

Golden Corn Fritters

1 cup flour
1 teaspoon baking powder
1 teaspoon sugar
1/2 teaspoon salt
2 eggs, beaten

1 cup fresh corn cut from cob
2/3 cup milk
1 teaspoon margarine, melted
Vegetable oil
Powdered sugar

Combine flour, baking powder, sugar, and salt; mix well. Combine eggs, corn, milk, and butter; mix well and stir into dry ingredients. Drop mixture by tablespoons into vegetable oil heated to 375°. Cook until golden, turning once. Drain on paper towels; sprinkle with powdered sugar. Serve hot. Yields about 2 1/2 dozen. —Jamie Overbay

O Thou who clothest the lilies
  And feedeth the birds of the sky,
Who leadest the lambs to the pasture
  And the hart to the waterside,
Who hast multiplied loaves and fishes
  And converted water into wine,
Do Thou come to our table
  As Guest and Giver to dine.

Spicy Apple Muffins

1 egg
1/2 cup milk
1/4 cup melted butter
1 cup grated raw apple
1 1/2 cups flour

1/2 cup sugar
2 teaspoons baking powder
1/2 teaspoon salt
1/2 teaspoon cinnamon

Nut-Crunch Topping:
1/3 cup brown sugar
1/3 cup chopped nuts
1/2 teaspoon cinnamon

Preheat oven to 400°. Beat egg; stir in milk, butter, and apples. Blend dry ingredients. Stir in just until flour is moistened. Spoon into greased muffin tins, filling 3/4 full. For topping, combine brown sugar, nuts, and cinnamon. Sprinkle on top of batter. Bake for 20-25 minutes. Makes 12 medium spicy muffins.

—Teresa Adkins

"Surprise" Muffins

1/3 cup shortening
1/3 cup sugar
1 teaspoon vanilla
1 egg

1 3/4 cups sifted self-rising flour
2/3 cup milk
3/4 cup jelly

Cream shortening and sugar; add vanilla and egg and beat well. Add milk and flour, and mix together just enough to thoroughly wet down. Don't over mix; let batter be rather lumpy. Place batter in well greased muffin tin. Indent muffin batter with spoon, and fill with 1/2 teaspoon of your favorite jelly. Bake in 400° oven for 20 minutes, or until golden brown. Makes 12 muffins.

—Thelma Joyce

Carrot Muffins

1 cup grated carrots
1 1/2 cups sifted flour
1/2 cup brown sugar
2 teaspoons baking powder
1/2 teaspoon salt

1 cup milk
1 beaten egg
1/4 cup oil
1/4 teaspoon cinnamon
1/4 teaspoon nutmeg

In bowl combine flour, baking powder, brown sugar, cinnamon, nutmeg, and salt. In another bowl combine egg, milk, and oil. Add egg mixture to flour. Blend in carrots. Grease 2 muffin tins liberally. Pour in batter to fill 3/4 of each cup. Bake at 375° for 35 minutes. Use toothpick to test for doneness. Remove tins to a rack. Let stand 5 minutes. With a greased knife cut around each cup. Invert and tap to remove muffins. Serve immediately with butter. Serves 6.

—Evelyn Altizer

Zucchini Bread

3 eggs
1 cup vegetable oil
1½ cups sugar
3 medium zucchini (2 cups), grated
  and drained
2 teaspoons vanilla
2 cups flour

¼ teaspoon baking powder
2 teaspoons baking soda
3 teaspoons cinnamon
1 teaspoon salt
1 cup chopped nuts (walnuts
  or pecans)
1 cup raisins

Beat eggs; stir in oil, sugar, zucchini, and vanilla. Sift flour, baking powder, soda, cinnamon, and salt together and add to above. Stir in raisins and nuts. Bake in 375° oven for 1 hour or until center springs back. Cool 10 minutes and remove from pan. Makes 2 loaves.   —Louise Freedman

Banana Bread

½ cup butter
1 cup sugar
2 eggs
3 bananas
2 cups flour

1 teaspoon salt
1 teaspoon soda
½-1 cup pecans
½-1 cup dates

Cream butter and sugar; beat eggs and fold in. Mash bananas, add to mixture. Sift flour, salt, and soda. Beat dry ingredients in quickly. Add dates and nuts. Pour into greased bread pan. Let stand for 20 minutes. Bake at 350° for 50 minutes. For variety, try substituting whole wheat flour.
          —Donna Davis

Banana-Date Nut Bread

1¾ cups flour
½ cup sugar
1 teaspoon baking powder
½ teaspoon salt
¼ teaspoon baking soda
½ cup shortening

1 cup mashed bananas (about 2
  medium)
1 cup coarsely chopped nuts
1 cup coarsely chopped dates
2 eggs, slightly beaten

Preheat oven to 350°. Grease and flour 8"x4½" pan. In large bowl with fork mix first five ingredients. With pastry blender (or two knives used scissor fashion) cut in shortening until mixture resembles coarse crumbs. With fork stir in bananas, dates, walnuts, and eggs just until blended. Spread batter evenly in pan. Bake 1 hour and 15 minutes. Cool in pan on wire rack 10 minutes. Remove from pan; cool on rack. Makes 1 loaf.
          —Evelyn Altizer

New Banana Bread

2 cups flour
1 teaspoon baking powder
$^1/_2$ teaspoon baking soda
$^1/_2$ teaspoon salt
$1^1/_2$ cups mashed ripe bananas

$1^1/_2$ cups flaked bran cereal
$^1/_2$ cup margarine, softened
$^3/_4$ cup sugar
2 eggs
$^1/_2$ cup coarsely chopped nuts

Stir together flour, baking powder, soda, and salt; set aside. In small mixing bowl, stir together mashed bananas and bran flakes. Let stand two or three minutes or until cereal is softened. In large mixing bowl beat margarine and sugar until well blended; add eggs, mix well. Add cereal mixture. Stir in flour mixture; stir in nuts. Spread batter evenly in greased 9"x5"x3" loaf pan. Bake in 350° oven for 1 hour, or until toothpick comes out clean. Let cool 10 minutes before removing from pan.

—Gladys Joyce

Whole Wheat Banana Bread

$^1/_2$ cup butter
1 cup sugar
2 eggs, slightly beaten
3 medium-sized bananas (1 cup,
    mashed)
1 cup sifted flour

$^1/_2$ teaspoon salt
1 teaspoon soda
1 cup whole wheat flour
$^1/_3$ cup hot water
$^1/_2$ cup chopped nuts

Melt butter and blend in sugar. Mix in beaten eggs and mashed bananas, blending until smooth. Sift flour again with salt and soda. Stir whole wheat flour. Add dry ingredients alternately with hot water. Stir in chopped nuts. Turn into a greased 9"x5" loaf pan. Bake at 325° for 1 hour and 10 minutes.

—Marilyn Wells

Delicious Pumpkin Bread

3 cups sugar
1 cup vegetable oil
4 eggs, beaten
2 cups cooked, mashed pumpkin or
    1 16-ounce can
$3^1/_2$ cups flour
1 teaspoon baking powder
2 teaspoons salt

2 teaspoons soda
$^1/_2$ teaspoon cloves
1 teaspoon cinnamon
1 teaspoon nutmeg
1 teaspoon allspice
$^2/_3$ cup water
1-$1^1/_2$ cups chopped pecans (optional)

Combine sugar, oil, and eggs; beat until light and fluffy. Stir in pumpkin. Combine dry ingredients, and stir into pumpkin mixture; add water and nuts, mixing well. Spoon batter into two well greased $9^1/_4$"x$5^1/_4$"x$2^3/_4$" loaf pans. Bake at 350° for 65-75 minutes.

—Evelyn Altizer, Louise Freedman,
Gladys Joyce, Thelma Joyce

Apple Cheese Loaf

½ cup butter
½ cup sugar
2 eggs
2 cups unsifted flour
1 teaspoon baking powder
½ teaspoon soda
½ teaspoon salt

1¾ cups finely chopped, tart cooking
   apples
2 tablespoons milk
1½ cups shredded sharp Cheddar
   cheese
½ cup chopped walnuts

In a large mixing bowl, cream butter and sugar until light and fluffy. Add eggs and continue beating until well mixed, scraping bowl occasionally. Combine flour, baking powder, baking soda and salt. Add flour mixture alternately with apples and milk and mix until well combined. Stir in remaining ingredients. Pour into greased 8"x4½" loaf pan. Bake in 350° oven for 70 minutes or until toothpick inserted in center comes out clean. Place on wire rack and cool 10 minutes; remove from pan and cool completely before slicing.
                                                              —Marilyn Wells

R·O·L·L·S & B·U·N·S

Ham 'n' Cheese Crescent Buns

1 3-ounce package thinly sliced ham
   (1 cup)
¾ cup shredded Cheddar cheese
2-4 tablespoons finely chopped onion

½ teaspoon garlic salt
1 8-ounce can crescent dinner rolls
2 teaspoons butter

Preheat oven to 375°. Grease 8 muffin tins. Combine first four ingredients. Separate crescent dough into 8 triangles. Spoon ham mixture on wide end of each triangle; top with ¼ teaspoon butter. Wrap dough around ham mixture; completely seal edges of dough tightly to prevent filling from leaking during baking. Place in muffin cups. Bake at 375° for 20-25 minutes, or until lightly browned.
                                                              —Wilma Matney

Dinner Rolls

1 cake yeast
2 cups warm water
1 teaspoon salt
1 teaspoon sugar

2 tablespoons shortening
6 cups flour
1 egg

Dissolve yeast in water, add egg; beat well. Add salt, sugar, and shortening; gradually add flour. Let rise 2 hours. Take out and knead and let rise again until doubled in bulk. Cut out with biscuit cutter. Place on cookie sheet. Bake in 400° oven until brown.
                                                              —Dora Abel

Instant Rolls

3 packages dry yeast
1/2 cup warm water
5 cups self-rising flour
1/4 cup sugar

1 teaspoon soda
1 cup shortening
2 cups lukewarm buttermilk

Dissolve yeast in warm water and set aside. Mix flour, sugar, and soda. Cut in shortening. Add buttermilk and yeast, and mix. Place dough, a portion at a time, on floured cloth; pat out or roll out. Cut with biscuit cutter. Bake in 350° oven for 10-15 minutes. No rising needed.

—Wilma Matney

Shredded Bran Cereal Rolls

1 cup shredded bran cereal
3/4 cup sugar
3/4 teaspoon salt
3/4 cup lard
1 cup boiling water

2 packages yeast
1/4 cup warm water
2 beaten eggs
6 cups flour
1 cup warm water

Put first four ingredients in bowl. Add the 1 cup of boiling water to mixture. Dissolve 2 packages yeast in 1/4 cup warm water and add. Stir in eggs. Add flour and 1 cup warm water; stir well. Make out in rolls; put in refrigerator. Bake when needed in 350°-400° oven until golden brown. You do not have to let rise before baking.

—Opal Honaker

Mayonnaise Rolls

2 cups self-rising flour
1 cup sweet milk
1/2 cup mayonnaise

Mix well and bake at 450°. Best when baked in muffin pans.

—Opal Burgess

Spoon Rolls

1 cake yeast
2 cups warm water (not hot)
1/4 cup sugar

3/4 cup shortening
4 cups flour

Dissolve 1 cake yeast in 2 cups of warm water. Cream shortening and sugar; add flour and yeast mixture. Mix as for biscuit dough. Grease lightly a large mixing bowl; put dough in. Let rise until doubled in bulk; then spoon out in well greased muffin pan. Bake at 400° until brown or done. Grease with butter.

—Teresa Adkins

Buttermilk Rolls

1 package yeast
4½ cups flour
¼ cup sugar
1 teaspoon salt
½ cup lukewarm water

1 cup buttermilk
¼ cup shortening
½ teaspoon soda
1 egg

Dissolve yeast in lukewarm water. Heat buttermilk to lukewarm; add salt, shortening, and sugar to buttermilk. Add dissolved yeast and one cup flour with soda and egg to milk mixture. Beat vigorously. Beat and fold in remaining flour until soft dough. Fold lightly, about five minutes, and place in lightly greased bowl. Cover and let rise in warm place until dough is double in bulk (about 1 hour). Make into rolls and let rise again for 1 hour. Bake in 375° oven for 20 minutes.   —Jamie Overbay

No-Knead Refrigerator Rolls

1 package dry yeast
½ cup shortening
1 teaspoon salt

½ cup sugar
1 egg, slightly beaten
3¼ cups flour

Dissolve yeast in a small amount of warm water. Place shortening in a large bowl and stir in ½ cup boiling water, until shortening is dissolved. Add salt and sugar; cool until lukewarm.

Add egg and mix well; stir in yeast mixture. Combine flour, one cup at a time. Mix ingredients well. Cover bowl and let the dough rise. Shape into rolls and place in greased pan. Let rise for two hours or until doubled in bulk.

Bake at 375° for about 15 minutes, or until lightly browned.

—Gladys Joyce

Cinnamon Rolls

2 cakes yeast
1 cup lukewarm water
½ cup lard
1 cup milk, scalded and cooled

⅔ cup sugar
2 teaspoons salt
2 eggs, beaten
7 cups flour (white or whole wheat)

Topping:
butter
brown sugar
cinnamon

Mix yeast in lukewarm water; mix rest of ingredients, then add flour. Let rise in bowl until doubled in size. Divide dough in half. Roll out on floured surface to ¼-inch thick. Spead heavily with butter, brown sugar, and cinnamon. Roll into long roll. Slice into 1-inch pieces. Let rise slightly. Bake 30 minutes at 350°.

—Donna Davis

APPALACHIAN

Onion-Rye Buns

1 cup milk
2 tablespoons honey
1 teaspoon salt
3 tablespons butter
2 packages dry yeast
½ cup lukewarm water

3 cups unbleached flour
2 tablespoons caraway seeds
6 tablespoons minced onion
½ cup wheat germ
1-1¼ cup rye flour
1 egg beaten with 2 teaspoons water

Scald the milk and combine it in a mixing bowl with the honey, salt, and butter. Stir well and cool to lukewarm. Dissolve the yeast in the warm water and combine with the milk mixture. Add the white flour and beat vigorously for 1 minute or until the batter is very smooth. Add the caraway seeds, onion, wheat germ, and enough rye flour so that the dough is firm enough to knead. Turn the dough out onto a floured surface and knead for 8 minutes. Wash out the mixing bowl. Dry it well and coat it with oil or butter. Place the dough in the bowl and turn it around so that the dough is coated on all sides. Cover and let rise in a warm place for 1 hour or until dough is doubled. Punch the dough down and roll it out with your hands into a long rope about 1½ inches thick. Cut into 1½-inch pieces and shape into buns. Place in oiled muffin tins or on an oiled baking sheet, placing them 2 inches apart. Cover with a towel and let rise until doubled. Preheat the oven to 400°. Beat the egg with the water and brush the tops of the buns.

Bake 12-15 minutes or until nicely browned.

—Marilyn Wells

S·P·E·C·I·A·L·T·Y B·R·E·A·D·S

Doughnuts

4 cups sifted flour
1 teaspoon soda
1 teaspoon salt
¼ teaspoon cinnamon
½ teaspoon nutmeg

1 cup sugar
2 eggs, well beaten
2 tablespoons shortening, melted
1 cup sour milk

Sift flour; measure. Add soda, salt, and spices, and sift again. Combine sugar, eggs, shortening, and sour milk; add flour mixture; beat well. Chill; turn out on floured board. Roll ¼-inch thick. Cut with doughnut cutter. Fry in deep fat at 375°. Turn once.

Drain on unglazed paper, then dip in syrup made of 2 cups brown sugar, 1 cup water, and 1 tablespoon butter. Let come to a boil and add 1 teaspoon vanilla.

—Vera Tatum

Dip the spoon in hot water before measuring
shortening, butter, etc. The fat will slip out more easily.

Hush Puppies I

2 cups corn meal
1 teaspoon baking powder
1/2 cup chopped onion
1/2 teaspoon sugar

1/2 cup sweet milk
3/4 cup water
1 egg

Mix all dry ingredients together; add onion, then milk, water, and egg. Roll into balls 3/4-inch thick. Cook in deep fat at 350° for 5-7 minutes. Makes 8-10 servings. —Vera Tatum

Hush Puppies II

2 cups corn meal
1 cup flour
1 egg
1/8 teaspoon salt

1/2 cup chopped onion
1 teaspoon sugar
1 1/2 cups milk
1 1/2 teaspoons melted butter

Mix all ingredients together. With teaspoon, form balls. Drop into hot deep fat until golden brown. —Evelyn Altizer

Hush Puppies III

1/2 cup sifted flour
1 tablespoon sugar
1/2 teaspoon salt
1 small onion, finely chopped

2 teaspoons baking powder
1 beaten egg
1 1/2 cups corn meal
3/4 cup milk

Mix dry ingredients and add onion. Combine eggs and milk; beat, and add dry ingredients. Drop teaspoonfuls of batter into hot deep fat which your fish has been fried in. Cook until golden brown. Serve with fish and eat while hot. Yields about 22. —Gladys Joyce

Hush Puppies IV

2 1/2 cups self-rising meal
3 tablespoons flour
1 beaten egg

1 cup buttermilk
1 chopped onion

Mix ingredients together, drop from spoon into hot oil, and deep-fat fry until golden brown. —Donna Davis

Hush Puppies V

1 cup self-rising meal
3 tablespoons flour
1/4 teaspoon soda

1 egg
1/2 cup buttermilk (approximately)
1 small chopped onion

Mix dry ingredients. Add egg and milk. Mix well. Batter must be thick. Add onion. Heat oil to about 375°. Spoon heaping teaspoons into oil and fry, turning when needed. Drain on paper towels and serve with fish.
—Margaret Matney

Butter Dips

1/4 cup butter
1 1/4 cups flour
2 teaspoons sugar

2 teaspoons baking powder
1 teaspoon salt
2/3 cup milk

Heat oven to 450°. Melt butter in square 9"x9"x1 3/4" pan in oven. Remove as soon as butter melts. Measure flour by dip-level-pour method or by sifting. In bowl, stir dry ingredients together. Add milk. Stir 30 strokes with fork until dough clings together. Turn out on floured board. Knead lightly about 10 times. Roll out 1/2-inch thick into 8-inch square. With floured knife, cut into strips 4 inches wide, then cut crosswise to make 18 sticks. Dip sticks in butter, place two rows in pan. Bake 15-20 minutes. Serve hot. Makes 18 butter dips.

—Jamie Overbay

Whole Wheat Pancakes

1 1/3 cups whole wheat flour
2 teaspoons baking powder
1/4 teaspoon salt
1 egg, slightly beaten

1 1/3 cups milk
1 tablespoon brown sugar, packed
1 tablespoon oil

Mix flour, baking powder, and salt. Beat egg, milk, sugar, and oil together. Add liquid mixture to flour mixture. Stir only until flour is moistened. Batter will be slightly lumpy. For each pancake, pour about 1/4 cup batter onto hot griddle. Cook until covered with bubbles and edges are slightly dry. Turn and brown other side.

Blueberry Sauce for Pancakes:

2 teaspoons cornstarch
1/2 cup water
3/4 cup frozen unsweetened blueberries, thawed, crushed

2 tablespoons honey
2 teaspoons lemon juice

Mix cornstarch with a small amount of water in a saucepan; stir until smooth. Add remaining water, blueberries, and honey. Bring to boil over medium heat, stirring constantly. Cook until thickened. Remove from heat. Stir in lemon juice. Serve warm over whole wheat pancakes. Try this recipe with blackberries or strawberries.

—Marilyn Wells

O, weary mothers mixing dough,
Don't you wish that food would grow?
Your lips would smile I know to see
A cookie bush or a pancake tree.

Favorite Waffles

2 eggs
2 cups buttermilk
1 teaspoon soda
2 cups flour

2 teaspoons baking powder
1/2 teaspoon salt
6 tablespoons melted shortening

Beat eggs well. Beat in remaining ingredients with beater until smooth. Pour onto center of hot waffle iron. Spread to cover surface. Bake until steaming stops. Serve hot with butter and syrup. Makes 8 waffles. *(See recipe for Homemade Maple Syrup, page 94.)*

—Teresa Adkins

Pizza Dough

1 package yeast
7/8 cup lukewarm water
1 1/2 tablespoons salad oil

1/4 teaspoon salt
2 2/3 cups sifted flour

Soften the yeast in the water; add the oil, salt, and 2 cups flour and mix well. The dough should be soft but not sticky. Add a little more flour if necessary. Turn onto floured surface and knead about 5 minutes. Place in a greased bowl; turn dough over so it will be greased on top. Cover bowl with a towel, and let rise in a warm place, one-half hour to an hour. Spread on a greased pizza pan, prick with a fork, bake in a 400° oven 10 minutes. Cool on wire rack.

—Dorothy Tatum

Y·E·A·S·T B·R·E·A·D·S

Light Bread

1 package yeast
1/4 cup water
3 tablespoons vegetable oil
2 tablespoons sugar

1 teaspoon salt
1 egg
1 3/4 cup warm water
6 cups flour (approximately)

Dissolve yeast in 1/4 cup water with a little sugar added. Mix oil, sugar, salt, and egg. Add to yeast mixture. Add flour, mix well, let rise until doubled in bulk. Knead well. Divide dough into 2 loaf pans. Let rise again until doubled. Bake at 400° for 35-40 minutes.

—Opal Honaker

APPALACHIAN

Tender Egg Bread

½ cup warm water
1½ packages yeast
3 tablespoons honey or brown sugar
1½ cups water
5¾ cups whole-wheat flour

⅔ cup oil
1 tablespoon salt
4 eggs
1 teaspoon water
Poppy sead or sesame seed

Mix together warm water, yeast, and 1 tablespoon honey or brown sugar; let stand until doubled. Mix water and 1 cup flour; cook, stirring constantly until thick and smooth. Add oil, salt, 2 tablespoons honey or brown sugar, 3 eggs and 1 egg white; these should cool the batter enough to add yeast. Mix in well. Add remaining flour and let rise until doubled, then turn onto floured board. Knead until smooth and elastic. Let stand 15 minutes; punch down, cut into two pieces and let stand another 15 minutes. Then shape into two loaves. Put in greased bread pans and let rise until doubled. Brush with 1 egg yolk beaten with 1 teaspoon water; sprinkle with poppy or sesame seed. Bake at 350° for 50-55 minutes.

—Marilyn Wells

Whole-Wheat Bread

1 package yeast
2 cups lukewarm water
2 tablespoons sugar
2 teaspoons salt
3 cups white flour

½ cup hot water
½ cup brown sugar
3 tablespoons shortening
3 cups whole-wheat flour

Soften yeast in lukewarm water. Add sugar, salt, and white flour; beat smooth. Set in warm place (82°) until light and bubbly (about an hour). Combine hot water with brown sugar and shortening; cool to lukewarm. Add to first mixture, then add whole-wheat flour; mix smooth; knead and let rise for about an hour. Knead again, place in greased pans; let rise until doubled. Bake at 375° for 50 minutes. Makes two 1-pound loaves.

—Marilyn Wells

BEST THINGS TO GIVE

To a friend .... Loyalty
To an enemy .... Forgiveness
To your boss .... Service
To a child .... A Good Example
To your father........................... Respect
To your mother .... Gratitude
To your wedded mate .... Love and Faithfulness

Hints From Our Cooks 1

— SUBSTITUTIONS IN BAKING —

Baking powder: 1 teaspoon equals ¼ teaspoon baking soda plus ½ teaspoon cream of tartar.

Buttermilk: 1 cup equals 1 cup yogurt; or 1 cup whole milk plus 1 tablespoon vinegar or lemon juice, let stand 5 minutes; or 1 cup milk plus 1¾ teaspoons cream of tartar.

Chocolate: 1 ounce unsweetened equals 3 tablespoons cocoa plus 1 tablespoon butter or other kind of fat.

Chocolate: 6 ounces semi-sweet (chips or squares) equal 6 tablespoons cocoa plus 7 tablespoons sugar and ¼ cup shortening.

Chocolate: premelted unsweetened, 1-ounce envelope equals 3 tablespoons cocoa plus 1 tablespoon oil or melted shortening.

Egg yolks: for thickening, 2 yolks equal 1 whole egg.

Flour: for thickening, 1 tablespoon equals 2 teaspoons quick-cooking tapioca or 1½ teaspoons cornstarch, potato starch, or arrowroot.

Cake flour: 1 cup equals 1 cup minus 2 tablespoons sifted all-purpose flour.

All-purpose flour: 1 cup equals 1 cup plus 2 tablespoons cake flour.

Self-rising flour: 1 cup equals 1 cup all-purpose flour plus 1¼ teaspoons baking powder plus ⅛ teaspoon salt.

Whole-wheat flour: ¾ cup whole-wheat flour equals 1 cup white flour. Reduce shortening by using 2 tablespoons for every 3 tablespoons called for. Add 1 or more tablespoons liquid for cakes, slightly more for bread.

Cakes

Funnel Cakes

3 eggs
2 cups milk
1/4 cup sugar
Cooking oil

3-4 cups flour
1/2 teaspoon salt
2 teaspoons baking powder

Beat eggs. Add sugar and milk. Sift half the flour, salt, and baking powder together and add to milk and egg mixture. Beat batter smooth and add only as much flour as needed. Batter should be thin enough to run through a funnel. Drop from funnel into deep, hot oil (375°). Spirals and endless intricate shapes can be made by swirling and criss-crossing while controlling the funnel spout with a finger. Serve hot with molasses, jelly, jam, or sprinkled with powdered sugar.　　　　　—Margaret Matney

Best Two-Egg Cake

1/2 cup shortening
1 1/2 cups sugar
1 teaspoon vanilla
2 eggs

2 1/4 cups sifted cake flour
2 1/2 teaspoons baking powder
1 teaspoon salt
1 cup plus 2 tablespoons milk

Stir shortening to soften. Gradually add sugar; cream thoroughly. Add vanilla. Add eggs. Sift dry ingredients; add to creamed mixture, alternating with milk. Beat well. Bake in two 9-inch cake pans at 375° for 23 minutes.
　　　　　—Donna Davis

Peanut Butter Cake

1/2 cup peanut butter
1/4 cup butter
1 1/2 cups brown sugar, packed
2 eggs
2 cups sifted flour

2 teaspoons baking powder
1/2 teaspoon soda
1 teaspoon salt
2/3 cup milk
1 teaspoon vanilla

Cream butter and peanut butter. Add brown sugar; beat until fluffy. Add eggs. Add dry ingredients gradually, alternating with milk. Add vanilla. Bake in two greased and floured 8-inch cake pans at 350° for 30 minutes.

Peanut Butter Icing:
　1/2 cup peanut butter
　1/4 cup softened butter
　2 1/2 cups sifted confectioners' sugar

1 teaspoon vanilla
3 or 4 tablespoons milk

Mix together and frost cake. Serves 12.　　　　　—Opal Honaker

Eggnog Cake

1 18½-ounce yellow cake mix
1 cup canned eggnog
¼ cup oil

3 eggs
2 tablespoons rum
¼ teaspoon nutmeg

Combine cake mix, eggnog, oil, eggs. Beat for 3 minutes. Add rum and nutmeg. Pour into three well greased and floured 8-inch cake pans. Bake at 350° for 20 minutes. Cool 10 minutes. Remove from pans. Frost with cream cheese frosting. —Gladys Joyce

Butterscotch Cake

1 18½-ounce yellow cake mix
1 3¾-ounce instant butterscotch
   pudding mix
2 eggs

2 cups milk
1 cup pecans, broken
1 6-ounce package butterscotch
   chips

Mix cake mix, pudding, and eggs. Slowly add milk. Beat for 2 minutes. Pour batter into greased 13"x9"x2" baking dish. Top with nuts and chips. Bake in 325° oven for 45 minutes. —Margaret Matney

Black Walnut Cake

½ cup butter, softened
½ cup shortening
2 cups sugar
5 eggs, separated
1 cup buttermilk
1 teaspoon soda

2 cups flour
1 teaspoon vanilla
1½ cups chopped black walnuts
1 3-ounce can flaked coconut
½ teaspoon cream of tartar

Cream butter and shortening; gradually add sugar, beating until light and fluffy and sugar is dissolved. Add egg yolks, beating well. Combine buttermilk and soda, stir until soda dissolves. Add flour to creamed mixture alternately with buttermilk mixture, beginning and ending with flour. Stir in vanilla. Add 1½ cups walnuts and coconut, stirring well. Beat egg whites (at room temperature) with cream of tartar until stiff peaks form. Fold egg whites into batter. Pour batter into three greased and floured 9-inch round cake pans. Bake at 350° for 30 minutes or until cake tests done. Cool layers in pans for 10 minutes; remove from pans, and cool completely. Frost cake with Cream Cheese Frosting (below); sprinkle remaining walnuts on top of cake.

Cream Cheese Frosting:

1 8-ounce package cream cheese,
   softened
½ cup butter or margarine, softened

1 16-ounce package powdered sugar
1 teaspoon vanilla

Combine cream cheese and butter; cream until smooth. Add powdered sugar, beating until light and fluffy. Stir in vanilla. —Gladys Joyce

Black and Gold Marble Cake

2½ cups flour
1½ teaspoons baking powder
½ teaspoon soda
1 teaspoon salt
1⅔ cups sugar
1 ounce unsweetened chocolate,
   melted

2 tablespoons hot water
¼ teaspoon soda
1 tablespoon sugar
¾ cup shortening
1 cup buttermilk
3 eggs
1 teaspoon vanilla

Sift the first five ingredients, then mix the next four ingredients in a small bowl and set aside. Stir shortening just to soften. Stir in dry ingredients. Add milk and mix until all flour is dampened. Beat 2 minutes in mixer; add eggs and beat 1 minute. Add chocolate mixture to ¼ of the batter, mixing only enough to blend. Put large spoonfuls of batter into 9-inch pans, alternating plain and chocolate mixtures. Then, with a knife, cut through batter in a wide zig-zag course. Bake at 350° for 35-40 minutes. Frost with a chocolate icing.

—Evelyn Altizer

Butter Cake

3 cups flour
1 teaspoon baking powder
1 teaspoon salt
½ teaspoon soda
1 cup butter

2 cups sugar
4 eggs
1 cup buttermilk
2 teaspoons vanilla

Sift together flour, baking powder, salt, and soda. In bowl, cream butter and sugar. Add eggs one at a time. Combine buttermilk and vanilla. Add alternately with the dry ingredients to creamed mixture. Turn into a 10-inch tube pan which has been greased on the bottom. Bake at 350° for 60-65 minutes or until it tests done. Prick cake with fork. Pour hot Butter Sauce over cake. Cool before removing from pan.

Butter Sauce:

1 cup sugar
¼ cup water

½ cup butter
1 tablespoon vanilla

Combine all ingredients, except vanilla, in saucepan. Heat until butter is melted; do not boil. Add vanilla. Pour over cake.

—Wilma Matney

When separating the yolk from the white of an egg,
if you drop a portion of egg yolk into the white,
moisten a cloth with cold water, touch to the yolk,
and it will adhere to the cloth.

Rum Cake

1 cup chopped pecans or walnuts	$^1/_2$ cup cold water
1 18$^1/_2$-ounce yellow cake mix	$^1/_2$ cup vegetable oil
1 3$^3/_4$-ounce vanilla instant pudding	$^1/_2$ cup dark rum (80 proof)
4 eggs	

Sprinkle nuts evenly in bottom of greased and floured 10-inch tube or Bundt pan. Combine cake mix, pudding mix, eggs, water, oil, and rum in a large mixer bowl. Blend; then beat at medium speed for 2 minutes. Pour into pan. Bake at 325° for 60 minutes or until cake springs back when lightly pressed. Cool in pan 15 minutes.

Glaze:

1 cup sugar	$^1/_4$ cup water
$^1/_2$ cup butter or margarine	$^1/_2$ cup rum

Combine sugar, butter or margarine, and water in a saucepan. Bring to a boil; boil 5 minutes, stirring constantly. Remove from heat. Stir in $^1/_2$ cup rum and bring to a boil. Remove cake from pan onto plate. Prick with cake tester. Spoon warm glaze over warm cake. Garnish if desired.

—Evelyn Altizer

Oatmeal Cake

1$^1/_2$ cups boiling water	1 teaspoon soda
1 cup oatmeal	$^1/_2$ teaspoon salt
$^1/_2$ cup margarine	1$^1/_2$ cups flour
1 cup brown sugar	1 teaspoon cinnamon
1 cup white sugar	1 teaspoon vanilla
2 eggs, well beaten	

Pour boiling water over oatmeal and let stand 20 minutes. Cream margarine, brown sugar, and white sugar; beat well. Add eggs. Sift together flour, soda, salt, and cinnamon. Add to sugar mixture. Add oatmeal mixture and mix well. Bake at 350° for 45 minutes in 9"x13" pan.

Icing:

1 cup brown sugar	$^1/_2$ cup evaporated milk
$^1/_2$ cup butter	$^1/_2$ cup chopped nuts

Bring to boil sugar, butter, and milk. Add nuts. Let stand 5 minutes. Pour over cake.

—Gladys Joyce

*Father, forgive our sins and give
us grateful hearts for these and
all thy blessings, and keep us
mindful always of the needs of others.*

Apple Butter Spice Cake

2 cups flour
1 teaspoon soda
¼ teaspoon salt
1 teaspoon apple pie spice
½ cup butter

1 cup sugar
1 egg
1 cup raisins
1¼ cups apple butter

Sift flour, salt, baking soda, and spice together. Set aside. In mixing bowl, cream butter; add sugar gradually, beating until light and fluffy. Add egg and beat well. Add flour alternately with apple butter, a small amount at a time, and beat. Add raisins. Bake in a greased shallow 11½"x7½"x2" pan. Bake 1 hour and 10 minutes in 350° oven. When cake is cool, cover with Apple Butter Icing.

Apple Butter Icing:
2 tablespoons butter
2 cups powdered sugar

2 tablespoons apple butter
1 cup nuts

Cream butter. Add half of sugar, half of apple butter. Beat well. Add remaining sugar and apple butter. Beat. Spread on cake and sprinkle nuts on top.
—Wilma Matney

Peanut Butter and Jelly Cake

2½ cups flour
⅔ cup sugar
4 teaspoons baking powder
½ teaspoon salt
1 cup brown sugar, firmly packed
⅓ cup shortening

⅓ cup peanut butter
1¼ cups milk
3 eggs, unbeaten
1 teaspoon vanilla
¼ cup peanut butter
½ cup red jelly

Sift together in bowl flour, sugar, baking powder, and salt. Add brown sugar, shortening, eggs, vanilla, peanut butter, and milk. Beat together 1½ minutes. Turn into two 9-inch round layer pans, well greased and lightly floured on the bottoms. Bake at 350° for 30-35 minutes until cake springs back when touched lightly in center. Cool. Place one layer top-side down on plate. Spread with peanut butter, then with jelly. Top with second layer; frost with Peanut Butter Frosting.

Peanut Butter Frosting:
3 tablespoons cream-style peanut butter
1 14-ounce can sweetened condensed milk

In top of double boiler, combine peanut butter and sweetened condensed milk. Cook over hot water; stir constantly, until thickened. Cool. Spread on cooled cake.
—Wilma Matney

Queen Elizabeth Cake

1 cup boiling water
1 cup chopped dates
1 cup sugar
1/4 cup butter
1 egg, beaten
1 teaspoon soda

1/2 teaspoon salt
1 teaspoon baking powder
1 1/2 cups flour
1 teaspoon vanilla
1/2 cup walnuts

Mix water and dates together. Set aside. Cream sugar and butter. Add egg. Mix together all dry ingredients. Add to creamed mixture alternately with date mixture. Add vanilla and nuts. Bake in 9"x12" well greased baking dish at 350° for 25 minutes. —Margaret Matney

Old-Fashioned Molasses Stack Cake

1 cup butter
1 cup brown sugar
2 cups molasses
1 teaspoon soda
1 cup buttermilk
1 tablespoon ginger

1 teaspoon cinnamon
1 teaspoon cloves
1 teaspoon nutmeg
4 eggs, beaten
5 cups flour

Cream butter and sugar; add eggs and molasses to the mixture. Add soda to buttermilk. Sift dry ingredients together and add alternately with buttermilk mixture to creamed mixture. Pour very thin layer in 8-inch or 9-inch round cake pans. Makes about six or seven layers. Bake in preheated oven at 350° for about 25 minutes.

Spread a mixture of cooked apples and molasses, or apple butter, or apple sauce between layers and stack. —Margaret Matney
Vera Tatum

Mom's Jam Cake

1 1/2 cups sugar
3/4 cup oil
3 eggs
1 cup buttermilk
2 cups flour
1 teaspoon soda

1/2 teaspoon salt
1 teaspoon cinnamon
1 teaspon allspice
1 teaspoon nutmeg
1 1/2 cups strawberry preserves
1 teaspoon vanilla

Mix sugar, oil, and eggs. Add buttermilk, flour, salt, and soda. Beat well. Add cinnamon, allspice, and nutmeg. Blend in preserves and vanilla. Bake in 10-inch tube pan at 350° for 1 hour and 15 minutes.

—Vera Tatum

Mrs. Johnson's Lemon Cake

¾ cup butter	¼ teaspoon salt
1¼ cups sugar	¾ cup milk
8 egg yolks	1 teaspoon vanilla
2½ cups cake flour	1 teaspoon grated lemon rind
3 teaspoons baking powder	1 teaspoon lemon juice

Preheat oven to 325°. Cream butter with sugar until light and fluffy. In separate bowl, beat 8 egg yolks until light and lemon colored; blend into creamed mixture. Sift together cake flour, baking powder, and salt. Add the sifted ingredients in thirds, alternating with the ¾ cup milk. Beat thoroughly after each addition. Add vanilla, lemon rind, and juice; beat 2 minutes. Bake in a greased 10-inch Bundt pan for 1 hour or until a straw inserted in the center comes out clean. Serves 16.

Lemon Icing (optional):

2 cups sifted powdered sugar	Juice of 1 lemon
¼ cup soft butter	2 teaspoons cream
Grated rind of 1 lemon	

Combine sugar with butter. Beat in juice and rind. Add 2 teaspoons cream (or a little more) to spreading consistency. —Marilyn Wells

Jam Cake

2 cups sugar	1 teaspoon allspice
½ cup shortening	1 teaspoon cinnamon
3 eggs	1 teaspoon nutmeg
3 cups flour	1 teaspoon vanilla
2 scant teaspoons soda	1 cup buttermilk
1 teaspoon cloves	1 cup thick jam

Cream sugar and shortening. Add eggs; beat well. Sift flour, soda, and spices; add to butter, sugar, and egg mixture. Add milk and jam. Beat well. Bake in three 9-inch pans at 350° for 25 or 30 minutes. Frost with Caramel Frosting.

Caramel Frosting:

2½ cups brown sugar	½ cup cream
¼ cup shortening	1 teaspoon vanilla

Boil sugar, shortening, and cream together until soft ball forms when tested in cold water. Beat with mixer until creamy. Add vanilla. Frost cooled layers. —Opal Honaker

Keep a powder puff in your flour bin
for dusting cake pans.

APPALACHIAN

Orange Slice Cake

1 cup margarine
2 cups sugar
4 eggs
1 teaspoon soda
1½ cups buttermilk
4 cups flour

1 pound chopped dates
1 pound candy orange slices,
  chopped
2 cups chopped nuts
1 3½-ounce can flaked coconut

Cream margarine and sugar until smooth. Add eggs, one at a time, beating well after each addition. Dissolve soda in buttermilk and add to creamed mixture. Place 1 cup flour in bowl; add dates, orange slices, and nuts. Stir to coat each piece. Add remaining flour to the creamed mixture. Beat well. Add coconut and flour mixture. Mix well. Bake in a greased, floured 10-inch tube pan at 250° for 2½ hours. Remove from oven; pour hot glaze over top of cake, and let sit in pan overnight.

Glaze:
  2 cups brown sugar
  1 6-ounce can frozen orange juice concentrate, undiluted

Combine sugar and juice concentrate; heat and pour over hot cake.

—Gladys Joyce

Gelatin Poke Cake

1 18½-ounce white cake mix
1 3-ounce package vanilla instant
  pudding and pie filling
4 eggs

1 cup water
¼ cup oil
1 3-ounce package raspberry gelatin

Combine first five ingredients in large mixer bowl. Blend, then beat at medium speed for 2 minutes. Pour into greased and floured 13"x9" pan. Bake at 350° for 40-45 minutes. Do not underbake. Cool in pan 15 minutes. Dissolve gelatin as directed on package. Poke holes in cake with big fork or candy thermometer. Pour warm gelatin over cake. Chill 4 hours. Spread whipped topping over cake.

—Gladys Joyce

During the week, keep a shopping list handy to write down items as you need them, to eliminate unnecessary trips to the store. Before your weekly shopping trip, make a complete shopping list. If the list is arranged according to the layout of the store, you'll save time and steps.

My Best Gingerbread

½ cup shortening
½ cup sugar
1 egg, beaten
2½ cups flour, sifted
1½ teaspoons soda
½ teaspoon salt

1 teaspoon ginger
1 teaspoon cinnamon
½ teaspoon cloves
1 cup molasses
1 cup hot water, not boiling

Cream shortening and sugar; add beaten egg. Measure and sift dry ingredients. Combine molasses and hot water. Add dry ingredients alternately with liquid, a small amount at a time, and beat after each addition until smooth. Bake in paper-lined 9"x9"x2" pan in 350° oven for 45 minutes. Yields 16 portions.

—Evelyn Altizer
Gladys Joyce

Lemon Nut Cake

2 cups margarine
2½ cups sugar
6 eggs
4 cups flour
1 pound whole pecans
1 pound candied cherries (half
    red, half green), whole

1 pound white raisins
1 teaspoon salt
1 teaspoon baking powder
4 ounces lemon extract

Dredge nuts, raisins, and cherries in ½ cup flour. Sift remaining flour with salt and baking powder. Cream margarine and sugar in a very large bowl. Add eggs one at a time. Beat well after each addition. Add dry ingredients. Add lemon extract, nuts, and fruits last. Bake in 10-inch tube pan at 325° for 2 hours. Cool well before removing from pan. Freezes well. Can also be baked in 2 loaf pans for 1 hour and 15 minutes at 325°.

—Margaret Matney

Honey Cake

¾ cup sugar
½ cup vegetable oil
½ cup honey
2 eggs
½ teaspoon vanilla

2 cups unsifted flour
2½ teaspoons baking powder
½ teaspoon salt
1 cup milk

Combine sugar, oil, honey, eggs, and vanilla. Mix until well blended, using electric mixer. Add combined dry ingredients to oil mixture, alternating with milk. Mix well after each addition. Pour batter into greased and floured 9-inch square pan. Bake in 350° oven 40-45 minutes. Cool. Frost with Honey-Cream Cheese Frosting.

—Donna Davis

Mayonnaise Cake

2 cups flour
1 cup white sugar
4 tablespoons cocoa
2 teaspoons soda

¾ cup mayonnaise
2 tablespoons blackberry jam or jelly
1 cup buttermilk
1 teaspoon vanilla

Sift together dry ingredients. Beat rest of ingredients together and gradually add dry flour mixture. Beat until well mixed. Pour into pans; bake at 350°. Frost with Buttermilk Frosting.

Buttermilk Frosting

2 cups sugar
½ cup brown sugar
1 cup buttermilk

1 teaspoon soda
4 tablespoons butter
1 teaspoon vanilla

Boil until syrup forms soft ball in cold water. Remove from heat and cool. Beat until thick enough to spread.

—Wilma Matney

A·N·G·E·L F·O·O·D

Angel Food Cake 1

½ teaspoon salt
1½ cups egg whites
1 teaspoon cream of tartar
1 tablespoon lemon juice
1½ cups sugar

½ teaspoon lemon extract
½ teaspoon almond extract
1 teaspoon vanilla
1¼ cups cake flour, sifted

Add salt to egg whites and beat until frothy. Add cream of tartar; beat until mixture begins to stiffen. Add lemon juice and beat until it will hold its shape. Gradually fold in sugar, the flavorings, and flour. Bake in large tube pan in oven at 375° for 1 hour.

—Donna Davis

Wonder Cake

1 angel food cake, any size
2 cups frozen strawberries with juice
1 6-ounce package instant vanilla
  pudding
2 cups milk

1 6-ounce package strawberry gelatin
1 quart vanilla ice cream
1 8-ounce carton non-dairy whipped
  topping

Prepare gelatin using 2 cups boiling water. Stir in thawed strawberries. Chill until syrupy. Prepare pudding using milk. Beat in softened ice cream. Break cake up in pieces and put in 13"x9" pan. Pour pudding mixture over cake pieces. Then pour on strawberry mixture.

Top with non-dairy whipped topping.

—Evelyn Wyatt

Angel Food Cake II

1 cup cake flour
1½ cups powdered sugar
1½ cups egg whites (about 12)
1½ teaspoons cream of tartar

1 cup sugar
¼ teaspoon salt
1½ teaspoons vanilla
½ teaspoon almond extract

Mix flour and powdered sugar. Beat egg whites and cream of tartar in large bowl on medium speed until foamy. Beat in sugar on high speed, 2 tablespoons at a time; beat until stiff and glossy. Add salt, vanilla, and almond extract. Sprinkle flour-sugar mixture, ¼ cup at a time, over meringue, folding in just until flour-sugar mixture disappears. Push batter into ungreased tube pan. Cut gently through the batter with metal spatula. Bake until cracks feel dry and top springs back when gently touched, 30-35 minutes. Invert pan on funnel; let hang until cake is cold.

—Donna Davis

C·H·E·E·S·E C·A·K·E·S

Chocolate Cream Cheese Cake

The frosting comes from part of the batter.

2 3-ounce packages cream cheese, softened
½ cup margarine, softened
1 teaspoon vanilla
6½ cups sifted powdered sugar
⅓ cup milk, room temperature
4 ounces unsweetened chocolate, melted and cooled

4 tablespoons margarine, softened
3 eggs
2¼ cups flour
1 teaspoon baking powder
1 teaspoon soda
1 teaspoon salt
1¼ cups milk

Cream together cream cheese, ½ cup margarine, and vanilla. Alternately beat in sugar and ⅓ cup milk. Blend in chocolate. Remove 2 cups of this mixture for frosting; cover and refrigerate. Cream together the remaining chocolate mixture and 4 tablespoons margarine. Add eggs and beat well. Stir together dry ingredients. Beat into creamed mixture alternately with 1¼ cups milk. Turn into two greased and floured 9-inch pans. Bake in 350° oven for 30 minutes. Cool. Remove frosting from refrigerator 15 minutes before frosting cake.

—Margaret Matney

When a recipe calls for softened butter but you have forgotten to take it out of the refrigerator in advance, measure the correct amount and shred it as you would a carrot. The small pieces will be soft enough to work with immediately.

APPALACHIAN

Cheese Cakes

2 8-ounce packages cream cheese
¾ cup sugar
2 eggs
1 teaspoon vanilla

1 box vanilla wafers
1 package lined cupcake holders
1 21-ounce can cherry pie filling

Beat together cream cheese and sugar. Add the eggs and vanilla. Place one vanilla wafer in each cup. Fill each cup one-third full of cheese mixture. Bake for 12-15 minutes in a 350° oven. Do not overcook. Cool; cover with pie filling. If you want to omit the pie filling, crumble vanilla wafers on top of cheese cakes. Chill until ready to serve.

—Wilma Matney

Cheese Cake
(For Microwave)

2 cups graham cracker crumbs
½ cup sugar
½ cup butter
½ teaspoon cinnamon
3 8-ounce packages cream cheese
5 eggs

1 cup sugar
½ teaspoon vanilla
2½ cups sour cream
1½ teaspoons vanilla
⅓ cup sugar

Combine crumbs, sugar, melted butter, and cinnamon; pat firmly onto bottom of dish. Cook two minutes on high. Beat cream cheese until smooth; stir in eggs one at a time. Mix in sugar and vanilla. Pour into crust. Bake 15 minutes on high, turning every 4 minutes. Combine sour cream, sugar, and vanilla; blend well. Pour over cheese cake. Cook 1 minute and 15 seconds on high. Chill. May top with cherries or strawberries if desired.

—Donda Kidd

C·H·O·C·O·L·A·T·E

Tunnel of Fudge Cake

1½ cups butter
6 eggs
1½ cups sugar
2 cups flour

1 18½-ounce Double Dutch Fudge
Buttercream Frosting Mix
2 cups chopped walnuts

Cream butter in large mixing bowl at high speed of mixer. Add eggs, one at a time, beating well after each. Gradually add sugar; continue creaming at high speed until light and fluffy. By hand, stir in flour, frosting mix, and walnuts until well blended. Pour batter into greased 10-inch Bundt pan. Bake at 350° for 60-65 minutes. Cool 2 hours. Remove from pan. Cool completely before serving.

—Gladys Joyce

Caramel In-Between Cake

1 18-ounce fudge cake mix
1 cup water
1 tablespoon solid shortening

3 eggs
1/3 cup almonds (if desired)

Filling:
28 light caramels
1 1/3 cups sweetened condensed milk
1 tablespoon butter or margarine

Caramel Frosting:
1/2 cup butter, softened
2 1-ounce premelted chocolate
3 tablespoons cream or milk

1 teaspoon vanilla
2 cups sifted powdered sugar

Grease and flour 13"x9" pan. Prepare filling. In top of double boiler, combine caramels, sweetened condensed milk, and butter. Cook over hot water, stirring constantly, until caramels are melted. Make cake; spread half of batter in prepared pan. Spread filling evenly over batter. Cover with remaining batter. Bake at 350° for 30-40 minutes. Cool completely. Frost.

Frosting: In small mixer bowl, combine butter, chocolate, cream, and vanilla. Blend well; gradually add powdered sugar. Beat 2 or 3 minutes. Spread on cake.

—Wilma Matney

Cola Cake

2 cups flour
2 cups sugar
1 cup margarine
3 tablespoons cocoa
1 cup cola

1/4 cup buttermilk
1 teaspoon soda
2 eggs, well beaten
1 teaspoon vanilla
1 1/2 cups miniature marshmallows

Mix flour and sugar. Heat to boiling margarine, cola, and cocoa, and pour over flour and sugar, mixing well. Add eggs, buttermilk, soda, and vanilla. Beat well. Add marshmallows last. The batter will be thin and the marshmallows will float on top. Pour batter into greased 9"x13" pan and bake 30 minutes at 350°.

Cola Cake Frosting:
1/2 cup margarine
3 tablespoons cocoa
6 tablespoons cola

1 box confectioners' sugar
1 cup toasted nuts

Boil margarine, cocoa, and cola. Add sugar. Mix well and add nuts. Pour over hot cake while icing is still hot.

—Margaret Matney

*For all the good things you have provided
for us, our Father, we are truly grateful. Amen.*

Wellesley Fudge Cake

4 ounces unsweetened chocolate
½ cup hot water
½ cup sugar
2 cups sifted cake flour
1 teaspoon soda
1 teaspoon salt

½ cup shortening
1¼ cups sugar
3 eggs
1 cup milk
1 teaspoon vanilla

Melt chocolate with water in top of double boiler over hot water, stirring until chocolate is melted and mixture thickens. Add ½ cup sugar to mixture; cook and stir 2 minutes longer. Cool to lukewarm. Sift flour with soda and salt. Cream shortening. Gradually add 1¼ cups sugar; cream until light and fluffy. Add eggs one at a time, beating thoroughly after each addition. Alternately add flour mixture and milk, beating after each addition until smooth. Blend in vanilla and chocolate mixture. Pour batter into three 9-inch layer pans that have been lined on bottoms with paper. Bake at 350° for 25 minutes, or until cake springs back when touched lightly. Cool in pans for 10 minutes.

—Gladys Joyce

Chocolate Syrup Cake

½ cup margarine
1 cup sugar
4 beaten eggs
1¼ cups flour

1 teaspoon baking powder
½ teaspoon salt
1 teaspoon vanilla
1 16-ounce can chocolate syrup

Cream margarine and sugar. Add beaten eggs and mix well. Mix flour, baking powder, and salt. Add alternately with chocolate syrup. Add vanilla. Bake in 7"x9" baking dish at 350° for 30 minutes. Top with frosting.

Chocolate Frosting:

1 cup sugar
⅓ cup cream
4 tablespoons margarine

2 1-ounce squares semi-sweet
    chocolate

Combine sugar, cream, and margarine. Cook over medium heat, stirring constantly. Boil for 2 minutes. Add chocolate; let melt. Beat until spreading consistency.

—Margaret Matney
Wilma Matney

To test cake for doneness, touch lightly in center. Cake will spring back if it has baked long enough. It should also pull away from sides of pan.

Chocolate Pudding Cake

1 cup flour
¾ cup wheat germ
¾ cup sugar
2 teaspoons baking powder
¼ teaspoon salt
⅔ cup milk

2 tablespoons butter
1 teaspoon vanilla
1 cup firmly packed brown sugar
½ cup cocoa
2 cups hot water

Combine flour, wheat germ, sugar, baking powder, and salt in ungreased 8-inch square pan. Stir well to blend. Add milk, butter, and vanilla to blended dry ingredients. Mix thoroughly. Combine brown sugar and cocoa, mixing well. Sprinkle evenly on batter. Pour hot water carefully on batter in pan. Do not stir. Bake at 350° for 40-45 minutes. Serve warm with whipped cream if desired. Makes 6 servings.   —Wilma Matney

Honey Chocolate Cake

2 cups sifted cake flour
1½ teaspoons soda
½ teaspoon salt
½ cup butter
1¼ cup honey

2 eggs, beaten
3 1-ounce squares unsweetened
  chocolate, melted
⅔ cup water
1 teaspoon vanilla

Sift flour once; measure. Add soda and salt and sift together three times. Cream shortening. Add honey very gradually, by tablespoons at first, beating very hard after each addition to keep mixture thick. Add one-fourth of flour and beat until smooth and well blended. Add eggs, one at a time, beating well after each. Add chocolate and blend. Add remaining flour alternately with water, beating well after each addition. Add vanilla. Bake in two greased 9-inch pans at 350° for 30 minutes, or until done.

—Louise Freedman

Prize Chocolate Cake

¼ cup butter
¼ cup shortening
2 cups sugar
1 teaspoon vanilla
2 eggs
¾ teaspoon soda

¾ cup cocoa
1¾ cups unsifted flour
¾ teaspoon baking powder
⅛ teaspoon salt
1¾ cups milk

Grease and flour two 9-inch round cake pans. Cream butter, shortening, sugar, and vanilla until light and fluffy; blend in eggs. Combine soda, cocoa, flour, baking powder, and salt in bowl; add alternately with milk to batter. Blend well. Pour into prepared pans. Bake at 350° for 30-35 minutes or until cake tester inserted in center comes out clean. Cool 10 minutes; remove from pans. Use cocoa in your favorite frosting recipe, too.

—Gladys Joyce

Chocolate Disappearing Cake

1/4 cup butter
1/4 cup shortening
2 cups sugar
1 teaspoon vanilla
2 eggs
3/4 cup cocoa

1 3/4 cups unsifted flour
3/4 teaspoon baking powder
3/4 teaspoon soda
1/8 teaspoon salt
1 3/4 cup milk

Generously grease and flour two 9-inch round cake pans. Cream butter, shortening, sugar, and vanilla until fluffy; blend in eggs. Combine cocoa, flour, baking powder, soda, and salt in bowl; add to batter alternately with milk. Blend well; pour into pans. Bake at 350° for 30-35 minutes. Cool 10 minutes; remove from pans.   —Gladys Joyce

White Chocolate Cake

1/4 or 1/2 pound white chocolate
  melted over hot water
1 cup butter
2 cups sugar
4 eggs
1 teaspoon vanilla

2 1/2 cups cake flour
1 teaspoon baking powder sifted with
  flour
1 cup buttermilk
1 cup chopped pecans
1 cup flaked coconut

Mix in order listed and bake at 350° for 30-45 minutes.

White Chocolate Cake Icing:
2 cups white sugar
1 cup butter

1 small can evaporated milk
1 teaspoon vanilla

Mix all ingredients. Let stand one hour, then cook until it forms a soft ball in cold water. Beat until ready to spread.   —Vera Tatum

Hot Fudge Cake

1/2 cup butter
1 cup sugar
4 eggs
Pinch salt

1 cup flour
1 teaspoon baking powder
1 16-ounce can chocolate syrup
1 teaspoon vanilla

Cream sugar and butter. Add eggs, flour, salt, baking powder, syrup, and vanilla; mix well. Bake in ungreased 13"x9"x2" pan at 350° for 30 minutes.

Hot Fudge Icing:
1 cup brown sugar
1/2 cup margarine

1/3 cup evaporated milk
1/2 cup chocolate chips

Bring to boil sugar, margarine, and milk. Boil for 2 minutes. Add chocolate chips; mix well. Pour on cake. Serve warm.

—Vonda Kidd

Chocolate Square Cake

2 cups flour	½ cup buttermilk
2 cups sugar	1 teaspoon soda
1 cup margarine	2 eggs
4 tablespoons cocoa	½ teaspoon salt
1 cup water	1 teaspoon vanilla

Sift together flour and sugar. Bring to full rolling boil the water, margarine, and cocoa. Pour over flour and sugar; mix well. Mix buttermilk and soda. Add to flour mixture. Add eggs, salt, and vanilla. Pour into well greased 13"x9"x2" pan. Bake 25 minutes at 400°. Let cool 10-15 minutes and remove from pan.

Chocolate-Pecan Icing:

4 tablespoons cocoa	1 box sifted powdered sugar
4 tablespoons milk	1 teaspoon vanilla
½ cup margarine	1 cup pecans, if desired

Bring to boil cocoa, milk, and margarine. Pour over powdered sugar. Add vanilla and pecans. Cool icing a few minutes and spread on cooled cake.

—Opal Honaker
Vonda Kidd

Helen's Delight Cake

2 cups sugar	½ cup buttermilk
2 cups flour	2 teaspoons cinnamon
½ cup butter	1 teaspoon vanilla
4 tablespoons cocoa	2 eggs
1 cup water	Dash salt
1 teaspoon soda	

Mix together sugar and flour in large bowl. In saucepan bring butter, cocoa, and water to boil. Pour over flour and sugar. Mix well. Add soda to buttermilk, cinnamon, vanilla, and eggs. Pour over dry ingredients. Add a dash of salt and beat well. Bake 20 minutes in preheated 400° oven. Makes 25 servings.

Helen's Delight Icing:

½ cup butter	1 1-ounce square chocolate
6 tablespoons milk	1 pound confectioners' sugar
1 teaspoon vanilla	

Bring butter, milk, vanilla, and chocolate to boil. Add confectioners' sugar. Mix well; spread over hot cake.

—Thelma Joyce

We hate to have some people give us advice
when we know how badly they need it themselves.

APPALACHIAN

Red Velvet Cake

2 cups sugar
1 cup butter
2 eggs
1 tablespoon vinegar
1 tablespoon cocoa
2½ cups flour

½ teaspoon salt
1½ teaspoons soda
2 ounces red food coloring
1 cup buttermilk
1 teaspoon vanilla

Cream butter and sugar. Add eggs and beat until fluffy. Make paste of cocoa and vinegar; add to butter mixture. Sift salt and soda with flour; add alternately with buttermilk. Add vanilla and coloring. Bake 25-30 minutes at 350°.

Icing for Red Velvet Cake:
¼ cup flour
1 cup milk
½ cup margarine

½ cup shortening
1 cup powdered sugar
1 teaspoon vanilla

Cook flour and milk over low heat until it is a smooth paste; cool. Cream margarine, shortening, sugar, and vanilla; add paste. Beat with mixer until fluffy. Spread on cool cake.
— Opal Honaker

C·O·C·O·n·U·T

Italian Cream Cake

1 cup margarine
2 cups sugar
5 egg yolks
2 cups flour
1 teaspoon soda

1 cup buttermilk
1 teaspoon vanilla
1 3-ounce can coconut
1 cup chopped nuts
5 egg whites, beaten

Preheat oven to 350°. Bake for 30 minutes. Cream margarine and sugar until fluffy. Add egg yolks and beat well. Combine flour and soda and add to creamed mixture alternately with buttermilk. Stir in vanilla. Add coconut and chopped nuts. Fold in stiffly beaten egg whites. Pour batter into three 9-inch cake pans. Cool and frost with Cream Cheese Frosting.

Cream Cheese Frosting:
1 8-ounce package cream cheese, softened
½ cup margarine

1 pound confectioners' sugar
2 teaspoons vanilla
1 cup chopped pecans

Beat cream cheese and margarine until smooth. Add sugar and mix well. Add vanilla and beat until smooth.
— Evelyn Wyatt

Hawaiian Cake

1/2 cup butter
5 eggs
1 teaspoon baking powder
1 can coconut
1 pound graham cracker crumbs

2 cups sugar
1 teaspoon soda
1 cup milk
1 cup chopped black walnuts

Mix together well. Bake in three 9-inch layer pans for 25-30 minutes at 350°.

Hawaiian Icing:

1 16-ounce can crushed pineapple,
   drained well
1/2 cup butter, melted

1/2 cup coconut
1 box confectioners' sugar

Mix well. Put between layers and on top of cake.

—Wilma Matney

Marvelous Coconut Cake
(Lemon Filled)

3/4 cup butter or vegetable shortening
1 cup sugar
2 3/4 cups sifted flour
3/4 teaspoon salt
4 teaspoons baking powder

1 cup coconut milk or sweet milk
1 teaspoon lemon extract
4 egg whites, room temperature
1/2 cup sugar

Cream butter or vegetable shortening. Add 1 cup sugar and beat until light and fluffy. Sift flour, salt, and baking powder together three times. Add alternately with milk and extract. Blend well after each addition. Beat egg whites until frothy. Gradually add, beating until stiff peaks form, 1/2 cup sugar. Fold carefully into cake batter. Bake in greased and floured layer cake pans (two 9-inch or three 8-inch). Bake 25-30 minutes at 350° (do not overbake). Put together with Lemon Filling.

Lemon Filling:

1 cup sugar
3 tablespoons cornstarch
1 cup boiling water
4 well beaten egg yolks

Juice of two lemons
2 tablespoons cream
2 tablespoons butter

Combine sugar and cornstarch. Gradually add boiling water. Slowly add egg yolks. Then add lemon juice, cream, and butter. Cook over medium heat, stirring constantly until thickened. Cool thoroughly before filling cake.

Frost cake and cover generously with frozen or canned coconut.

—Gladys Joyce

APPALACHIAN

Coconut Cake I

1 15-ounce package frozen coconut
2 cups sour cream
2 cups sugar

Mix together and let sit overnight in the refrigerator.

The next day, bake a white or yellow cake mix according to directions on package. Split layers and spread with coconut mixture. Frost top and sides. Place in airtight container. Keep in refrigerator.

—Emma Jane Hale
Opal Honaker

Coconut Cake II

1 18¹/₂-ounce white cake mix
¹/₄ cup oil
3 eggs

1 8-ounce carton sour cream
1 8¹/₂-ounce can cream coconut

Mix together all ingredients for two or three minutes. Pour into 11"x14" pan. Bake at 350° for 30 minutes. Top with frosting.

Frosting:

1 8-ounce package cream cheese
1 pound confectioners' sugar, sifted

2 tablespoons milk
1 3¹/₂-ounce can coconut

Mix cheese, sugar, milk, vanilla, and half of coconut. Spread on cake. Sprinkle remainder of coconut on top.

—Gladys Joyce

C·U·P·C·A·K·E·S

Peanut Butter Cupcakes

¹/₂ cup peanut butter
¹/₃ cup margarine
1 teaspoon vanilla
1¹/₂ cups brown sugar
2 eggs

2 cups flour, sifted
2 teaspoons baking powder
¹/₂ teaspoon salt
³/₄ cup milk
Confectioners' sugar

Cream together peanut butter, shortening, and vanilla. Add brown sugar; beat until fluffy. Add eggs; beat well. Sift together dry ingredients; add alternately with milk. Place paper baking cups in muffin pans; fill half-full. Bake at 375° for about 20 minutes. Frost with peanut butter. Sift confectioners' sugar atop each. Makes 2 dozen.

—Donna Davis

Everyday Cupcakes

1/3 cup margarine
2 cups cake flour, sifted
1 cup sugar
2 1/2 teaspoons baking powder

3/4 teaspoon salt
3/4 cup milk
1 egg, beaten
1 teaspoon vanilla

Stir shortening until softened. Sift in dry ingredients. Add half the milk and the egg. Mix well. Beat two minutes on low speed with mixer. Add remaining milk and vanilla; beat one minute longer. Place paper baking cups in muffin pans; fill half-full. Bake at 375° about 20 minutes. Makes 20.

—Donna Davis

F·R·U·I·T C·A·K·E·S

Fruit 'n Cream Cake

1 18 1/2-ounce yellow cake mix
2 eggs
1/2 cup oil
1 3-ounce box instant vanilla
   pudding
1 20-ounce can crushed pineapple,
   undrained

1 11-ounce can mandarin oranges,
   undrained
1 4-ounce maraschino cherries,
   undrained
1 8- or 9-ounce carton whipped
   topping

Prepare cake mix as directed, adding the eggs and oil to mix. Bake in 9"x13" pan according to package directions. Let cool. Combine undrained fruits, pudding mix, and whipped topping. Spread on cake and refrigerate. Serves 12-15.

—Opal Honaker

Fruit Cocktail Cake

1 1/2 cups sugar
2 cups flour
2 teaspoons soda
1/2 teaspoon salt

1 egg, slightly beaten
1 teaspoon vanilla
1 16- to 17-ounce can fruit cocktail
   (use juice also)

Sift flour, sugar, soda, and salt in mixing bowl. Add egg, vanilla, and fruit cocktail; mix well. Bake in 9"x11" greased pan at 350° for 30-40 minutes.

Frosting:
3/4 cup evaporated milk
1/2 cup margarine

1 cup white sugar
1 cup flaked coconut

Cook milk, margarine, and sugar to full boil, about five minutes, stirring constantly. Cool. Add flaked coconut. Frost cake. Serves 12.

—Opal Honaker

Rhubarb Cake

1 cup sugar	3 cups rhubarb
1 3-ounce package strawberry	1 package mini-marshmallows
gelatin	1 18½-ounce cake mix

Mix sugar with gelatin; sprinkle over rhubarb in 9"x13" pan. Sprinkle with marshmallows; then pour in cake batter made according to directions. Bake 1 hour at 350°.

—Opal Honaker

Fruit Cake

1 pound butter	1 pound red candied cherries
2½ cups sugar	1 pound green candied cherries
1 dozen eggs	1 pound candied pineapple
5 cups flour	2 pounds raisins—1 dark, 1 golden
1 heaping teaspoon cinnamon	1 pound pecans
1 teaspoon cream of tartar	3 tablespoons vanilla

Beat butter, sugar, and eggs, until creamy. Add dry ingredients. Cut up fruits, nuts, and raisins. Add to batter; add vanilla. Grease two 10-inch tube pans. Line sides and bottom with wax paper, then grease wax paper. Put batter in pans and cover top of pan with aluminum foil. Put two inches of boiling water in pressure cooker. Put rack in cooker to set cakes on. Steam in pressure cooker for three hours. Check water after each hour of cooking time so you will maintain two inches of water in cooker. Bake cakes at 250° for 15 or 20 minutes. Yields two 5-pound cakes.　　　—Louise White

White Fruit Cake

4 cups sifted flour	½ pound red candied cherries
2 teaspoons baking powder	1 cup butter
½ teaspoon salt	2 cups sugar
2 cups seedless raisins	6 eggs, well beaten
1 pound mixed fruit	1 cup orange juice
½ pound chopped almonds	1 teaspoon orange or lemon extract

Mix and sift flour, baking powder, and salt; add fruits and nuts. Cream shortening; add sugar slowly and cream until fluffy. Stir in well beaten eggs. Add fruit and flour mixture alternately with fruit juice, stirring well after each addition. Add flavoring. Bake in a greased and floured 9-inch tube cake pan in a 300° oven for 2½-4 hours or till done. One half-hour before cake is done, remove from oven and decorate with cherries and almonds. Return to oven to finish baking.　　　—Gladys Joyce

Orange Slice Fruit Cake

2 cups sugar
1 cup butter or other shortening
4 eggs
1 pound orange slices, cut fine
1 cup flour

1⅓ cups buttermilk
2½ cups flour
1 teaspoon soda
1 8-ounce package dates, cut fine
1 cup pecans, chopped

Cream butter and sugar. Add eggs and mix well. Dredge orange slices with 1 cup flour and add to creamed mixture. Combine flour, buttermilk, soda, dates, and pecans and add. Mix well. Bake in 300° oven for 1½ hours in a tube pan. Serves 12.　　　　　　　　　　　　　—Opal Honaker

Easy Fruit Cake

2½ cups flour
1 teaspoon soda
2 eggs, slightly beaten
1 can sweetened condensed milk

2⅔ cups ready-to-use mincemeat
2 cups mixed candied fruit
1 cup coarsely chopped walnuts

Grease 9-inch tube pan; line with wax paper. Butter again. Sift together flour and soda; set aside. In large bowl combine eggs, sweetened condensed milk, mincemeat, fruits, and nuts. Mix well. Fold in sifted dry ingredients. Turn into prepared pan. Bake in a 300° oven for 2 hours or until center springs back when lightly touched with finger and top is golden brown. Cool in pan for five minutes. Turn out of pan; remove paper. Cool. Decorate with candied fruits and walnut halves.　　　　　　　　　　—Wilma Matney

Apple Swirl Cake

1 18½-ounce yellow cake mix
¼ cup sugar
2 teaspoons cinnamon

1⅔ cups applesauce
3 eggs

Blend sugar and cinnamon. Grease 10-inch Bundt or tube pan and dust with about 1 tablespoon of sugar-cinnamon mixture; save remainder for cake. Blend cake mix, applesauce, and eggs until moistened. Beat as directed on package. Reserve 1½ cups batter. Pour remaining batter into pan. Sprinkle with remaining sugar-cinnamon mixture; then top with reserved batter. Bake at 350° for 35-45 minutes, or until done. Cool cake in pan, top-side up, for 15 minutes, then invert on serving plate.　　　　—Gladys Joyce

The yolks of eggs, left over when baking requires the whites only, if dropped into a pan of boiling and salted water, will cook and be ready for your noon salad.

Fresh Apple Cake I

6 medium-size firm apples, peeled
   and sliced

2 teaspoons cinnamon
2 tablespoons sugar

Mix the above and set aside until the following is mixed.

3 cups sugar
1 cup oil
4½ cups flour
3 teaspoons vanilla

6 eggs
3 teaspoons baking powder
¾ teaspoon salt

Mix and beat as well as possible with a spoon. The batter will be stiff. Put in 10-inch tube pan a layer of batter, then a layer of apples, alternately, until all ingredients are used. Bake at 350° for 1½ hours.

—Wilma Matney

Fresh Apple Cake II

1½ cups oil
3 eggs
2 cups sugar
2 cups flour
1 teaspoon salt

1 teaspoon soda
1 teaspoon vanilla
3 cups diced raw apples
1 cup raisins
1 cup chopped walnuts

Dust apples, raisins, and nuts with some of the flour; set aside. Blend oil, sugar, and slightly beaten eggs. Sift together remaining flour, salt, and soda; add to egg mixture. Fold in coated apples, nuts, and raisins. Turn into 10-inch greased tube pan and bake in 325° oven for 1 hour and 15 minutes.

Sauce for Cake:

½ cup buttermilk
½ cup margarine
1 cup sugar

1 teaspoon vanilla
½ teaspoon soda

Combine buttermilk, margarine, sugar, vanilla, and soda; boil rapidly for 2 minutes, stirring constantly. Pour over cake in pan while the cake is still hot. Leave in pan for several hours before removing.

—Gladys Joyce

Tinted coconut makes a child's cake more festive. Fill a pint jar a third to half full of coconut. Add a few drops of cake coloring to 1-2 tablespoons water, and add to coconut; cover jar, and shake well to distribute color evenly.

Apple Cake

6 medium-tart apples, pared and sliced	4 eggs
2 teaspoons cinnamon	2 teaspoons baking powder
2 cups + 2 teaspoons sugar	1/2 teaspoon salt
1 cup salad oil	2 teaspoons vanilla
3 cups flour	1 tablespoon orange juice
	1 cup confectioners' sugar

Fold in cinnamon, 2 teaspoons sugar, and apples. Set aside. Mix together remainder of sugar, oil, flour, eggs, baking powder, salt, and vanilla. Beat well.

Line 9-inch tube pan with wax paper, and grease well. Spoon a layer of batter on the bottom, then a layer of apples. Repeat until all of batter is used. End with apples on top.

Bake at 350° for 1½ hours. When cake is done, mix orange juice and confectioners' sugar. Pour over cake. —Thelma Joyce

Apple Dapple Cake

1½ cups oil	1 teaspoon soda
2 cups sugar	2 teaspoons vanilla
3 eggs	3 cups Golden Apples, chopped
3 cups flour	1 cup nuts
1 teaspoon salt	

Beat eggs, sugar, and oil together; add sifted dry ingredients. Add vanilla, nuts, and apples. Mix well. Bake in 9"x13" pan at 350° for 1 hour and 15 minutes.

Icing:

Mix together ½ cup margarine, 1 cup brown sugar, and ¼ cup milk. Place in saucepan on medium heat. When it comes to a boil, cook for 3 minutes. Remove from heat, cool, then pour on cake.

—Teresa Adkins

Virginia Tatum's Applesauce Cake

2½ cups applesauce	1 teaspoon nutmeg
4 teaspoons soda	1 teaspoon allspice
2 cups brown sugar	1 teaspoon cinnamon
1 cup margarine	1 cup raisins
4 cups flour	½ pound chopped dates
1/8 teaspoon salt	½ cup walnuts

Warm applesauce and add soda; then set aside and let cool. Cream margarine and sugar until creamy. Add applesauce-soda mixture. Add flour, spices, and salt. Mix well. Fold in nuts, dates, and raisins. Grease and flour 10-inch tube pan. Pour in mixture. Bake in 350° oven for 1 hour.

—Donna Davis

Old-Time Applesauce Cake

1 quart applesauce, unsweetened
1 cup shortening
2 cups sugar
4 cups flour
3 teaspoons soda
1 teaspoon allspice
1 teaspoon cinnamon

1 teaspoon cloves
1 teaspoon ginger
1 teaspoon nutmeg
1 egg
1/8 teaspoon salt
1 box raisins
1 cup nuts, chopped

Sift together flour, soda, salt, and spices. Add nuts and raisins to flour mixture, making sure each piece is coated with flour. Cream butter and sugar. Add egg to this mixture; add applesauce alternately with flour mixture. Bake in 10-inch tube pan that has been greased and floured. Bake at 300° for 1 hour.

—Thelma Joyce

Applesauce Cake I

1 pound brown sugar
1 cup margarine
2 eggs
2 1/2 cups applesauce
1/2 cup strawberry preserves

4 cups flour
3 teaspoons soda
1 teaspoon allspice
1 1/2 teaspoons cinnamon
1 teaspoon nutmeg

Cream sugar and margarine. Add eggs and beat well. Add applesauce and preserves. Mix soda, spices, and flour. Blend into applesauce mixture. Beat well for 3 minutes. Add raisins and nuts. Bake in 10-inch tube pan at 350° for 1 1/2 hours.

—Vera Tatum

Applesauce Cake II

1/2 cup shortening
2 cups sugar
2 eggs
1 1/2 cups applesauce
2 1/2 cups flour
2 teaspoons soda
1 teaspoon cinnamon

1 teaspoon allspice
1/4 teaspoon salt
1 teaspoon cloves
1/2 cup boiling coffee
1 cup raisins
Other fruits if desired: candied
    cherries, dates, figs

Cream shortening and sugar; add well beaten eggs, then applesauce. Sift flour once before measuring; use a little to dredge fruits and nuts. Sift remaining flour with salt and spices. Dissolve soda in boiling coffee and add alternately with flour to creamed mixture. Then add nuts and fruits. Bake in a greased 10-inch tube pan at 350° for 1 hour, or until well done.

—Evelyn Altizer

Applesauce Cake III

2 cups brown sugar
2 cups hot apples or applesauce
½ cup butter
½ cup melted lard
¼ teaspoon nutmeg
2 teaspoons soda

1 teaspoon cinnamon
½ teaspoon cloves
1 pound raisins, chopped
1 cup nuts
4½ cups flour

Cream sugar and butter. Add melted lard, then hot apples. Mix a little flour with raisins. Sift spices with flour and soda. Add to butter mixture. Mix well; then add raisins and nuts. Bake in 10-inch tube pan at 350° for 45 minutes to an hour. —Mrs. Vernie Crawford

Banana Split Cake I

2 cups graham cracker crumbs
5 tablespoons butter, melted
2 cups powdered sugar
1 teaspoon vanilla
½ cup butter
2 eggs

3 bananas
1 16-ounce can crushed pineapple
Large container non-dairy whipped
  topping
Crushed peanuts

Mix crumbs and melted butter. Press into the bottom of a 9"x13" dish. Beat powdered sugar, vanilla, and ½ cup butter together for 10 minutes; this step is important. Add eggs; continue to beat. Spread over crumb layer. Peel bananas and cut in half lengthwise. Place over creamed layer. Drain pineapple thoroughly; spoon over bananas. Cover with whipped topping; sprinkle with nuts. Chill four hours. If desired, garnish each serving with a cherry. To serve, cut into squares. Makes 20 servings. —Jamie Overbay

Banana Split Cake II

1 cup margarine, melted
2 cups graham cracker crumbs
2 egg whites
2 cups powdered sugar
1 16-ounce can crushed pineapple,
  drained

5 bananas
1 9-ounce container whipped
  topping
¼ cup pecans, chopped

Mix ½ cup margarine with graham cracker crumbs and press evenly onto bottom and sides of buttered 9"x13" pan. Combine egg whites, ½ cup of margarine, and powdered sugar. Beat 10 full minutes. Pour evenly over crust. Spread drained pineapple over egg white mixture. Split bananas lengthwise and place on pineapple. Spread whipped topping over bananas and sprinkle with chopped nuts. Refrigerate 30 minutes.

—Margaret Matney

APPALACHIAN

Banana Cake

¾ cup shortening
1½ cups sugar
2 eggs
4 medium bananas, crushed
2 cups flour

½ teaspoon salt
1 teaspoon soda
4 tablespoons buttermilk
1 teaspoon vanilla
½ cup chopped pecans

Cream shortening and sugar. Add eggs and beat well. Add bananas. Combine salt with flour; set aside. Combine soda with buttermilk; set aside. Add both mixtures alternately to the banana mixture. Add vanilla and pecans. Pour in 9"x13" baking pan and bake at 350° for 25 minutes. Top with frosting while cake is hot.

Coconut Frosting:

¾ cup brown sugar
4 tablespoons margarine
6 tablespoons milk

1 cup coconut
½ teaspoon vanilla

Mix and let come to a full boil. Pour over cake.

—Evelyn Altizer
Vera Tatum

Carrot Pineapple Cake

1½ cups flour, sifted
1 cup sugar
1 teaspoon baking powder
1 teaspoon soda
1 teaspoon cinnamon
½ teaspoon salt

⅔ cup cooking oil
2 eggs
1 cup finely shredded raw carrot
½ cup crushed pineapple with syrup
1 teaspoon vanilla

In large mixing bowl stir together dry ingredients. Add oil, eggs, carrots, pineapple, and vanilla. Mix until all ingredients are moist. Then beat with electric mixer 2 minutes at medium speed. Pour batter into greased and lightly floured 9"x9"x2" baking pan. Bake in 350° oven for 35 minutes. Cool and frost with Cream Cheese Frosting.

Cream Cheese Frosting:

1 3-ounce package cream cheese
4 tablespoons softened butter
1 teaspoon vanilla

2½ cups sifted powdered sugar
½ cup chopped pecans

Cream cheese and softened butter. Beat in vanilla and gradually add sugar. Blend well, then stir in nuts. Spread over cake. Makes nine servings.

—Evelyn Altizer

You can't lose weight by talking about it.
You have to keep your mouth shut.

Fresh Apple Nut Cake

2 eggs
1 cup cooking oil
1¾ cups sugar
2½ cups sifted self-rising flour

1 cup chopped nuts
3 cups pared chopped apples
1 teaspoon cinnamon
1 teaspoon vanilla

Cream eggs, oil, and sugar. Add flour and cinnamon, mixing well. Add nuts, apples, and vanilla. Turn batter into greased 13"x9"x2" baking dish. Bake for 1 hour and 10 minutes at 300°. Frost with Cream Cheese Icing.

—Margaret Matney

Carrot Applesauce Cake

2¾ cups flour
3 teaspoons soda
1 teaspoon salt
3 teaspoons cinnamon
1 teaspoon nutmeg
4 eggs
¾ cup oil

2 cups sugar
1 teaspoon vanilla
1 15-ounce jar applesauce (about 1⅔ cups)
3 cups shredded carrots
1 cup golden raisins
1 cup chopped walnuts, divided

In large bowl, mix flour, soda, salt, cinnamon, and nutmeg; set aside. Beat eggs. Stir in oil, sugar, and vanilla. Add applesauce and carrots; mix well. Add to flour mixture, stirring just to moisten. Fold in raisins and ½ cup walnuts. Pour into greased 12-cup tube pan (with remaining nuts sprinkled in bottom). Bake in preheated 350° oven for about 65 minutes or until done. Cool in pan on rack for 15 minutes before removing. Yields 18 servings.

—Janette Newhouse

Cherry Chocolate Cake

1 18½-ounce chocolate cake mix
3 eggs
1 21-ounce can cherry fruit filling

Combine cake mix, eggs, and cherry fruit filling. Mix until well blended. Pour into greased and floured 9"x13" pan. Bake at 350° for 35-40 minutes. Frost when cool.

Chocolate Frosting:

1 cup sugar
5 tablespoons butter
⅓ cup milk

1 6-ounce package semi-sweet chocolate pieces

In small saucepan combine sugar, butter, and milk; bring to a boil, stirring constantly, and cook 1 minute. Remove from heat; stir in chocolate pieces until melted and smooth. Spread over cake.   —Wilma Matney

Brazil Nut Cake

3 cups Brazil nuts (2 pounds)
1 pound whole pitted dates
1 cup maraschino cherries, drained
¾ cup flour
¾ cup sugar

½ teaspoon baking powder
½ teaspoon salt
3 eggs
1 teaspoon vanilla

Put dates, nuts, and cherries in a large bowl and mix. Sift dry ingredients on top. Beat eggs and vanilla in bowl and add to other ingredients. Mix well. Grease loaf pan. Line with paper. Bake at 300° for 1 hour and 45 minutes. Let cool. Turn out and peel off paper. Slice with very sharp knife.

—Margaret Matney

Carrot Cake

2 cups flour
2 cups sugar
1½ cups oil
4 eggs

2 teaspoons soda
2 teaspoons cinnamon
1 teaspoon salt
3 cups grated carrots

Mix flour, sugar, oil, eggs, soda, cinnamon, and salt well. Blend carrots in mixture. Bake in two 9-inch cake pans at 350° for 60 minutes. Spread Cream Cheese Frosting on cooled cake.

—Opal Honaker
Dora Abel

Pineapple Upside-Down Cake

½ cup brown sugar
3 tablespoons butter
1 15½-ounce can crushed pineapple,
    drained
2 cups cake flour
3 teaspoons baking powder

¼ teaspoon salt
¼ cup shortening or butter
1 cup sugar
1 egg, beaten
1 teaspoon vanilla
¾ cup milk

Sprinkle brown sugar in bottom of well greased 9"x9"x2" pan. Dot with butter. Melt mixture over very low heat. Place pineapple evenly over this mixture. Sift together flour, baking powder, and salt. Cream shortening. Add sugar gradually and beat until fluffy. Add egg and vanilla; beat well. Add flour mixture, a little at a time, alternately with milk. Pour batter over fruit. Bake 1 hour, or until light brown, at 350°. Turn upside down on serving plate at once. Makes 9 servings.

—Donna Davis

For a successful cake, measure ingredients
accurately, follow recipe without substitutions, and
use the pan size recommended.

Refrigerator Cake

1¹/₃ cups sweetened condensed milk
¹/₂ cup crushed pineapple,
  well drained

¹/₄ cup lemon juice
¹/₂ cup diced orange sections
Vanilla wafers

Blend lemon juice with milk. Fold in fruit. Line a spring form with waxed paper. Cover with a layer of wafers, then fruit mixture. Repeat until fruit mixture is used. Top with a layer of wafers. Cover and chill in refrigerator 6-8 hours. Serve with fresh fruit and whipped cream or whipped topping. Serves 6-8.

—Gladys Joyce

Fourteen Karat Cake

2 cups flour
2 teaspoons baking powder
1¹/₂ teaspoons soda
1 teaspoon salt
2 teaspoons cinnamon
2 cups sugar

1¹/₂ cups oil
4 eggs
2 cups grated raw carrots
1 8¹/₂-ounce can crushed pineapple,
  drained
¹/₂ cup chopped nuts

Sift together dry ingredients. Add sugar, oil, and eggs; mix well. Add remaining ingredients. Pour mixture into tube pan. Bake at 325° for 1 hour or until done. Top with Cream Cheese Frosting.

—Wilma Matney

Pineapple Cake

1 18¹/₂-ounce pineapple cake mix
1 3-ounce box instant pudding mix
4 eggs

³/₄ cup oil
1 10-ounce bottle lemon-lime
  beverage

Mix together cake mix, pudding mix, eggs, and oil; add beverage slowly. Bake in three 9-inch pans at 350° for 20-25 minutes.

Filling:
1¹/₂ cups white sugar
2 heaping tablespoons cornstarch
¹/₂ cup margarine

1 20-ounce can crushed pineapple
2 eggs, well beaten

Cook these ingredients until thick. Cool; spread between layers and on top of cake.

—Vernelle Herrin

Fall is the time to check your spices to see if they have lost their aroma. The spice should smell strong and clear as soon as you open the container. If it doesn't, now is the time to replace it. This is the peak time of the year for using spices, and you'll want to get the most in flavor and aroma.

APPALACHIAN

Pineapple Icebox Cake

½ cup butter
1 cup confectioners' sugar
2 eggs, well beaten
2 cups vanilla wafer crumbs

1 cup whipping cream
1 cup crushed pineapple, well
   drained
1 cup chopped pecans

Cream butter and sugar; add eggs, beat well. Spread over 1 cup of crumbs that have been placed in the bottom of a 9"x15" dish. Whip cream; add pineapple and nuts; spread over butter mixture. Top with remaining crumbs. Place in refrigerator for at least 12 hours.　　—Gladys Joyce

---

P·O·U·N·D　C·A·K·E·S

Sour Cream Pound Cake

1 cup softened butter
2¾ cups sugar
6 eggs
3 cups sifted cake flour

¼ teaspoon soda
1 cup sour cream
1 tablespoon vanilla
1 tablespoon lemon extract

Cream butter and sugar together until well blended and light and fluffy. Add eggs one at a time, beating well after each addition. Sift flour and soda together three times. Add flour mixture to sugar alternately with sour cream, beating until smooth. Blend in extracts. Pour into greased and floured 9-inch tube cake pan. Bake in preheated 350° oven for 1 hour and 20 minutes, or until done.　　—Gladys Joyce

Buttermilk Pound Cake

½ cup butter
½ cup shortening
2½ teaspoons vanilla
2 cups sugar
5 eggs

3 cups sifted flour
½ teaspoon salt
½ teaspoon baking powder
½ teaspoon soda
1 cup buttermilk

Grease and dust with flour a 10-inch tube pan. Cream butter and shortening together; add vanilla, and gradually cream in sugar. Add eggs one at a time, beating well after each addition. Sift dry ingredients together and add to creamed mixture alternately with buttermilk. Pour batter into prepared pan and bake 1¼ hours at 325°.　　—Donna Davis

Cream Cheese Pound Cake

3 cups sugar
1 8-ounce package cream cheese
1/2 cup butter
1 cup margarine

6 eggs
1/4 teaspoon salt
1 tablespoon lemon extract
3 cups flour

Cream shortening, salt, cheese, and sugar. Add eggs and flour alternately. Add flavoring. Bake in a well greased and floured 10-inch tube or Bundt pan. Start in a cold oven and bake 1 1/2 hours at 325°. Do not open the oven door while the cake is baking. Cool in pan for 10 minutes. Makes 20 servings.

—Louise Freedman
Margaret Matney

Butternut Pound Cake

1 cup shortening
2 cups sugar
4 eggs
2 tablespoons butternut flavoring

2 cups flour
1/2 cup self-rising flour
1 cup milk

In large mixer bowl cream shortening and sugar. Add eggs and beat on low speed for 10 minutes. Add sifted flour alternately with milk; add flavoring, and mix well. Pour into a well-greased and floured 10-inch tube pan. Bake in preheated 325° oven for 1 hour.

—Mattie Stilwell
Evelyn Wyatt

Icing for Butternut Pound Cake:
1 box powdered sugar
1 egg, whole

1/2 cup margarine
1 tablespoon butternut flavoring

Combine ingredients, using half the sugar, and stir until smooth. Add rest of sugar gradually; stir until smooth.

—Evelyn Wyatt

Coconut Pound Cake

1 cup butter
1/2 cup shortening
3 cups sugar
6 eggs
1/2 teaspoon almond flavoring

1 teaspoon coconut flavoring
3 cups flour
1 cup milk
1 3 1/2-ounce can flaked coconut

Cream shortening, butter, and sugar until light and fluffy. Add eggs, one at a time, beating well after each addition. Add flavoring and mix well. Alternately add flour and milk, beating after each addition. Stir in coconut. Spoon into 10-inch greased tube pan. Bake at 350° for 1 hour and 15 minutes.

—Evelyn Altizer

APPALACHIAN

Cold Oven Pound Cake

1 cup butter
3 cups sugar
½ cup shortening
5 eggs
1 teaspoon salt

3 cups flour
1 cup milk
½ cup cocoa
½ teaspoon baking powder
1 teaspoon vanilla

Cream butter, sugar, and shortening together. Add one egg at a time until all five eggs have been added. Combine flour, salt, baking powder, and cocoa and add alternately with milk. Add vanilla. Pour into large tube pan. Bake at 325° for 1½ hours.

Do not turn oven on until cake has been mixed.

—Margaret Matney

Never-Fail Pound Cake

1½ cups margarine
3 cups sugar
5 large eggs, beaten
3 cups flour

1 cup milk
2 teaspoons lemon extract
1 4-ounce package coconut

Cream margarine and sugar. Add eggs and beat well. Add flour and milk alternately. Fold in extract and coconut. Pour into large tube pan and bake at 300° for 1½ hours.

—Margaret Matney

Brown Sugar Pound Cake

1 cup shortening
½ cup margarine
1 pound brown sugar
1 cup white sugar
5 eggs

3½ cups flour
½ teaspoon baking powder
½ teaspoon salt
1 cup milk
2 teaspoons maple flavoring

Cream shortening, margarine, brown sugar, and white sugar; add eggs, one at a time. Sift flour, baking powder, and salt. Add alternately with milk and flavoring. Bake in 10-inch tube cake pan at 350° for 1½ hours. Serves 18.

—Opal Honaker

... The tree and I abide. Our birds can go
And come, and all that we can do is hold
Our arms out wide to mark a place they know
Whenever they want shelter from the cold.

—"Welcome" by Cecil Mullins

Frostings & Sauces

Honey Cream Cheese Frosting

2 tablespoons butter or margarine,
  softened
1 3-ounce package cream cheese,
  softened

½ cup confectioners' sugar
3 tablespoons honey
Dash salt

In small bowl with electric mixer at medium speed, blend butter, cream cheese, confectioners' sugar, honey, and salt. Use to frost 9-inch square or round cake or cupcakes. Makes 1 cup. —Donna Davis

Economical Frosting

¼ cup flour
1 cup milk
1 stick margarine

½ cup shortening
1 cup powdered sugar
2 teaspoons vanilla

Cook flour and milk until very thick; cool. Cream together margarine, shortening, sugar, and vanilla. Beat all together until smooth and well blended. This is like whipped cream in flavor. Very good!
—Opal Honaker

Vanilla Frosting

¼ cup shortening
½ teaspoon salt
2 teaspoons vanilla

3 cups confectioners' sugar (sift if
  lumpy)
¼ cup milk

In a bowl mix shortening, salt, vanilla, and about one-third of the sugar. Add milk and remaining sugar alternately. Mix until smooth and creamy. Add more sugar to thicken or milk to thin frosting if needed for good consistency. —Gladys Joyce

Snow White Frosting

2 cups sugar
1 cup water
1 teaspoon vinegar

⅛ teaspoon salt
3 egg whites
½ teaspoon vanilla

Boil sugar, water, vinegar, and salt, stirring until clear. Without stirring, cook until mixture forms a thin thread when dropped from spoon (242°). Beat until stiff 3 egg whites. Add hot syrup, beating constantly until frosting holds its shape. Add ½ teaspoon vanilla. Spread between layers.
—Gladys Joyce

APPALACHIAN

White Fluffy Icing

1 cup light corn syrup
2 egg whites

2 tablespoons white sugar

Bring corn syrup to boil on medium heat. Remove from heat and cool 1 minute. Place in bowl 2 egg whites. Beat until foamy. Gradually add 2 tablespoons sugar; beat until stiff peaks form. Pour hot syrup into egg whites gradually. Beat until stiff enough to spread. —Evelyn Wyatt

White Cloud Icing

1½ cups sugar
⅓ cup water
¼ teaspoon cream of tartar

Dash salt
3 egg whites
1 teaspoon vanilla

Combine sugar, water, cream of tartar, and salt in a saucepan. Cook covered for 3 minutes. Remove cover and boil to a soft ball stage (242°). Beat egg whites until stiff but not dry. Slowly add hot syrup to egg whites, beating all the time. Add vanilla and beat until mixture will hold straight peaks. —Donna Davis

Hot Milk Icing

2 cups sifted confectioners' sugar
¼ cup hot milk

2 tablespoons melted butter or margarine
½ teaspoon vanilla

Combine all ingredients and spread over warm cake.

—Donna Davis

Mocha Butter Frosting

1 pound unsifted confectioners' sugar
¼ cup cocoa
⅛ teaspoon salt

¼ cup butter or margarine
¼ cup vegetable shortening
⅓ cup (about) cold brewed coffee
½ teaspoon vanilla

Sift sugar with cocoa and salt. Cream butter and shortening. Gradually add part of sugar mixture, blending after each addition until light and fluffy. Add remaining sugar alternately with coffee until of right consistency to spread, beating after each addition until smooth. Blend in vanilla. Makes about 3 cups. —Gladys Joyce

Hot Fudge Sauce

⅔ cup evaporated milk
1 cup semi-sweet chocolate pieces

Combine evaporated milk and chocolate pieces in top of double boiler. Cook over hot water until chocolate is melted. Serve hot. Makes about 1 cup.
—Donna Davis

Chocolate Frosting

1/4 cup shortening, melted
1/2 cup cocoa
1/4 teaspoon salt
1/3 cup milk

1 1/2 teaspoons vanilla
3 1/2 cups confectioners' sugar (sift if lumpy)

In a saucepan, melt shortening. Remove from heat after melting and add cocoa and salt. Stir in milk and vanilla. Put all sugar in a bowl. Add chocolate mixture to sugar. Mix at medium speed until smooth and creamy. Add 1 tablespoon more milk, if needed for good spreading consistency. Frosts two 8- or 9-inch layers or a 13"x9" cake.   —Gladys Joyce

Magic Chocolate Frosting

1 can sweetened condensed milk
1 tablespoon water
1/8 teaspoon salt

2 1-ounce squares unsweetened chocolate
1/2 teaspoon vanilla

In top of double boiler, combine sweetened condensed milk, water, salt, and chocolate. Cook over hot water; stir frequently until thickened. Remove from heat. Cool. Stir in vanilla. Spread on cooled cake.
                                        —Wilma Matney

Easy Fudge Icing

2 1-ounce squares unsweetened chocolate
3 tablespoons shortening
5 tablespoons milk

2 cups sifted confectioners' sugar
1/4 teaspoon salt
1 teaspoon vanilla

Melt chocolate and shortening in milk; blend in confectioners' sugar, salt, and vanilla. Stir until thick enough to spread. If necessary to thicken, stir over ice water; to thin, stir over hot water. Makes frosting for 9-inch layer cake.   —Wilma Matney

Chocolate-Cheese Frosting

1 3-ounce package cream cheese, softened
1/4 cup soft butter or margarine
3 1/4 cups confectioners' sugar
Dash of salt

2 1-ounce squares unsweetened chocolate, melted
2-3 tablespoons milk
1/2 teaspoon vanilla

Blend cream cheese and butter. Stir in sugar, salt, melted chocolate, 2 tablespoons milk, and vanilla. Add just enough additional milk to make a spreading consistency. Frost tops and sides of cake. Yields frosting for one 8-inch square or round cake.   —Wilma Matney

Easy Caramel Frosting

1 cup brown sugar, firmly packed
Pinch of salt
5 tablespoons milk or cream

1 tablespoon butter
1 teaspoon vanilla
1 pound powdered sugar

In saucepan, mix brown sugar, salt, cream, and butter. Heat to boiling, stirring constantly. Cool and stir in vanilla. Add powdered sugar, a little at a time. Beat until smooth and creamy. If mixture seems too firm, add additional cream.
—Wilma Matney

Caramel Butter Frosting

½ cup butter
1 cup brown sugar

¼ cup milk
3¼ cups confectioners' sugar, sifted

Melt butter in saucepan; add brown sugar. Bring to a boil; stir 1 minute or until slightly thick. Cool slightly. Add ¼ cup milk; beat smooth. Beat in confectioners' sugar until of spreading consistency. Makes enough to frost two 8-inch layers.
—Donna Davis

Lemon Sauce

2 tablespoons cornstarch
1 cup sugar
2 teaspoons grated lemon peel
2 cups water

¼ cup lemon juice
¼ cup butter
¼ teaspoon salt

Combine cornstarch, sugar, and lemon peel in one-quart saucepan. Add water slowly. Stir over medium heat until thickened. Remove from heat; add remaining ingredients. Makes about 3 cups.
—Donna Davis

Lemon Butter Sauce

1 cup sugar
¼ cup butter
3 egg yolks

¼ cup boiling water
¾ tablespoon fresh lemon juice

Add sugar to melted butter in top of double boiler. Beat in one egg yolk at a time until completely blended. Add boiling water and cook over low heat until sauce thickens. Add lemon juice and mix well.
—Gladys Joyce

Use baking soda on a damp cloth
to shine up your kitchen appliances.

~ MEASURING METHODS ~

Dry Ingredients: Use a measure holding exactly one cup when top-leveled with a straight knife or spatula. For part-cup amounts, use measuring sets having $1/4$-, $1/3$-, or $1/2$-cup capacities.

Liquids: Use graduated glass measure for full measure without overflow. The transparency lets you see when the liquid reaches the right mark.

Baking Pans: Baking-pan capacity should be correct in relation to the amount of batter. Use pan size suggested in recipe. To measure pans with sloping sides, hold ruler across the top from inside rim to inside rim. Measure straight-sided pans across the bottom.

Flour: Sift flour (except whole wheat or rye) before measuring. Spoon lightly into measuring cup until heaping; level with edge of spatula.

Sugars: Brown sugar should be packed firmly enough to retain shape of cup when turned out. Granulated sugar may be piled in a measuring cup and leveled.

Hints From Our Cooks II

Use the water-displacement method for measuring shortening if the water that clings to the shortening will not affect the product. Do not use this method for measuring shortening for frying. To measure $1/4$ cup shortening using this method, put $3/4$ cup water in a measuring cup; add shortening until the water reaches the 1-cup level. Be sure that the shortening is completely covered with water. Drain off the water before using shortening.

Use shiny cookie sheets and cakepans for baking rather than darkened ones. Dark pans absorb more heat and cause baked products to overbrown.

When baking a layer cake, don't let pans touch each other or sides of oven; stagger their placement so that heat can circulate evenly around pans.

Confections

... She and I took physics together, too.
   She would whisper "I love you"
   down a tube and I would time how long it took
   the words to reach my ear.

... We grew up.
   Now I can't even remember her name.
   —"When I Took High-School Chemistry" by Preston Newman

Confections

— CANDY & FROSTING CHART —

230 degrees - 234 degrees	Thread
234 degrees - 240 degrees	Soft Ball
244 degrees - 248 degrees	Firm Ball
250 degrees - 266 degrees	Hard Ball
270 degrees - 290 degrees	Soft Crack
300 degrees - 310 degrees	Hard Crack

Sweetened Condensed Milk

1 cup instant nonfat dry milk solids
²/₃ cup sugar

¹/₃ cup boiling water
3 tablespoons melted margarine

Combine all ingredients in container of blender; process until smooth. Store in refrigerator until ready to use. Makes about 1¼ cups or 14 ounces.

—Margaret Matney
Opal Honaker

Fudge Truffles

1 12-ounce package semi-sweet
  chocolate pieces
³/₄ cup sweetened condensed milk

Pinch salt
1 cup chopped walnuts
1 teaspoon vanilla

Melt chocolate on lowest heat. Stir in condensed milk, salt, chopped nuts, and vanilla. Pour into waxed paper-lined 9"x5"x3" loaf pan. Cool for a few hours. When firm, cut into squares. Makes 1¼ pounds.

—Margaret Matney

Pralines

4³/₄ cups sugar
4 cups pecans, broken in large pieces
2 cups water

¹/₈ teaspoon salt
2 tablespoons butter

Put 4 cups sugar, pecans, water, and salt in a pan and bring to a boil; meanwhile, melt ¾ cup sugar in an iron skillet and let it brown slightly but not scorch. When it is caramel-colored, pour it into first mixture. Cook until it forms a firm ball when dropped in cold water. Put wax paper over newspaper laid out on a flat surface or table. Add butter; beat until it cools a little. Then drop by spoonfuls any size desired on the wax paper. When cool and hard, pralines will easily lift from paper. —Marilyn Wells

Fudge

5 cups white sugar
2 sticks margarine
1 13-ounce can evaporated milk
3 6-ounce packages chocolate chips

1½ cups peanut butter (crunchy or
  smooth)   .
1 cup nuts (if desired)
1 tablespoon vanilla

Combine first three ingredients and let come to a boil. Boil 8 minutes, stirring constantly. Add rest of ingredients; stir well. Pour into buttered 9"x13"x2" pan. Cool. Cut into squares.　　　　　—Dorothy Tatum

White Chocolate Fudge

2 cups sugar
⅔ cup milk
½ cup margarine
12 large marshmallows

1 cup crushed white chocolate
½ cup chopped nuts
1 teaspoon vanilla

Combine and bring to a full bubbly boil: sugar, milk, margarine, and marshmallows, stirring constantly. Start timing and boil and stir for five minutes. Remove and stir in chocolate, nuts, and vanilla. When chocolate is completely melted and mixed well, pour into a 9-inch buttered dish. It hardens as it cools.　　　　　—Margaret Matney

Peanut Butter Fudge I

2 cups sugar
¾ cup milk
2 tablespoons butter

½ teaspoon salt
4 tablespoons peanut butter
1 teaspoon vanilla

Cook sugar, milk, and butter together until they reach the soft ball stage; add vanilla, salt, and peanut butter; beat. Pour into 8-inch square buttered pan and cool.　　　　　—Donna Davis
　　　　　Helen Steele

Peanut Butter Fudge II

1 cup brown sugar
1 cup sugar
½ cup cream

2 tablespoons white corn syrup
2 tablespoons butter
½ cup peanut butter

Add sugars, cream, syrup; bring to a boil. Add butter; cook to soft ball stage. Remove from heat; add peanut butter and beat until creamy.
　　　　　—Jennie Tatum

Creamy Peanut Butter Fudge

2 cups sugar
1 cup packed light brown sugar
1 cup heavy cream
3 tablespoons light corn syrup

¼ teaspoon salt
⅓ cup creamy peanut butter
1½ teaspoons vanilla
nuts (optional)

In large heavy saucepan mix sugar, cream, corn syrup, and salt. Bring to boil over medium heat, stirring to dissolve sugars. Set candy thermometer in pan and cook syrup without stirring to 254° (soft ball stage). Cool to 110° (lukewarm). Add peanut butter and vanilla; beat until mixture thickens and begins to lose its gloss. Pour into greased 8"x8"x2" pan. When firm, cut in small squares. Decorate each square with chopped nuts. Store airtight in cool dry place. Makes 2½ pounds.　　　　　　　　　　　—Evelyn Altizer

Easy Peanut Butter Chocolate Fudge

1 12-ounce package peanut butter-
　flavored chips
1 14-ounce can sweetened
　condensed milk (not evaporated)

¼ cup butter
½ cup chopped peanuts (optional)
1 6-ounce package semi-sweet
　chocolate morsels

In large saucepan, melt peanut butter chips, 1 cup sweetened condensed milk, and 2 tablespoons butter; stir occasionally. Remove from heat, stir in peanuts. Spread mixture into wax paper-lined 8-inch square pan. In small saucepan, melt chocolate morsels, remaining sweetened condensed milk, and butter. Spread chocolate mixture on top of peanut butter mix. Chill 2 hours or until firm. Turn fudge onto cutting board; peel off paper, and cut into squares. Tightly cover any leftovers.　　　　　　　—Gladys Joyce

Two-Flavor Fudge

2 cups brown sugar, firmly packed
1 cup sugar
1 cup evaporated milk
½ cup margarine
1 10-ounce jar marshmallow creme

1 6-ounce package butterscotch
　morsels
1 6-ounce package chocolate morsels
1 cup walnuts, chopped
1 teaspoon vanilla

Combine the two sugars, milk, and margarine. Bring to full boil over moderate heat, stirring frequently. Boil for 15 minutes. Remove from heat and add marshmallow creme, butterscotch and chocolate morsels. Stir till melted and smooth. Blend in walnuts and vanilla. Pour into greased 9-inch square pan. Chill.　　　　　　　　　　—Margaret Matney

The top drawer in a kitchen cabinet can make an extra "shelf" to use while cooking. Open the drawer, and place across it a large tray or a cookie sheet.

Chocolate Fudge

4½ cups sugar
1 13-ounce can evaporated milk
1 cup margarine
1 8-ounce jar marshmallow creme

2 6-ounce packages semi-sweet
  chocolate chips
Pinch salt
1 cup nuts (if desired)

Cook together sugar, milk, margarine, and salt. Bring to a boil and cook 10-12 minutes, stirring constantly. Add chips and creme. Pour in greased pan after beating until smooth. —Teresa Adkins

Favorite Cocoa Fudge

⅔ cup cocoa
3 cups sugar
⅛ teaspoon salt

1½ cups milk
¼ cup butter
1 teaspoon vanilla

Combine the first three ingredients with milk. Bring to a bubbly boil on high heat, stirring continuously. Turn heat down to medium and continue to boil without stirring, until it reaches the soft ball stage (approximately 1 hour). Remove saucepan from heat; add butter and vanilla. Set saucepan in cold water to hasten cooling. Beat until fudge thickens and loses some of its gloss. Quickly pour and spread fudge in lightly greased 8"x8"x2" pan. Cool; cut into squares. —Wilma Matney

Fudge Candy

2 cups sugar
4 tablespoons cocoa
½ cup milk

⅓ cup white syrup
2 tablespoons butter
1 teaspoon vanilla

Cook first five ingredients until they form a soft ball in water. Take off and add vanilla. Let stand 10 minutes and beat and pour into buttered dish. When set cut into blocks. —Dora Abel

Festive Fudge

2 cups sugar
⅔ cup evaporated skimmed milk
12 regular marshmallows
½ cup margarine

Few grains salt
1 cup semi-sweet chocolate pieces
1 cup cut-up nuts
1 teaspoon vanilla

Cook in heavy pan sugar, milk, marhsmallows, margarine, and salt, stirring constantly over medium heat to boil. Boil and stir 5 minutes more. Take off heat. Stir in chocolate pieces until melted. Stir in nuts and vanilla. Spread in a buttered 8-inch square pan. Cool. —Margaret Matney

Homemade Fudge with Marshmallow Creme

3 cups sugar
¾ cup margarine
⅔ cup evaporated milk
1 12-ounce package semi-sweet
chocolate pieces

1 7-ounce jar marshmallow creme
1 cup chopped nuts
1 teaspoon vanilla

Combine sugar, margarine, and milk in heavy 2½-quart saucepan. Bring to a full rolling boil, stirring constantly. Continue boiling 5 minutes over medium heat, stirring constantly to prevent scorching. Remove from heat. Stir in chocolate pieces until melted. Add marshmallow creme, nuts, and vanilla; beat until well blended. Pour into greased 13"x9" pan. Cool at room temperature, cut into squares. Makes 3 pounds.

—Gladys Joyce

Fabulous Fudge

2¼ cups sugar
¼ cup margarine
16 large marshmallows or 1 cup
marshmallow creme
¼ teaspoon salt

1 cup evaporated milk
1 teaspoon vanilla
1 cup semi-sweet chocolate chips
1 cup chopped nuts
30 nut halves

Mix first five ingredients in heavy 3-quart saucepan. Stir over medium heat until mixture boils and is bubbly all over top. Boil and stir over medium heat 5 minutes. Remove from heat. Stir in vanilla and chocolate chips until melted. Stir in nuts. Spread in buttered 9-inch square dish. Press nut halves on top. Cool. Cut into about 30 pieces.

—Margaret Matney

Peanut Butter Roll

4 cups sugar
1 cup light corn syrup
1 cup hot water

3 egg whites
1 teaspoon vanilla
Peanut butter

Pour hot water over 3 cups sugar and syrup; boil until mixture spins a thread from spoon.

Mix 1 cup sugar and 1 cup water; boil until it forms a hard ball in water.

Beat egg whites until stiff; add first syrup and beat. Add second syrup and beat.

Add vanilla and continue beating until stiff enough to roll. Sprinkle with flour and flatten on floured board until about ¼" in thickness. Spread with peanut butter and roll up. Put aside to harden and slice.

—Thelma Joyce

Uncooked Peanut Butter Roll

4 tablespoons margarine, melted
1 egg white, slightly beaten
Dash salt
1 teaspoon vanilla

1 pound confectioners' sugar
  (approximately)
Peanut butter

Mix margarine, egg white, salt, and vanilla. Add sugar and work until mixture becomes stiff like dough.

Spread dough between wax paper. Sprinkle confectioners' sugar on wax paper to keep from sticking. Roll to about ⅛" thick. Spread with peanut butter. Roll up from one side. Wrap in wax paper. Refrigerate until stiff. Cut into slices.

—Margaret Matney

Peanut Butter Cups

1 pound margarine
2 cups peanut butter
2½-3 pounds confectioners' sugar
3 tablespoons vanilla

1 6-ounce package semi-sweet
  chocolate chips
¼ pound paraffin

Cream margarine and peanut butter. Add sugar until the consistency to form into balls the size of large marbles. Add vanilla. Mix thoroughly; this is best done with hands. Melt chocolate chips and paraffin in a small double boiler. Dip balls in the chocolate, using a toothpick to dip with, and place on wax paper to cool. This candy will freeze well. Yields 125 pieces.

—Dorothy Tatum

Sea Foam Candy

2 cups brown sugar
½ cup water
1 stiffly beaten egg white

½ cup nuts
1 teaspoon vanilla

Boil sugar and water together until soft ball stage—238°. Pour hot mixture over beaten egg white, beating while pouring. Add ½ cup nuts and 1 teaspoon vanilla. Beat vigorously until candy stiffens. When nearly set, drop by spoonfuls onto paper.

—Gladys Joyce

Dropped Penuche

1 cup brown sugar
2 cups white sugar
1 cup cream
⅔ cup light corn syrup

Pinch salt
1 tablespoon butter
1 teaspoon vanilla

Boil until soft ball forms—240°. Let sit until cool. Beat until creamy. Drop on wax paper. Put half of a nut on top of each piece.

—Jennie Tatum

APPALACHIAN

Broken Glass Candy

2 cups sugar
1 cup water
¾ cup white syrup

Food Coloring & Flavoring as follows:
Red—Cinnamon   Orange—Orange
Green—Wintergreen   Yellow—Lemon
Clear—Peppermint

Mix first three ingredients and boil to 300°. Remove from heat and add ½ teaspoon flavoring and a few drops of color. Mix well and quickly. Pour on marble slab and let set a minute. Cut with pizza cutter in about 1-inch squares. When set, break into pieces.   —Thelma Joyce

Strawberry Divinity

3 cups sugar
¾ cup light corn syrup
¾ cup water

2 egg whites, stiffly beaten
1 3-ounce package strawberry gelatin
1 cup chopped nuts

Combine sugar, syrup and water. Bring to boil stirring constantly. Cook to 252°. Combine gelatin with egg whites gradually. Beat until mixture forms peak. Pour the hot syrup in a thin stream into egg whites, beating until candy loses gloss and holds shape. Fold in nuts. Drop onto waxed paper with teaspoon. May put a nut on top.

Other flavors of gelatin may be used.   —Gladys Joyce

Pecan Turtles

2 cups pecan halves
36 individually wrapped caramels
3 tablespoons margarine

½ teaspoon vanilla
⅔ cup semi-sweet chocolate chips
1½ teaspoons shortening

Cover baking sheet with waxed paper. Arrange pecan halves in clusters spread 1 inch apart.

Place caramels in top of double boiler with butter. Set over boiling water and heat until caramels are completely melted. Remove from heat and stir until butter and vanilla are completely mixed with caramels. Drop by teaspoonfuls onto center of each pecan cluster, making sure caramel touches each pecan piece to hold them together. Allow to cool.

Melt chocolate with shortening over hot (not boiling) water. Spread over caramel on cluster and allow to set before removing from waxed paper.
—Teresa Adkins

Date Confection

1 cup flour
¼ cup butter
1 egg white, unbeaten
1 3-ounce package cream cheese

1 pound pitted dates
1 cup walnuts (chopped)
½ cup sugar

Mix flour, butter, and softened cream cheese into a pastry. Wrap pitted dates with pastry. Dip each wrapped date in unbeaten egg white. Roll in ½ cup sugar and finely chopped walnuts. Bake on ungreased cookie sheet at 325° for 15 minutes.

This is a delicious tea-time confection.   —Thelma Joyce

Maple Cream Candy

½ cup margarine
1½ teaspoons water (more if needed)

1½ teaspoons maple flavoring
1 pound confectioners' sugar

Cream margarine, water, and maple flavoring well. Add confectioners' sugar. Add chopped nuts if desired. Form into balls and dip in chocolate candy coating or caramel candy coating.   —Evelyn Altizer

Caramel Candy

6 cups sugar
2 cups light syrup
1 16-ounce can evaporated milk
1 cup butter

2 teaspoons vanilla
1 cup coconut
1 cup nuts

Cook sugar, syrup, milk, and butter to hard-boil stage over low heat. Beat until stiff. Add nuts, coconut, and vanilla. Pour into greased pan. Makes 5 pounds.   —Thelma Joyce

Caramels

1 14-ounce can sweetened
    condensed milk
1 cup white syrup
2 cups brown sugar

1 cup butter
1 teaspoon vanilla
1 cup chopped pecans

Combine milk, syrup, sugar, and butter in heavy pan. Heat, stirring constantly, until mixture comes to a boil. Boil 15 minutes, stirring constantly. Remove from heat. Add vanilla and nuts. Pour into 9"x9" square dish and cool 12 hours. Cut into 1-inch squares. Wrap each piece in plastic wrap.   —Margaret Matney
                         Vera Tatum

Peanut Brittle

1 cup light corn syrup
1 cup sugar
¼ cup water

2 tablespoons margarine
1½ cups salted peanuts
1 teaspoon soda

Combine corn syrup, sugar, water, and margarine in a heavy 3-quart saucepan. Cook over medium heat, stirring constantly, until sugar is dissolved, and mixture comes to a boil. Continue cooking without stirring until temperature reaches 280°.

Gradually stir in nuts so mixture continues to boil. Cook, stirring until temperature reaches 300°. Watch and don't let it scorch. Remove from heat. Add 1 teaspoon soda; blend quickly but thoroughly. Immediately turn onto heavily greased baking sheets. Spread evenly with greased metal spatula. Cool; break into pieces. Store in airtight container.   —Margaret Matney

Frosted Strawberries

⅔ cup sweetened condensed milk
2⅔ cups flaked coconut
1 3-ounce package strawberry gelatin
½ cup ground blanched almonds
½ teaspoon almond extract

Red food coloring
1 cup sifted confectioners' sugar
2 tablespoons heavy cream
Green food coloring

In medium bowl, combine condensed milk, coconut, 3 tablespoons gelatin, almond extract, and enough red food coloring to tint mixture a strawberry shade. Form small amounts (about ½ tablespoon) into strawberry shapes. Sprinkle remaining gelatin in a flat dish, roll each strawberry to coat. Place on waxed paper; refrigerate. *To make strawberry hull:* combine sugar, cream, and green food coloring. Spoon into pastry bag with open star tip. Pipe small amount atop each strawberry.

Other fruits and vegetables may be made from the above recipe by using the appropriate color and flavor of gelatin.   —Ruth Bales

Mrs. Horton's Candy

1 cup brown sugar
2 cups sugar
1 cup cream
⅔ cup corn syrup

Pinch of salt
1 tablespoon butter
1 tablespoon vanilla

Boil first five ingredients until soft ball forms in cold water—238°. Let stand until cooler. Add butter and vanilla. Beat until creamy. Drop on waxed paper by spoonfuls. Put half of a nut on top of each drop.

—Gladys Joyce

Mints

2 cups sugar
1 cup boiling water

7 tablespoons margarine
¼ teaspoon oil of peppermint

Boil sugar, water, and margarine to 260°. Pour on ice-cold marble slab. Pull as soon as you can handle it. Add coloring and flavoring; cut into small pieces.

—Thelma Joyce

Molded Mints

2 tablespoons margarine, softened
1 large egg white, slightly beaten
1 pound confectioners' sugar, sifted

Food Coloring & Flavoring as follows:
¼ teaspoon extract of

Peppermint—Red	Strawberry—Pink
Spearmint—Green	Wintergreen—Green
Lemon—Yellow	

Blend well, adding a small amount of sugar at a time. Knead in all of sugar. Divide in half and add ¼ teaspoon extract for flavoring and a drop of coloring. Knead well, making smooth. Put each color in a bowl covered with a damp cloth. Make small balls and roll in bowl of granulated sugar. Press into mold and flip out.

—Margaret Matney

Chocolate Leaves

Paint melted semi-sweet chocolate on the backs of ivy, rose, or other small leaves; chill until hardened. Gently and quickly remove leaves from chocolate. Discard leaves.

Homemade Maple Syrup

1 cup white sugar
1 cup brown sugar
1 cup boiling water

1 teaspoon maple flavoring
1 teaspoon butter flavoring

Combine all ingredients. Stir until sugar is dissolved. Bring to a rolling boil. Cool, Serve warm.

—Teresa Adkins

APPALACHIAN

Cookies

Cinnamon Jumbles

1/2 cup shortening	2 cups flour
1 cup sugar	1/2 teaspoon soda
1 egg	1/2 teaspoon salt
3/4 cup buttermilk	1/4 cup sugar
1 teaspoon vanilla	1 teaspoon cinnamon

Mix shortening, 1 cup sugar, and egg thoroughly. Stir in buttermilk and vanilla. Blend together flour, soda, and salt; stir in. Chill dough. Shape into balls; roll in mixture of 1/4 cup sugar and cinnamon. Bake 8-10 minutes in a 375° oven. Makes 4 dozen. —Donna Davis

Gumdrop Cookies

1 cup shortening	1 teaspoon cinnamon
1 cup sugar	1 9-ounce package mincemeat
1 cup brown sugar	1 cup finely chopped walnuts
2 eggs	2/3 cup finely cut green and
2 1/2 cups sifted flour	red gumdrops
1 teaspoon salt	6 6-ounce frozen juice cans
1/2 teaspoon soda	

Cream shortening, sugar, and eggs together. Sift together dry ingredients. Dredge mincemeat, nuts, and gumdrops in 1/2 cup flour mixture. Stir remaining mixture into creamed mixture. Mix in floured gumdrops, nuts, and mincemeat. Pack firmly into six 6-ounce frozen juice cans and freeze or chill well. Cut in 1/8-inch slices. Place 3/4" apart on ungreased cooky sheet. Top each with pecan half. Bake at 375° for 6-8 minutes. Makes 7-8 dozen.
—Evelyn Altizer

Jelly Bean Cookies

1/2 cup butter	1 egg
1/3 cup sugar	1 cup jelly beans, chopped
1/3 cup brown sugar	1/2 teaspoon soda
3/4 cup flour	1 teaspoon salt
1/2 cup rolled oats	1/2 teaspoon vanilla

Cream together butter and sugar. Beat in egg, soda, salt, and vanilla. Stir in flour and oats. Add chopped jelly beans. Heat oven to 375°. Drop spoonfuls of batter about 2 inches apart on lightly greased cooky sheet. Bake 10-12 minutes or until lightly browned. Makes 3-3 1/2 dozen cookies.
—Vera Tatum

Marshmallow Treats

¼ cup margarine or butter
1 6- to 10-ounce package regular marshmallows
   or 4 cups miniature marshmallows
5 cups crisp rice cereal

Melt margarine in 3-quart saucepan. Add marshmallows and cook over low heat, stirring constantly until marshmallows are melted and mixture is very syrupy. Remove from heat. Add cereal and stir until well coated. Press warm mixture evenly and firmly into buttered 13"x9"x2" pan. Cut into squares when cool. —Gladys Joyce

Southern Cookies

1 cup brown sugar
½ teaspoon vanilla
1 egg white, beaten stiff

2 cups pecan halves
¼ teaspoon salt

Cut pecan halves into one-quarter size. Allow two pieces per cookie. Stir brown sugar into egg white. Add remaining ingredients. Drop by teaspoonful on well greased baking sheet. Bake in preheated 250° oven about 30 minutes. Check with knife to see if done.

Cool cookies on sheet, then tap table and they will slip off. Makes about 36 cookies. —Teresa Adkins

Walnut Clusters

½ cup sifted flour
¼ teaspoon baking powder
½ teaspoon salt
¼ cup soft butter
½ cup sugar

1 egg
1½ teaspoons vanilla
1½ 1-ounce squares unsweetened
   chocolate, melted
2 cups broken walnuts

Start heating oven to 350°. Sift together flour, baking powder, and salt. Mix butter and sugar until creamy. Add egg and vanilla; mix well. Mix in chocolate, then flour mixture. Fold in walnuts. Drop by teaspoonfuls, 1" apart, onto greased cookie sheet. Bake just 10 minutes, no longer. Makes 2½ dozen. —Gladys Joyce

When a recipe calls for softened butter but you have forgotten to take it out of the refrigerator in advance, measure the correct amount and shred it as you would a carrot. The small pieces will be soft enough to work with immediately.

APPALACHIAN

Tom Thumb Cookie Bars

¹/₂ cup margarine, creamed
¹/₂ cup brown sugar
1 cup sifted flour

Filling:

1 cup brown sugar
1 teaspoon vanilla
2 eggs, well beaten
2 tablespoons flour

¹/₄ teaspoon salt
¹/₂ teaspoon baking powder
1¹/₂ cups coconut
1 cup chopped nuts

Cream shortening and sugar. Add flour and blend. Spread in 9-inch square pan and bake at 325° for 5 minutes.

For filling, add sugar and vanilla to beaten eggs. Beat until foamy. Add flour, baking powder, salt, coconut, and nuts. Spread over baked mixture. Return to oven and bake at 325° for 25 minutes. Cool and cut into small rectangles.

—Evelyn Altizer
Opal Honaker

Ice Box Cookies

1 cup butter
1 cup brown sugar
1 cup sugar
3 eggs
4 cups flour

1 teaspoon soda
¹/₄ teaspoon salt
1 teaspoon cinnamon
1 cup nuts, chopped

Cream shortening and sugar; add unbeaten eggs, one at a time. Beat hard after each addition. Sift flour, soda, salt, and cinnamon together. Add nuts; mix all into a dough. Place dough on a floured board and mold into a large roll; make two rolls if necessary. Roll in wax paper; put in refrigerator overnight. Cut in thin slices and bake at 375° for about 10-12 minutes.

—Gladys Joyce

Jane's Cookies

1 cup butter
1¹/₂ cups powdered sugar, sifted
1¹/₂ cups flour, sifted

1 teaspoon vanilla
³/₄ cup nuts, finely chopped

Beat butter with ¹/₂ cup sugar until fluffy. Stir in flour, vanilla, and nuts. Form into 1-inch balls. Place on greased cookie sheet. Bake at 350° for 15 minutes. While hot, roll in rest of powdered sugar.

—Jane Smith

Slice ice-box cookie dough
with string held taut in both hands.

Butterscotch Squares

1/2 cup butter	1/2 teaspoon salt
2 cups brown sugar	2 teaspoons baking powder
2 eggs	2 teaspoons vanilla
2 cups flour	1/2 cup chopped nuts

Preheat oven to 350°. Grease 13"x9"2" pan. Melt butter in saucepan. Stir in sugar until soft; cool slightly. Add eggs and mix well. Add dry ingredients; mix. Add vanilla and nuts; mix well. Spread in pan. Bake 30 minutes. Cool; cut into squares.

—Wilma Matney

Congo Bars

1 1-pound box brown sugar	1 3/4 cups self-rising flour
3/4 cup butter	1 8-ounce box chopped dates
4 eggs	1 6-ounce package butterscotch bits

Melt butter; pour over sugar. Mix well. Add eggs and flour; beat. Fold in butterscotch bits and pour into greased 13"x9½"x2" pan. Bake at 350° for 25 minutes. Serves 25-30 people.

—Thelma Joyce

Butterscotch Refrigerator Cookies

1/2 cup butter	1 egg, well beaten
1 cup brown sugar	1½ cups sifted flour
1½ teaspoons baking powder	1/2 cup chopped nuts
1/4 teaspoon salt	1 teaspoon vanilla

Cream butter and brown sugar together until light. Stir in egg, then add sifted dry ingredients. Add nuts and vanilla and mix thoroughly. Place mixture on waxed paper and form in a roll. Roll up and seal edges. Chill for several hours, or overnight, until firm. Slice with sharp knife into thin slices about 1/8" thick. Bake on cookie sheet in 400° oven for about 8-10 minutes. Makes 5-6 dozen cookies.

—Jamie Overbay

Come, Lord Jesus, our Guest to be,
Bless these gifts bestowed by Thee,
And may there be a goodly share
On every table everywhere.

Chocolate Chip Cookies

2¼ cups flour
1 teaspoon soda
½ teaspoon salt
½ cup margarine or butter, softened
½ cup shortening
¾ cup sugar

¾ cup brown sugar
2 eggs
1 teaspoon vanilla
1 cup shredded bran cereal
1 6-ounce package semi-sweet
   chocolate morsels

Sift together flour, soda, and salt. Beat margarine, shortening, sugar, and brown sugar until well blended. Beat in eggs and vanilla. Mix dry ingredients. Stir in cereal and chocolate morsels. Drop by level measuring tablespoon onto greased baking sheet. Bake at 350° about 12 minutes or until lightly browned. Makes 5 dozen. —Gladys Joyce

Michelle's Chocolate Chip Oatmeal Cookies

1 cup butter
¾ cup brown sugar
¾ cup sugar
1½ teaspoons vanilla
2 eggs

1½ cups flour
1 teaspoon soda
1 teaspoon salt
2 cups oats
2 cups semi-sweet chocolate pieces

Beat butter, sugars, and vanilla together until creamy. Beat in eggs. Sift together flour, soda, and salt. Add to creamed mixture; beat well. Stir in oats and chocolate pieces. Drop by rounded teaspoonfuls onto lightly greased cookie sheets. Bake in preheated 375° oven for 8-10 minutes.

—Wilma Matney

Magic Cookie Bars

½ cup butter or margarine
1½ cups graham cracker crumbs
1 14-ounce can sweetened
   condensed milk

1 6-ounce package semi-sweet
   chocolate morsels
1 3½-ounce can flaked coconut
1 cup chopped nuts

Preheat oven to 350°. In 13"x9" baking pan melt butter. Sprinkle crumbs over butter. Pour sweetened condensed milk evenly over crumbs. Top evenly with remaining ingredients; press down gently. Bake 25-30 minutes or until brown. Cool thoroughly before cutting. Store loosely covered at room temperature. Makes 24 bars. —Teresa Adkins
Evelyn Altizer

Fudge Peanut Butter Bars

1 18-ounce package yellow cake mix
1 cup peanut butter

½ cup butter or margarine, melted
2 eggs

In large bowl, combine cake mix, peanut butter, margarine, and eggs. By hand, stir until dough holds together. Press two-thirds of dough into bottom of ungreased 13"x9" baking pan. Reserve remaining dough for topping. Prepare filling.

Filling:

1 cup semi-sweet chocolate pieces
1 14-ounce can sweetened
   condensed milk

2 tablespoons butter or margarine
1 box coconut pecan frosting

In saucepan, combine chocolate pieces, milk, and butter. Melt over low heat, stirring until smooth. Remove from heat; stir in dry frosting mix.

Spread filling over dough in pan. Crumble reserved dough over filling. Bake at 350° for 20-25 minutes. Cool. Cut into 36 bars.

—Vera Tatum

Cream Cheese Brownies

1 4-ounce package sweet chocolate
5 tablespoons butter, divided
1 3-ounce package cream cheese
1 cup sugar
3 eggs

½ teaspoon baking powder
¼ teaspoon salt
1½ teaspoons vanilla
¼ teaspoon almond extract
½ cup chopped nuts

Melt chocolate and 3 tablespoons butter over very low heat. Stir, then cool. To make cheese layer, cream the cream cheese with 2 tablespoons butter. Gradually add ¼ cup sugar, creaming until fluffy. Blend in 1 egg, 1 tablespoon flour, and ½ teaspoon vanilla. Set aside. To make chocolate layer, beat 2 eggs until light. Slowly add ¾ cup sugar; beat until thickened. Add baking powder, salt, and ½ cup unsifted flour. Blend in chocolate mixture, 1 teaspoon vanilla, almond extract, and nuts. To bake, spread half the chocolate batter in greased 9-inch square pan. Top with cheese mixture. Spoon remaining chocolate batter over top. Zig-zag knife through batter to marble. Bake at 350° for 35 minutes. Cool.   —Margaret Matney

How to measure sweetened condensed milk: Pour it into a measuring cup or spoon and allow the milk to level itself. If a full can of condensed milk is called for, it saves work to pour it directly from the can. Remember you must remove the whole lid, because condensed milk is too thick and creamy to pour through a hole.

Brownies

4 1-ounce squares unsweetened
    chocolate
²/₃ cup shortening or butter
2 cups sugar
4 eggs

1 teaspoon vanilla
1¼ cups flour
1 teaspoon baking powder
1 teaspoon salt
1 cup chopped nuts

Melt chocolate and shortening over low heat. Beat in sugar, eggs, and vanilla. Stir flour, baking powder, and salt together; blend in. Mix in nuts. Spread in 13"x9½"x2" pan. Bake in 350° oven for 30 minutes.

—Jennie Tatum

Crunchy Bars

½ cup margarine
1 cup brown sugar
1 egg
1 teaspoon vanilla
1¼ cups flour

½ teaspoon soda
½ teaspoon salt
1½ cups quick oats
¼ cup nuts

Combine all ingredients. Press one-third of mixture into a 7"x11"x2" pan.

Filling:

1 cup chocolate bits
1 teaspoon margarine
½ cup sweetened condensed milk

¼ teaspoon salt
1 teaspoon vanilla
½ cup nuts

Melt chocolate bits, margarine, condensed milk, and salt over low heat. Stir in vanilla and nuts. Spread over bottom layer. Cover with remaining first mixture. Bake at 350° for 30 minutes.

—Wilma Matney

Milk Chocolate Bars

¼ cup butter
1 cup sugar
1 teaspoon vanilla
2 eggs
½ cup milk

1 cup flour, sifted
2 tablespoons cocoa
¼ teaspoon salt
½ cup chopped walnuts

Cream butter and gradually add sugar. Add vanilla. Beat in eggs one at a time. Add milk; stir in dry ingredients. Spread in 9-inch square pan and bake at 375° for 20-25 minutes. Remove from oven and immediately frost.

Icing:

1½ teaspoons soft butter
1 tablespoon milk
¼ teaspoon vanilla

1½ tablespoons cocoa
²/₃ cup sifted confectioners' sugar

Blend all ingredients. Put on hot cake. Cool and cut into bars.

—Wilma Matney

Chocolate Thumbprint Cookies

½ cup butter
⅔ cup sugar
1 egg yolk
2 tablespoons milk
1 teaspoon vanilla

1 cup flour
⅓ cup cocoa
¼ teaspoon salt
Vanilla filling (below)
Sugar

Cream butter, sugar, egg yolk, milk, and vanilla. Combine flour, cocoa, and salt; blend into creamed mixture. Chill dough about one hour. Roll dough into 1-inch balls. Roll in sugar. Place on lightly greased cookie sheet. Press thumb gently into center of each cookie. Bake at 350° for 10-15 minutes. As soon as cookies are removed from oven, spoon about ¼-teaspoon filling into "thumbprint." You can also top with walnut half.

Vanilla Filling:

½ cup confectioners' sugar
1 tablespoon butter

2 teaspoons milk
¼ teaspoon vanilla

Combine thoroughly.

—Wilma Matney

Chocolate Drop Cooky

¼ cup butter
¼ cup margarine
¾ cup sugar
1 egg
2 1-ounce squares unsweetened
    chocolate, melted
1¾ cups flour

½ teaspoon soda
½ teaspoon salt
½ cup milk
1 teaspoon vanilla
½ cup chopped pecans
Pecan halves (optional)

Cream butter and margarine; add sugar gradually. Beat well and add egg. Stir in chocolate. Add the flour sifted with soda and salt alternately with the milk. Mix this and stir in vanilla and pecans. Drop cooky dough by teaspoons on ungreased baking sheet, leaving about 1″ between, as cookies will spread. Bake in 350° oven for 7-8 minutes; remove from oven at once. Makes 25-30.

Icing:

Milk or cream
2 cups powdered sugar

⅛ teaspoon salt
1 teaspoon vanilla

Mix to easy spreading consistency. Swirl 1 teaspoon on each cooky. Top each with pecan half if desired.

—Marilyn Wells

A failure is someone who can't put things over
because he's always putting things off.

Applesauce Cookies

1¾ cups sifted cake flour
1 teaspoon salt
1 teaspoon cinnamon
½ teaspoon nutmeg
½ teaspoon ground cloves
1 cup canned applesauce

1 teaspoon soda
½ cup shortening
1 cup sugar
1 egg
1 cup seedless raisins
1 cup ready-to-eat bran flakes

Start heating oven to 375°. Sift together flour, salt, cinnamon, nutmeg, and cloves. Combine applesauce and soda. Mix shortening with sugar and egg until creamy. Mix in flour mixture alternately with applesauce. Fold in raisins and bran. Drop by teaspoonfuls, about 2 inches apart, onto greased cookie sheet. Bake about 20 minutes or until brown. If desired, frost cookies with butter or cream cheese frosting. Makes 3 dozen.

—Gladys Joyce

Applesauce Refrigerator Cookies

¾ cup shortening
1 cup sugar
1 egg
2½ cups sifted flour
1 teaspoon soda

¼ teaspoon salt
½ teaspoon cinnamon
¼ teaspoon cloves
½ cup chopped nuts
½ cup applesauce

Cream shortening and sugar; stir in egg. Sift together dry ingredients; mix in nuts. Add in thirds to creamed mixture alternately with applesauce. Form dough in rolls. Wrap in waxed paper and chill in refrigerator. When ready, slice, then bake on greased cookie sheet in 375° oven for 10 minutes. Makes 5 dozen.

—Gladys Joyce

Date Balls

3 cups rice cereal
½ cup chopped nuts
1 tablespoon margarine
¾ cup sugar

2 eggs, beaten
1 8-ounce box chopped dates
1 7-ounce can flaked coconut

Mix together cereal and nuts. Melt margarine; add sugar, eggs, and dates. Stir constantly until smooth and thickened, about 8-10 minutes. Pour hot mixture over cereal and nuts. Drop by teaspoon into coconut. Roll into balls. Makes about 5 dozen.

—Evelyn Altizer
Opal Honaker

Date Squares

Pastry:
1 8-ounce package cream cheese
1 cup butter
2 cups flour

Mix cheese, butter, and flour together. Roll out thin. Cut in 2-inch squares.

Filling:
1 8-ounce pasckage pitted dates   ¹/₂ cup sugar
Juice of one lemon   ¹/₂ cup water

Mix dates, lemon juice, sugar, and water together. Cook until thick. Cool and add one teaspoon to pastry. Bake at 350° for 10-12 minutes, or until pastry is done. Makes 50-60.   —Opal Honaker

Holiday Fruit Cookies

1 cup shortening   1 teaspoon soda
2 cups brown sugar   1 teaspoon salt
2 eggs   1¹/₂ cups broken pecans
¹/₂ cup sour milk or buttermilk   2 cups candied cherries, chopped
3¹/₂ cups flour   2 cups dates, chopped

Mix shortening, sugar, and eggs. Stir in milk. Sift dry ingredients and stir in mixture. Mix fruits and nuts. May be worked with hand. Chill 1 hour. Drop rounded teaspoons about 2 inches apart on lightly greased baking sheet. Bake at 375° for 8 minutes.   —Evelyn Altizer
                                                    Margaret Matney

Lizzies

¹/₄ cup margarine   1 pound white raisins
¹/₂ cup light brown sugar   ¹/₂ cup bourbon
2 eggs   1 pound pecans
1¹/₂ cups flour   1 pound candied cherries
1¹/₂ teaspoons soda   ¹/₂ pound candied citron
1¹/₂ teaspoons cinnamon   ¹/₂ pound candied pineapple
¹/₂ teaspoon cloves

Soak raisins in bourbon overnight. Cream margarine with sugar. Add eggs one at a time. Beat well. Sift flour with soda and spices. Add raisins, chopped nuts, and chopped fruit mixture. Mix all together. Drop from teaspoon onto a greased cookie sheet. Bake at 325° for 15 minutes. Makes 100-120 cookies.   —Margaret Matney

Lemon Bars

2 cups flour
1 cup butter, softened
½ cup powdered sugar
4 eggs
2 cups sugar

Dash salt
5 tablespoons lemon juice
¼ cup flour
1 teaspoon baking powder
Powdered sugar

Preheat oven to 350°. Lightly spoon flour into measuring cup; level off. Combine flour, butter, and ½ cup powdered sugar. Mix thoroughly and press into ungreased 13"x9"x2" pan. Bake 20 minutes. Meanwhile, mix sugar, egg, salt, and lemon juice. Fold in ¼ cup flour and baking powder. Pour into hot crust; bake 25 minutes longer. Cool; cut into squares and sprinkle with powdered sugar. Makes 2 dozen.　　　　—Wilma Matney

Lemon-Cheese Pressed Cookies

1 cup butter or margarine, softened
1 3-ounce package cream cheese,
　softened
1 cup sugar
1 egg

1 teaspoon grated lemon peel
1 tablespoon lemon juice
2½ cups flour
1 teaspoon baking powder

Cream butter, cheese, and sugar until fluffy. Blend in remaining ingredients. Cover. Chill 1 hour.

Heat oven to 375°. Fill cookie press with one-fourth of dough at a time. Form desired shapes on ungreased baking sheet. Bake 8-10 minutes or until lightly browned on edges. Makes 6 dozen.　　　　—Janette Newhouse

Miniature Thumbprint Pastries

2 cups Master Mix Baking Mix *(see page 21)*
1 cup sour cream
½ cup preserves

Mix Master Mix and sour cream until a soft dough forms. Beat vigorously 20 strokes. Turn dough onto a well-floured surface. Shape into a ball and knead 20 times. Divide in half. Roll each half ⅛" thick. Cut with a floured 1-inch cutter. Place on ungreased cookie sheets. With a floured finger, make a deep indentation in the center of each pastry. Press finger all the way to surface of cookie sheet but not through pastry. Fill indentation with a level ¼ teaspoon of preserves. Bake at 450° for 8-10 minutes or until slightly browned. Sift lightly with powdered sugar, if desired. Makes 7 dozen.

—Jennie Tatum

Pineapple-Oatmeal Cookies

½ cup butter, softened
½ cup sugar
½ cup brown sugar
1 egg
1 9-ounce can crushed pineapple,
    drained
1½ cups rolled oats

1 cup sifted flour
½ teaspoon soda
½ teaspoon salt
½ teaspoon cinnamon
¼ teaspoon nutmeg
½ cup chopped nuts

Cream butter; add sugar and beat until light. Add eggs and beat. Add pineapple, oats, sifted dry ingredients, and nuts; mix well. Drop by teaspoon onto ungreased cookie sheet. Bake 15 minutes in a 375° oven. Makes 4 dozen.

—Evelyn Altizer

Spicy Pumpkin Cookies

1 cup shortening
2 cups sugar
4 eggs
4 cups flour
8 teaspoons baking powder
2 teaspoons salt

5 teaspoons cinnamon
½ teaspoon ginger
1 teaspoon nutmeg
2 cups pumpkin
2 cups raisins
2 cups chopped nuts

Cream together shortening, sugar, and eggs. Mix together dry ingredients. Add pumpkin to creamed mix, then fold in dry ingredients. Mix well. Fold in raisins and nuts. Bake for 12-15 minutes at 375° on cookie sheet. Makes about 8 dozen.

—Donna Davis

Raisin Cookies

1 14-ounce box of raisins
1 cup water
2 cups sugar
1 cup butter
4 cups flour
1 egg

4 teaspoons baking powder
1 teaspoon soda
1 teaspoon nutmeg
1 teaspoon cinnamon
1 teaspoon cloves

Boil raisins and water for 5 minutes. Cream sugar and butter; add egg. Stir in raisins and dry ingredients. Mix thoroughly. Drop by teaspoon on greased cookie sheet. Bake at 400° for 10 minutes.

—Evelyn Altizer

Using kitchen shears for cutting foods saves time and gives a neat-looking cut. When cutting sticky foods, such as marshmallows or dates, dip the shears in hot water.

APPALACHIAN

Raspberry Bars

2¼ cups flour
1 cup sugar
1 cup chopped pecans

1 cup butter, softened
1 egg
1 10-ounce jar raspberry preserves

Preheat oven to 350°. Grease an 8"x8"x2" pan. Combine all ingredients in a mixing bowl, except preserves. Beat at low speed, until mixture is crumbly. Reserve 1½ cups crumb mixture; set aside. Press remaining crumb mixture into greased baking dish. Spread preserves to within ½ inch of edge of unbaked crumb mixture. Crumble remaining crumb mixture over preserves. Bake near center of 350° oven for 40-50 minutes, or until lightly browned. Cool. Cut into bars.　　　　　　　　　　—Wilma Matney

Zucchini Cookies

¾ cup shortening (part margarine)
½ cup dark brown sugar
½ cup sugar
1 egg, slightly beaten
1 cup grated zucchini, peeled
1 teaspoon vanilla

2 cups sifted flour
2 teaspoons baking powder
½ teaspoon salt
1 teaspoon cinnamon
½ teaspoon ginger
½ teaspoon nutmeg

Cream shortening together with sugar. Stir in egg, zucchini, and vanilla. Sift dry ingredients together and beat in. Drop by teaspoon on cookie sheet. Bake at 375° for 10-12 minutes, until light brown. Makes about 4 dozen.
　　　　　　　　　　—Evelyn Altizer

M·O·L·A·S·S·E·S

Molasses Crinkles

¾ cup soft shortening
1 cup brown sugar
1 egg
¼ cup molasses
2½ cups sifted flour

2 teaspoons soda
¼ teaspoon salt
½ teaspoon cloves
1 teaspoon cinnamon
1 teaspoon ginger

Combine shortening, sugar, egg, and molasses; mix thoroughly. Sift together the dry ingredients; add to first mixture. Chill the dough. Roll chilled dough into balls the size of walnuts; dip tops in sugar, and bake at 375° for 10 minutes. Makes about 4 dozen.　　　　—Donna Davis

Molasses Filled Cookies

1/2 cup shortening	3 teaspoons baking powder
1/3 cup sugar	1/2 teaspoon salt
1 egg	1 teaspoon ginger
2/3 cup molasses	1/2 teaspoon cinnamon
1 3/4 cups sifted flour	1 cup mincemeat or other filling

Cream shortening and sugar. Add egg and molasses; beat well. Sift flour, baking powder, salt, ginger, and cinnamon. Add to shortening mixture and mix well. Roll in wax paper and chill. Roll 1/8-inch thick on floured board. Cut with cookie cutter or biscuit cutter. Put 1 teaspoon filling on half of the rounds and cover each with another round. Bake at 375° for 10 minutes. Makes 3 dozen. —Evelyn Altizer

Moravian Christmas Cookies

1 quart molasses	4-5 pounds flour (approximately
1 pound dark brown sugar	4 cups per pound)
3/4 cup lard	2 tablespoons mace
3/4 cup butter	2 tablespoons ground cloves
7 teaspoons soda	2 tablespoons ginger
1/4 cup boiling water	2 tablespoons cinnamon

In a 4-quart pan mix molasses, lard, and butter over low heat. Add brown sugar and dissolve. Sift spices with 4 pounds of flour. Dissolve soda in boiling water; add to molasses mixture. Remove from stove and add enough flour to make a stiff dough. Roll paper thin, cut to desired shape, and bake at 300° on a greased cookie sheet until golden brown. Dough may be refrigerated or frozen. Makes about 800 2-inch cookies. —Janette Newhouse

O·A·T·M·E·A·L

Oatmeal Cookies

1 tablespoon cocoa	3 cups oats, quick or old fashioned
2 cups sugar	1/2 cup peanut butter
1 stick butter	1 teaspoon vanilla
1/2 cup milk	

Mix the first four ingredients and bring to a rolling boil; boil for 1 minute. Add oats, peanut butter, and vanilla. Drop teaspoonfuls on wax paper. Makes 4 dozen.

Vary by adding nuts, raisins, or coconut. —Evelyn Altizer

Oatmeal Refrigerator Cookies

¾ cup + 2 tablespoons sifted
  cake flour
½ teaspoon soda
½ teaspoon salt
½ cup soft shortening
½ cup sugar

1 egg
1½ teaspoons grated lemon rind
1½ tablespoons molasses
½ teaspoon vanilla
1½ cups uncooked quick rolled oats

Sift together flour, soda, and salt. Thoroughly mix shortening with sugars, egg, rind, molasses, and vanilla. Mix in flour mixture, then oats. Press and mold into two rolls. Wrap and refrigerate several hours or overnight. Slice dough ⅛" to ¼" thick. Slice off only what you need; return unsliced portion to refrigerator and bake later as needed. Place on ungreased cookie sheet. Bake at 375° about 10 minutes or until golden brown.

—Gladys Joyce

P·E·A·N·U·T B·U·T·T·E·R

Peanut Butter Cookies I

1¼ cups flour
½ cup wheat germ
1 teaspoon soda
¼ teaspoon salt
¾ cup peanut butter

½ cup butter
½ cup brown sugar
½ cup sugar
2 eggs
1 teaspoon vanilla

Measure dry ingredients together. Stir to blend. Cream peanut butter, butter, sugar, eggs, and vanilla thoroughly. Add dry ingredients to creamed mixture. Mix well. Shape dough into 1-inch balls. Place on greased baking sheet. Flatten with fork. Bake at 350° for 10-12 minutes. Makes 4½-5 dozen cookies.

—Wilma Matney

Peanut Butter Cookies II

1⅔ cups sifted flour
1 teaspoon baking powder
½ teaspoon salt
1¾ cups sugar
¾ cup butter or vegetable shortening

2 eggs
1 teaspoon vanilla
½ cup peanut butter
1 cup rolled oats

Sift together flour, baking powder, salt, and sugar. Blend shortening, eggs, vanilla, and peanut butter; add gradually to flour mixture. Add oats. Drop on cookie sheet. Bake at 365° for 6 minutes.

—Evelyn Wyatt

Simple Peanut Butter Cookies III

1 cup peanut butter
1 cup sugar
1 egg

Mix well. Roll into balls. Bake in 350° oven for 10 minutes.

—Wilma Matney

Peanut Butter Cookies IV

2 cups sugar
1/2 cup milk
1/2 cup butter
3 tablespoons cocoa

2 1/2 cups quick oats
2 teaspoons vanilla
1/2 cup peanut butter

Mix sugar, milk, butter, and cocoa together; boil 1 1/2 minutes. Add oats, vanilla, and peanut butter; mix. Drop by teaspoon on waxed paper.

—Teresa Adkins

Peanut Butter Chips

1 1/2 cups flour
1/2 teaspoon soda
1/4 teaspoon salt
1/2 cup shortening
1/2 cup sugar
1/2 cup brown sugar

1/2 cup creamy peanut butter
2 eggs
1/2 teaspoon vanilla
1 6-ounce package semi-sweet
    chocolate pieces
1/4 cup chopped nuts

Cream shortening and sugar. Add peanut butter and eggs and then sifted dry ingredients. Add vanilla, chocolate bits, and nuts. Form into balls. Place on greased cookie sheet. Bake at 350° for 10 minutes.

—Margaret Matney

Peanut Butter Crinkles

1 cup margarine
1 cup peanut butter
1 cup sugar
1 cup brown sugar
2 eggs
1 teaspoon vanilla

2 1/2 cups unsifted flour
1 teaspoon baking powder
1 teaspoon soda
1 teaspoon salt
Sugar
6 dozen chocolate kisses

In bowl cream first six ingredients until fluffy. Beat in next four ingredients. Shape into 1-inch balls; roll in sugar. Place 2″ apart on ungreased cookie sheets. Bake in 350° oven for 10 minutes. Immediately press kiss into each cookie. Cool. Makes 6 dozen.

—Thelma Joyce

Chewy Charlies

½ cup butter
2 cups sugar
⅓ cup cocoa
½ cup milk

⅓ cup peanut butter
3 cups rolled oats
1 teaspoon vanilla

Mix together butter, sugar, cocoa, and milk. Boil 1 minute. Stir in peanut butter, rolled oats, and vanilla. Refrigerate 1 hour. Drop by teaspoon on greased cookie sheet. Bake in 350° oven for 10-12 minutes, or until done. —Opal Honaker

S·U·G·A·R

Brown Sugar Cookies

1 cup brown sugar
¼ cup butter
2 eggs
1 cup flour

¼ teaspoon baking powder
¼ teaspoon salt
½ cup pecans
1 teaspoon vanilla

Mix sugar and butter; put on low heat and let melt. Add eggs; add flour, baking powder, salt, and pecans. Mix well. Drop by teaspoons onto greased cookie sheet. Bake at 325° until brown. Makes 2½ dozen.

—Opal Honaker

Honey-Sugar Cookies

⅔ cup honey
⅓ cup margarine, softened
⅓ cup brown sugar
1 egg, beaten

1 teaspoon vanilla
2¾ cup sifted flour
1 teaspoon salt
1 teaspoon soda

Cream shortening, sugar, and honey together. Add beaten egg and vanilla. Sift together flour, soda, and salt; add to creamed mixture. Roll dough to ¼" thickness. Cut out designs with cookie cutters. Place on greased cookie sheet and bake at 350° for 8-10 minutes. Cookies may be frosted, sprinkled with sugar, or decorated. —Donna Davis

Out-of-Sugar Cookies

1 cup biscuit mix
1 4-ounce box pudding mix, any flavor (not instant)
½ cup water

Mix all ingredients. Drop by teaspoonfuls onto a greased cookie sheet. Bake at 350° for 10 minutes. This recipe is very inexpensive since it uses no sugar, no eggs, and no butter. —Wilma Matney

Christmas Cookies

3 cups flour
3 teaspoons baking powder
1 cup sugar
2 tablespoons grated lemon rind

1/2 teaspoon salt
1 cup soft shortening
2 eggs

Sift flour with salt and baking powder. Cut in shortening until mealy. In another bowl, cream sugar and eggs. Add lemon rind to egg mixture. Add all to flour. Chill. Roll dough about 1/4" thick. Cut in desired shapes. Bake 5-8 minutes at 425°.

—Wilma Matney

Molded Party Cookies

2 1/2 cups flour
3 tablespoons cornstarch
1/4 teaspoon salt
1 cup margarine
1 1/3 cups confectioners' sugar, sifted

1 egg
1 teaspoon almond extract
1 teaspoon vanilla
Sugar

Stir together flour, cornstarch, and salt. Cream margarine and confectioners' sugar together. Add egg; beat until fluffy. Add flavoring. Add dry ingredients; mix well. Chill dough for one hour.

Pinch off a small amount of dough. Form a small ball. Dip one side in granulated or sanding sugar in a small bowl. Place, sugar-side down, into cavity of mold, pressing firmly; level off top. Unmold at once onto lightly greased cookie sheet. Bake in 300° oven for 20 minutes until cookies are a light straw color on bottom. Do not brown. Makes 10 dozen cookies.

—Margaret Matney

Whole Wheat Sugar Cookies

1 cup sugar
1 teaspoon baking powder
1/2 teaspoon salt
1/2 teaspoon soda
1/2 teaspoon nutmeg
1/2 cup butter, softened

2 tablespoons milk
1 teaspoon vanilla
1 egg
2 cups whole wheat flour
2 tablespoons sugar
1/2 teaspoon cinnamon

Combine first nine ingredients in large bowl; blend well. Lightly spoon flour into measuring cup; level off. Stir in flour. Shape into 1-inch balls. Place on ungreased cookie sheets, 2" apart; flatten slightly. Combine sugar and cinnamon; sprinkle over cookies. Bake at 375° for 8-10 minutes, until light golden brown. Cookies will be soft in center. Makes 2-3 dozen.

—Marilyn Wells

Desserts

Butter Pecan Delight

1 cup crushed pecans
1 cup self-rising flour
½ cup butter
1 cup powdered sugar
1 8-ounce package cream cheese

1 9-ounce carton frozen whipped
 topping
4 cups milk
2 3-ounce packages butter pecan or
 butterscotch instant pudding mix

First Layer:
Combine flour, butter and ¾ cup pecans. Bake at 350° for 15 minutes in a 9″x11″ dish.

Second Layer:
Combine cream cheese, powdered sugar, and 1 cup whipped topping.

Third Layer:
Mix pudding mix as directed on package.

Use remainder of the whipped topping on top and sprinkle with the remainder of the pecans. Serves 12. —Opal Honaker

Humdingers for New Year

½ cup butter
¾ cup sugar
1 8-ounce package dates, chopped

1½ cups crisp rice ereal
1 cup pecans, chopped

Mix dates, sugar, and butter in saucepan. Cook 5 minutes, stirring constantly. Remove from heat; add cereal and nuts. Mix well. When cool enough to handle, roll in pieces about the size of a date, then roll in powdered sugar. —Gladys Joyce

Minute Mousse

1 6-ounce package chocolate chips
4 teaspoons dark rum (sherry, creme
 de menthe, or Grande Marnier)

¾ cup scalded milk
2 tablespoons strong coffee
2 eggs

Put all ingredients in blender for 1½ minutes. Pour into 4 large or 6 small molds or sherbet glasses. Top with whipped topping.
 —Teresa Adkins

Burned food can be removed from an enamel saucepan by using the following procedure: Fill the pan with cold water containing 2-3 tablespoons salt, and let stand overnight. The next day, cover and bring water to a boil.

Popcorn Balls

¼ cup oil
½ cup popcorn
½ cup sugar

½ cup white corn syrup
⅓ cup molasses
½ teaspoon salt

Pop corn in oil in 4-quart kettle. Mix sugar, molasses, corn syrup, and salt together in a small saucepan and bring to a boil, stirring occasionally. Pour over popcorn; mix until all popcorn is coated. Shape into balls with hands. Use butter on hands. —Donna Davis

C·O·B·B·L·E·R·S & D·U·M·P·L·I·N·G·S

Blackberry Dumplings

1 quart fresh or frozen blackberries
1 cup sugar
2 cups biscuit mix

¼ cup sugar
1 egg
Milk or water, enough to moisten

Bring berries and 1 cup sugar to boil. Mix biscuit mix with ¼ cup sugar. Add beaten egg and milk or water to moisten. Drop by spoonfuls on the boiling berries. Cover and steam slowly for 20 minutes. Good warm with ice cream or whipped topping. Serves 6. —Opal Honaker

Fruit Cobbler

½ cup margarine
1 cup milk
1 cup sugar

1 cup flour
1 teaspoon baking powder
1 quart berries or other fruits

Melt margarine in 9"x13"x2" pan. Make batter of milk, sugar, flour, and baking powder. Pour over melted margarine. Spoon berries or other fruits over batter. Bake at 350° until done. —Evelyn Wyatt

Peach Cobbler

1 quart peaches, approximately
½ cup butter
½ cup milk
½ cup sugar
1 cup flour

1 teaspoon baking powder
¼ teaspoon salt
½ teaspoon vanilla
½ cup water
½ cup sugar

Make batter of butter, milk, ½ cup sugar, flour, baking powder, salt, and vanilla. Line a greased 8"x8"x2" pan with lots of sliced fresh peaches. Spread batter over peaches. Mix ½ cup sugar with ½ cup water and pour over batter. Bake at 350° for 1 hour. —Wilma Matney

APPALACHIAN

Easy Apple Dumplings

2-3 apples, chopped fine
1 can of 10 biscuits

Flatten individual biscuits. Place one well rounded teaspoon of chopped apples on each biscuit; fold over and seal. Place dumplings in greased casserole dish and pour syrup over them. Bake covered at 350° for 40 minutes.

Syrup:

1 stick butter
1 12-ounce can lemon-lime beverage

1 cup sugar
1 teaspoon cinnamon

Bring to a boil; pour over apple dumplings before baking.

—Teresa Adkins

C·U·S·T·A·R·D·S & P·U·D·D·I·N·G·S

Boiled Custard

1 quart milk
¾ cup sugar
3 eggs, beaten

Pinch salt
1 teaspoon vanilla

Mix milk, sugar, eggs, and salt. Cook on very low heat until thick. Add vanilla. Chill in refrigerator. If this gets too warm it will curdle.

—Margaret Matney

Banana Pudding

2 cups milk
⅓ cup sugar
1 tablespoon cornstarch
¼ teaspoon salt
½ teaspoon vanilla

2 eggs, separated
12 ounces vanilla wafers (82-84 wafers by count)
2 tablespoons sugar
¼ teaspoon vanilla

Mix ⅓ cup sugar, cornstarch, and salt. Add egg yolks and then pour on scalded milk. Cook in double boiler until custard sets. Add ½ teaspoon vanilla. Line bottom and sides of baking pan with vanilla wafers and then put alternate layers of bananas, custard, and vanilla wafers, repeating twice. Make meringue of egg whites, 2 tablespoons sugar, and ¼ teaspoon vanilla. Spread on top. Sprinkle with three finely crumbed vanilla wafers. Bake in a 300° oven for 20 minutes. Makes 6 servings.

—Gladys Joyce

Quick Creamy Chocolate Pudding

⅔ cup sugar
¼ cup cocoa
3 tablespoons cornstarch
¼ teaspoon salt

2¼ cups milk
2 tablespoons butter
1 teaspoon vanilla

Combine sugar, cocoa, cornstarch, and salt in medium saucepan; gradually stir in milk. Cook over medium heat, stirring constantly, until mixture boils; boil and stir 1 minute. Remove from heat; blend in butter and vanilla. Pour into individual serving dishes. Carefully press plastic wrap onto surface. Chill. Garnish with whipped topping and chopped nuts, if desired. Makes 4 or 5 servings.   —Marilyn Wells

Butterscotch Spectacular

1 cup flour
½ cup margarine, softened
1 cup chopped pecans
1 8-ounce package cream cheese,
   softened
1 cup powdered sugar

1 13-ounce carton frozen whipped
   topping, thawed
2 3¾-ounce packages butterscotch
   instant pudding mix
3 cups cold milk
1 teaspoon vanilla

Mix flour, margarine, and pecans as for pie crust. Pat into 9"x13" pan and bake at 350° for 15 minutes. Let cool. Cream sugar and cream cheese together and fold in half of whipped topping. Spread over cooled crust. Beat together pudding mix and milk for two or three minutes. Stir in vanilla. Spread over cream cheese mixture. Then spread remaining whipped topping over butterscotch layer and sprinkle with a few additional chopped pecans. Refrigerate 2 or 3 hours.   —Margaret Matney

Vanilla Custard

1 quart milk
3 eggs
3 tablespoons cornstarch

¾ cup sugar
1 teaspoon vanilla

To cornstarch add ½ cup of milk; stir until smooth. Add beaten eggs, then sugar; stir until smooth again. Add rest of the milk. Cook over double boiler (this is important). When thickened, set in pan of cold water. When cooled, add vanilla. Set in refrigerator.

Note: If no double boiler is handy, use a 3-pound coffee can set down in kettle or pot of boiling water.   —Dora Abel

Table salt rubbed inside cups
removes those stubborn tea stains.

Rhubarb Pudding

1 quart rhubarb cut into small pieces
2 cups sugar (approximately)
2 eggs
²/₃ cup sugar

1 cup cream
2 teaspoons baking powder
1 cup flour (approximately)

Place rhubarb in bottom of 9"x13"x2" pan. Sprinkle sugar over. Make batter of eggs, ²/₃ cup sugar, cream, baking powder, and flour. This should be as thick as cake batter. Pour over rhubarb and bake in 350° oven until lightly browned and set.   —Dora Abel

Old-Fashioned Banana Pudding

¾ cup sugar
2 tablespoons flour
¼ teaspoon salt
2 cups milk

3 eggs, separated
1 teaspoon vanilla
Vanilla wafers
6 bananas

Combine ¹/₂ cup sugar, flour, and salt in top of double boiler; stir in milk. Cook over boiling water, stirring constantly, until thickened. Cook, uncovered, 15 minutes more, stirring occasionally. Beat egg yolks; gradually stir in hot mixture. Return to double boiler; cook 5 minutes, stirring constantly. Remove from heat; add vanilla. Line bottom of casserole with vanilla wafers. Top with a layer of sliced bananas. Pour a portion of custard over the bananas. Continue to layer wafers, bananas, and custard, ending with custard on top. Beat egg whites until stiff, but not dry; gradually add remaining ¹/₄ cup sugar and beat until mixture forms stiff peaks. Pile on top of pudding in casserole. Bake in 425° oven for 5 minutes or until delicately browned.   —Wilma Matney

Deluxe Banana Pudding

3 3-ounce boxes instant vanilla
   pudding
5 cups milk
1 cup sour cream

1 9-ounce carton frozen whipped
   topping
1 box vanilla wafers
6 or 8 bananas

Layer in 9-inch or 11-inch dish, starting with coarsely crumbled vanilla wafers, then a layer of sliced bananas. Mix the pudding mix, milk, sour cream, and one-half of the whipped topping. Pour one-half of this mixture over the bananas and wafers. Repeat the three layers—crushed vanilla wafers, then sliced bananas, then pudding mix. Cover with remaining half of the whipped topping and chill. Serves 12.   —Opal Honaker

Frosty Strawberry Square

2 egg whites
3/4 cup sugar
1 10-ounce package frozen strawberries or 2 cups sliced fresh
   strawberries

2 tablespoons lemon juice
1 14-ounce carton frozen whipped
   topping

In a large mixer bowl, combine egg whites, sugar berries, and lemon juice. Beat at low speed with electric mixer until mixture begins to thicken, about 2 minutes. Then beat at high speed until stiff peaks form, about 10 minutes. Fold in whipped topping. Pour into square pan (or pie shells) and freeze. Freeze 8 or 10 hours. Makes two 9-inch pies.

—Thelma Joyce

Lemon Sherbet

2 eggs, separated
1 teaspoon grated orange and lemon
   rind
1/4 cup orange juice

1/4 cup lemon juice
1/2 cup sugar
2 cups milk
1/8 teaspoon salt

Beat egg yolks; add rinds, juices, and 5 tablespoons sugar. Stir until sugar dissolves; add milk. Add salt to egg whites and beat stiff, then add 5 tablespoons sugar while beating. Fold into fruit mixture. Freeze until almost firm. Take out and beat with fork. Return and freeze firm.

—Donna Davis

Lemon Fruit Freeze

2/3 cup butter
1/3 cup sugar
3 cups crushed rice biscuit cereal
   (7 cups uncrushed)
1 14-ounce can sweetened condensed
   milk

1/2 cup lemon juice
1 21-ounce can lemon pie filling
1 17-ounce can fruit cocktail, well
   drained
2 cups whipped topping

Melt butter; stir in sugar, then crumbs. Pat crumbs firmly on bottom of 13"x9"x2" pan. Bake at 300° for 12 minutes. Cool. In large bowl mix milk and lemon juice; stir in pie filling and fruit cocktail. Pour over cooled crust. Top with whipped topping and freeze for 4 hours. Remove from freezer 20 minutes before cutting. Makes 12-15 servings. —Evelyn Altizer

Tropical Fruit Freeze

1 3-ounce package orange gelatin
1½ cups water
1 11-ounce can Mandarin oranges, drained
1 8¼-ounce can crushed pineapple
½ cup pecan pieces
1½ cups miniature marshmallows

1 6-ounce can frozen orange juice concentrate
⅔ cup sweetened condensed milk
1 4-ounce container frozen whipped topping
¼ cup flaked coconut

Dissolve gelatin in 1 cup boiling water. Drain pineapple, saving juice. Add water to juice to make ½ cup liquid; stir into dissolved gelatin. Mix pineapple, oranges, marshmallows, and pecans; chill. Beat together frozen orange juice concentrate, condensed milk, and whipped topping. Fold into thick gelatin mixture and pour into 11¾"x7½"x1¾" glass dish. Sprinkle flaked coconut over top and freeze. Cut into squares to serve. Makes 12 servings. *Note:* Set out of freezer a few minutes before serving.

—Evelyn Altizer

Raspberry Cream

1 3-ounce package raspberry gelatin
1 cup hot water

1 10-ounce package frozen raspberries, unthawed
½ pint vanilla ice cream

Dissolve gelatin in hot water; stir in frozen raspberries. Add ice cream, stirring until melted. Refrigerate until set, about 20 minutes. Serves 6.

—Vera Tatum

Raspberry Ice Cream

1 3-ounce package raspberry gelatin
½ cup boiling water
1 10-ounce package frozen raspberries, thawed and sieved
2 eggs
1 cup whipping cream

1 3¾- or 3⅝-ounce package instant vanilla pudding mix
⅔ cup sugar
2 teaspoons vanilla
1 quart milk

Dissolve gelatin in boiling water; stir in raspberries. Beat eggs; add whipping cream, dry pudding mix, sugar, and vanilla. Stir into raspberry mixture. Pour into 1-gallon ice cream freezer container; add milk and stir till blended. Freeze according to freezer manufacturer's directions. Makes 2 quarts.

—Margaret Matney

Why heat a kettle of water when all you need is a cup?

Pineapple-Orange Squares

6 tablespoons butter or margarine
$^{3}/_{2}$ cup flour
$^{3}/_{4}$ cup flaked coconut
2 tablespoons brown sugar
1 quart vanilla ice cream

1 8-ounce package cream cheese, softened
$^{1}/_{3}$ cup frozen orange juice concentrate, thawed
1 8$^{1}/_{4}$-ounce can crushed pineapple, drained

In a medium saucepan melt the butter or margarine. Stir in flour, coconut, and brown sugar. Press mixture into bottom of an 8"x8"x2" baking pan. Bake in 325° oven for 20 minutes. Cool. Stir ice cream to soften. In large mixing bowl beat cream cheese and orange juice till fluffy. Add ice cream by spoonfuls; beat smooth. Stir in pineapple. Spoon into prepared crust. Freeze 8 hours or overnight. To serve, let stand 10-15 minutes; cut into squares. Garnish with quartered pineapple slices and orange peel strips. Serves 8 or 9.

—Teresa Adkins

Strawberry Ice Cream

1 14-ounce can evaporated milk
1 14-ounce package frozen strawberries, undrained

Using a chilled bowl, beat milk with a mixer until it's the consistency of thick whipped cream. Add strawberries. Beat together and freeze solid.

—Gladys Joyce

Strawberry Mousse

1 10-ounce package frozen strawberries
$^{1}/_{2}$ pint sour cream

$^{1}/_{2}$ cup sugar
1 tablespoon vanilla

Mix all ingredients in blender. Freeze. Serve in sherbet dishes. Serves 4-6.

—Teresa Adkins

Special Treat. Here's a low-calorie "glamor dessert" that serves eight, is delicious, lovely to look at, and can be easily prepared in five minutes at a small cost per serving. Stir together the following ingredients and place in refrigerator to cool: 1 large carton of frozen whipped topping, 1 package of instant pistachio pudding mix (as it comes from the package), 1 cup crushed and drained pineapple, 1 cup miniature marshmallows, and $^{1}/_{2}$ cup chopped nuts.

APPALACHIAN

Blueberry Dessert I

1 pound vanilla wafers	1 cup blueberry pie filling
1/2 cup butter	1 cup whipped cream or frozen
2 eggs	whipped topping
1 cup sugar	1 teaspoon vanilla
1 8-ounce package cream cheese	1/2 cup chopped pecans

Crush wafers until very fine. Sprinkle over bottom of greased 9"x11"pan. Reserve some crumbs for top. Cream egg yolks, butter, sugar, cream cheese, and vanilla. Fold in beaten egg whites. Spread over crumbs; sprinkle pecans over top. Spread blueberry filling over mixture. Top with whipped topping and wafer crumbs. Chill overnight. Serves 12.   —Opal Honaker

Blueberry Dessert II

Crust:

1 cup flour	1/4 cup brown sugar
1/2 cup chopped nuts	1/2 cup butter

Melt butter; add other ingredients to make crust. Pat in a 9"x13"x2" pan. Bake 10 minutes at 400°.

Filling:

1 package whipped topping	3/4 cup sugar
1 8-ounce package cream cheese,	1/2 teaspoon vanilla
softened	Blueberry pie filling

Prepare packaged whipped topping; mix with softened cream cheese, sugar, and vanilla. Spread over crust. Cover with blueberry pie filling.

—Dollie Warburton

Cherry Delight

Crust:

2 cups graham cracker crumbs	1 tablespoon confectioners' sugar
2 tablespoons unflavored gelatin	1/2 cup margarine, melted

Blend ingredients to make crust. Put into bottom of 9"x13"x2" pan.

Filling:

2 1 1/2-ounce envelopes whipped	1 8-ounce package cream cheese
topping mix	1 teaspoon vanilla
1 cup milk	2 21-ounce cans cherry pie filling
1 cup sugar	

Whip topping mix, milk, and sugar until stiff. Add cream cheese and vanilla. Continue beating until well blended. Pour mixture over crust in pan. Top with cherry pie filling. Chill overnight.   —Dora Abel

Rhubarb Dessert

½ cup sugar	1 egg
½ cup chopped nuts	2 cups flour
1 tablespoon butter, melted	1 teaspoon baking soda
1 teaspoon cinnamon	½ teaspoon salt
1½ cups brown sugar	1 cup sour cream
½ cup shortening	1½ cups rhubarb, cut into ½" pieces

Mix sugar, nuts, butter, and cinnamon till crumbly; set aside. Cream together brown sugar, shortening, and egg. Thoroughly stir together flour, soda, and salt; add to creamed mixture alternately with sour cream. Stir in rhubarb. Turn into greased and floured 13"x9"x2" baking pan. Sprinkle with reserved topping. Bake in 350° oven for 45-50 minutes. Cut into squares. Serve warm or cool.

—Evelyn Altizer

Oatmeal Rhubarb Crunch

1 cup flour	½ cup butter, melted
¾ cup uncooked oatmeal	1 teaspoon cinnamon
1 cup brown sugar	4 cups rhubarb, diced

Mix flour, oatmeal, brown sugar, melted butter, and cinnamon until crumbly. Press half of mixture into greased 9-inch baking pan. Cover crumb mixture with diced rhubarb. Sprinkle remaining crumb mixture over rhubarb.

Topping:

1 cup sugar	2 tablespoons cornstarch
1 cup water	1 teaspoon vanilla

Combine all ingredients and cook until thick. Pour this sauce over rhubarb. Bake at 350° for 1 hour. Serve warm, plain or with whipped cream.

—Donna Davis

Strawberry Shortcakes

1 quart strawberries	3 teaspoons baking powder
1 cup sugar	1 teaspoon salt
⅓ cup shortening	¾ cup milk
2 cups flour	Margarine or butter, softened
2 tablespoons sugar	Non-dairy whipped topping

Mix strawberries with 1 cup sugar; let stand 1 hour (may use prepared frozen strawberries). Cut shortening into flour, 2 tablespoons sugar, baking powder, and salt until mixture resembles fine crumbs. Stir in milk until blended. Knead 20-25 times on lightly floured surface. Roll to ½" thickness; cut with 3-inch cutter. Place on ungreased cookie sheet. Bake at 450° until golden brown, 10-12 minutes. Split crosswise while hot. Spread with margarine; fill and top with topping and strawberries. Makes 6 servings.

—Jennie Tatum

Raspberry Torte

1 cup butter
1½ cups sugar
5 eggs, separated
2 tablespoons milk
2 teaspoons vanilla
½ teaspoon baking powder

¾ teaspoon salt
2 cups flour
1 cup raspberry preserves
1 3½-ounce can flaked coconut
(2½ cups)
2 cups sour cream

Cream butter. Add ½ cup sugar, creaming well. Blend in egg yolks, milk, 1 teaspoon vanilla, baking powder, and ½ teaspoon salt; beat well. Stir in flour. Spread evenly into bottoms of three 9-inch round layer pans that have been greased on bottoms. Spread ⅓ cup raspberry preserves on each layer to within 1″ of edge. Beat egg whites and ¼ teaspoon salt until mounds form. Add 1 cup sugar, a little at a time. Continue beating until stiff peaks form. Fold in coconut and 1 teaspoon vanilla. Spread over preserves. Bake at 350° for 35-40 minutes until light golden brown. Cool 15 minutes; remove from pans. Cool completely. Spread sour cream between layers, leaving top plain. Chill several hours or overnight.　　　　　—Wilma Matney

Strawberry Fluff

Strawberry Fluff is made in three layers, and the layers must be made in sequence.

First Layer:

1 cup flour
¼ cup brown sugar

1 cup chopped pecans
1 cup melted butter or margarine

Mix and spread in 9″x13″ pan. Bake 10-15 minutes at 350° and cool layer completely.

Second Layer:

1 8-ounce package cream cheese
1 cup confectioners' sugar

1 8-ounce carton frozen whipped
topping
1 teaspoon vanilla

Cream cheese and sugar; add vanilla and whipped topping. Spread over cooled crust (first layer).

Third Layer:

4 cups strawberries
1 cup sugar

4 tablespoons cornstarch
Few drops red food coloring

Heat two full cups of strawberries with juice along with sugar, red food coloring, and cornstarch. Stir over low heat until thick. Add other two cups of drained berries but don't cook any longer. Cool completely before you spread over second layer. Chill 12 hours before serving. Serves 18.

　　　　　—Margaret Matney

Strawberry Roll

¾ cup cake flour
1 teaspoon baking powder
¼ teaspoon salt
4 eggs, separated
¾ cup sugar

1 teaspoon vanilla
2 tablespoons water
6 tablespoons confectioners' sugar
2 cups whipping cream
1 quart strawberry halves

Sift flour; measure. Add baking powder and salt; sift again. Beat egg whites until stiff; gradually beat in half the sugar, adding 2 tablespoons at a time. Beat egg yolks until thick. Add remaining sugar, vanilla, and water. Continue beating until very thick. Gently fold in beaten egg whites. Fold in dry ingredients gradually, one-fourth cup at a time. Pour mixture into well greased and floured 15½"x10½"x1" jelly roll pan. Bake in 375° oven for 15-20 minutes. Remove cake from pan onto clean cloth. Quickly roll up cake like jelly roll. Cool on rack while wrapped in cloth. Combine confectioners' sugar and whipping cream; whip until stiff. Unroll cake, spread whipped cream mixture, top with half the strawberries. Roll cake up again; spread outside with remaining whipped cream. Top with remaining strawberry halves. Makes 10 servings.
—Wilma Matney

S·A·U·C·E·S

Butterscotch Sauce

⅔ cup milk
2 tablespoons butter
1 cup sugar

1 cup light brown sugar
½ teaspoon vanilla

Heat milk to boiling point; add butter and sugar. Cook to a thick syrup, about 224°. Remove from fire; add vanilla, but do not stir. Serve hot or cold.
—Vera Tatum

Hot Fudge Sauce

1 6-ounce package semi-sweet chocolate pieces
½ cup evaporated milk

Put ingredients in heavy 1-quart saucepan. Stir over low heat until chocolate melts completely. Serve over ice cream or cake. Can be reheated.
—Wilma Matney

Main Dishes &
Side Dishes

B · E · E · F

Beef Cubes in Wine Sauce

¼ cup vegetable oil
3 pounds boneless chuck roast,
    cut into 1″ cubes
1½ cups water
3 tablespoons flour
1 1⅜-ounce envelope onion soup
    mix
1 bay leaf
½ teaspoon garlic powder
½ teaspoon ground thyme

5 carrots, cut into 1″ slices, cooked
    and drained
½ 16-ounce jar boiled onions,
    drained
1 4-ounce can button mushrooms,
    drained, or 12 small fresh
    mushrooms sauteed in butter
2½ cups red cooking wine
Hot cooked noodles or rice
    (optional)

Heat oil in heavy medium skillet; brown beef slowly on all sides. Place beef in a 4-quart casserole; reserve pan drippings. Stir flour into pan drippings; cook over low heat 1 minute, stirring constantly. Gradually stir in water; add onion soup mix. Cook over medium heat, stirring constantly, until thickened and bubbly. Pour over meat and stir in bay leaf, garlic powder, and thyme. Bake at 300° for 2 hours or until meat is tender. Add carrots, onions, mushrooms, and cooking wine; bake an additional 15 minutes, or until vegetables are thoroughly heated. Serve over noodles or rice, if desired. Yields 6-8 servings.   —Jamie Overbay

Beef Jerky

1 pound top round steak
Salt

Pepper
Liquid smoke

Remove all fat from steak. Freeze round steak until icy. Cut in very thin strips. Cut across the meat grain for crisp jerky, and with the grain for chewy jerky. Place beef strips in bowl or crock in ½″-thick layer. Sprinkle with salt, pepper, and liquid smoke. Repeat layers until all beef is used. Weight down meat with plate or heavy object; cover and refrigerate overnight. Drain and pat strips with paper toweling. Arrange strips on rack in shallow baking pan. Bake at 250° for 3½-4 hours, until of desired dryness. Cool. Store in airtight plastic bag or jar with tight-fitting lid in the refrigerator, or at cool room temperature until used.   —Wilma Matney

Skillet Steak

Round steak
Flour
2 1³/₈-ounce packages dried onion
  soup

1 10³/₄-ounce can cream of
  mushroom soup
1 10³/₄-ounce can water

Cut round steak and roll in flour. Brown in skillet; sprinkle with dried soup mix. Mix cream of mushroom soup with water. Pour over steak and let simmer for 2 hours.　　　　　　　　　　　—Evelyn Altizer

Steak Rolls
With Sour Cream Sauce

1 pound tenderized steak or
  4 4-ounce minute steaks
¹/₄ cup flour
¹/₄ teaspoon salt
¹/₈ teaspoon pepper
2 tablespoons shortening

3 tablespoons finely chopped
  mushrooms
3 tablespoons finely chopped onions
1 can refrigerated crescent dinner
  rolls

Cut steak into four rectangular pieces. Coat with mixture of flour, salt, and pepper. Brown in shortening. Drain. Sauté mushrooms and onions. Place 1½ tablespoons of mixture on one end of browned meat; fold over other end, covering mushroom mixture. Unroll dough, leaving two triangles joined to form a rectangle. Press perforation to seal. Place meat in center of dough. Fold, sealing sides and ends of dough. Place seam-side down on cookie sheet. Bake at 400° for 10-12 minutes, until golden brown. Serve hot with Sour Cream Sauce.

Sour Cream Sauce:
1 cup sour cream
1 tablespoon butter

½ teaspoon parsley flakes
¹/₄ teaspoon salt

Combine all ingredients. Heat thoroughly, but do not boil.

　　　　　　　　　　　—Wilma Matney

Hoagies

2 pounds sirloin steak, cut in thin
  strips
1 large onion, chopped
2 green peppers, sliced thin

1 8-ounce can tomato sauce
1 6-ounce can tomato paste
6 Hoagie buns
Pasteurized process cheese

Brown meat, onions, and green peppers in skillet until tender. Add tomato sauce and paste to mixture; simmer ½ hour. Butter inside of buns; put meat sauce inside; top with cheese. Wrap in foil; heat in oven until cheese is melted.

　　　　　　　　　　　—Yvonne Johns

Marinated Steak

1/4 cup vegetable oil
1/2 cup barbecue sauce with onions
1/4 cup lemon juice

1 tablespoon brown sugar
1 1 1/2-pound flank steak or round
steak, pierced

In small bowl combine oil, barbecue sauce, lemon juice, and brown sugar. Place steak in shallow bowl; cover with sauce. Refrigerate 6 hours or overnight; turn occasionally. Remove from sauce. Broil 5-7 minutes on each side, or until desired doneness. Baste occasionally with remaining sauce. Season with salt and pepper if desired.
—Wilma Matney

Japanese Steak

1 1/2 pounds round steak
1/2 cup onions, chopped
1/2 cup green peppers
1/2 cup celery, chopped
2 tablespoons margarine
1 15 1/2-ounce can Chinese vegetables

1 4-ounce can mushrooms, drained
1 15 1/2-ounce can zucchini, Italian
style
Slivered almonds
Rice
Soy Sauce

Cut steak into small strips and marinate in soy sauce 3 hours or overnight. Sauté onions, green peppers, and celery in margarine. Drain steak; reserve sauce. Brown steak. Add onions, reserved sauce, celery, and pepper. Cook slowly, covered, for 45 minutes, or until steak is tender. Drain and rinse Chinese vegetables; add to meat along with drained sliced mushrooms and zucchini. Cover and simmer 15 minutes; add almonds and serve over rice. don't use too much salt as soy sauce is very salty. Add a little water if necessary.
—Wilma Matney

Pepper Steak

2 tablespoons oil
1 pound round steak
1 teaspoon salt
1/8 teaspoon pepper
1/4 cup water
3 tablespoons onions, minced
1/2 cup mushrooms, chopped

1 clove garlic, minced
2 green peppers, diced
1 cup beef bouillon
1 1/2 cups stewed tomatoes
2 tablespoons cornstarch
2 teaspoons soy sauce

Cut meat into 1" strips; sprinkle with salt and pepper. Place meat, onion, and garlic in frying pan with oil. Brown all sides. Add peppers and bouillon; cover and cook 35 minutes. Add tomatoes and mushrooms. Simmer 15 minutes or until meat is very tender. Combine cornstarch, soy sauce, and water; add to meat mixture. Cook for about 8 minutes, stirring until thickened.
—Margaret Matney

Skillet Hash

2 tablespoons butter
2 cups cooked beef roast cut in
 1/2" cubes
2 cups raw potatoes cut in 1/2" cubes

1/3 cup finely diced onions
1/2 cup beef broth
1/2 teaspoon salt

Melt butter in skillet. Add remaining ingredients; mix well. Cover. Cook over low heat, stirring often, until potatoes are tender, about 15 minutes. Uncover and cook 5 minutes more. Makes 4 servings.

—Evelyn Altizer

Tommy's Pepper Steak

2 pounds thin steak, cut into strips
3 tablespoons shortening
Salt and pepper
2 cups water
2 beef bouillon cubes

2 teaspoons soy sauce
2 green peppers, cut into strips
2 red peppers, or a small jar of
 pimientos, cut into strips
2 tablespoons cornstarch

Brown strips of steak in shortening. Sprinkle lightly with salt and pepper. Add water and bouillon cubes. Simmer until beef is tender, about 1 hour. Add soy sauce and peppers; cook about 10 minutes longer, or until peppers are crisp tender. Thicken broth with cornstarch mixed with a little water, stirring constantly until thickened. Serve with rice, if desired. Serves 6.

—Evelyn Wyatt

C·A·S·S·E·R·O·L·E·S

Chicken Casserole 1

1 1/4 cups raw rice
1 10 3/4-ounce can cream of
 mushroom soup
1 10 3/4-ounce can cream of celery
 soup
1 10 3/4-ounce can cream of chicken
 soup

1/4 cup margarine
1/4 cup dry sherry wine
10 pieces of chicken
1/2 cup slivered almonds
1/3 cup grated Parmesan cheese

Sprinkle rice over bottom of 3-quart baking dish. In a bowl combine undiluted soups, margarine, and sherry. Spread and mix 2 cups of soup mixture over rice. Salt and pepper chicken pieces and place skin-side up in a single layer on top of soup and rice mixture. Spread remaining soup mixture over chicken. Sprinkle with almonds and cheese. Cover and bake at 300° for about 2 hours, or until fork tests done. When done, remove cover and increase temperature to 400°. Let cook about 20 minutes or until brown.

—Margaret Matney

Chicken Casserole II

1 2½- to 3-pound chicken
1 stalk celery, chopped
2 tablespoons butter
1 tablespoon onion, finely chopped

1 10¾-ounce can cream of chicken
  soup
¼ cup milk
1 8-ounce package dressing
1 quart chicken broth

Cook chicken with celery. Remove bones and skin. Place chicken in bottom of baking dish. In skillet add butter and onion. Cook slowly until onions are tender. Mix in soup and milk. Pour over chicken. Add dressing mix to chicken broth; stir well and cover chicken. Bake at 350° for 30 minutes. Serves 8.

—Pearl Barnes

Chicken Casserole III

1 package stuffing mix
4 cups cooked chopped chicken
½ cup chopped onions
½ cup chopped celery
1 cup mayonnaise
¾ teaspoon salt

1 teaspoon pepper
2 eggs
½ cup milk
1 10¾-ounce can cream of
  mushroom soup

Generously moisten stuffing mix with chicken broth. Press lightly into bottom of 8"x12" baking dish. Combine chicken, onions, celery, mayonnaise, salt, and pepper; pour over dressing. Beat eggs with milk; pour over chicken mixture. Cover with foil; refrigerate overnight. When ready to bake, spoon soup over mixture. Bake at 325° for 1 hour. Serves 6-8.

—Opal Honaker

Baked Chicken or Turkey Casserole

1 7-ounce package herb-seasoned
  croutons
1 10¾-ounce can mushroom soup
2½-3 cups cooked chicken or turkey
2 cups chicken or turkey broth

2 eggs, beaten
½ cup milk
1 2-ounce can pimientos, chopped
  (optional)

Pour broth over croutons; let stand a few minutes. Mix beaten eggs, mushroom soup, milk, and pimientos. Pour mixture over croutons. Add chicken or turkey; mix lightly together. Bake in greased casserole dish at 350° for 45-55 minutes.

—Evelyn Altizer

Chopped onions have the best flavor
if they are browned in shortening
before being added to casserole dishes.

Easy Chicken Casserole

2 cups cooked rice
1 broiler-fryer chicken, stewed and
cut into chunks

2 10¾-ounce cans cream of chicken
soup

Layer rice in greased 9"x9" casserole dish; cover with chicken chunks, then with chicken soup. Bake uncovered at 350° for 30 minutes.

—Teresa Adkins

Jean's Chicken Casserole

Chicken breasts
1 8-ounce package dressing mix
1 10¾-ounce can cream of
mushroom soup

1 10¾-ounce can cream of chicken
soup
1 14-ounce can evaporated milk
½ cup melted butter

Cook chicken breasts tender and cut up. Lay ½ bag of dressing in bottom of baking dish, then put cut-up chicken on the dressing. Mix together soups, evaporated milk, and melted butter; pour over chicken. Pour the remaining dressing over all. Cook at 350° 25 or 30 minutes until it bubbles.

—Gladys Joyce

Chicken-Broccoli Bake

4 boned chicken breasts
4 tablespoons butter
1 10-ounce package frozen broccoli

1 10¾-ounce can cream of chicken
soup
½ cup milk
½ cup shredded cheese

Brown chicken breasts lightly in butter. Arrange in casserole dish. Cover with broccoli. Mix soup, milk, and cheese. Pour over chicken and broccoli. Sprinkle with paprika. Bake at 400° for about 35-45 minutes.

—Evelyn Wyatt

Turkey Casserole

2 cups turkey, cooked and cut into
bite-sized pieces
1 cup diced celery
1 cup cooked rice
1 10¾-ounce can cream of chicken
soup, undiluted

1 small onion, chopped
⅔ cup sour cream
1 can water chestnuts, sliced and
drained
½ cup slivered almonds
1 cup crushed cornflakes

Mix all ingredients except the cornflakes and put into greased casserole. Top with 1 cup crushed cornflakes. Pour ½ cup melted butter over casserole. Bake at 350° for 45 minutes.

—Thelma Joyce

Country Casserole

½ pound ground beef
½ cup chopped onions
⅓ cup diced green peppers
1 16-ounce can home-style beans
2 cups cooked elbow macaroni

½ cup tomato juice
½ teaspoon salt
1 1-ounce slice sharp cheese cut into
    4 triangles

Brown beef in skillet. Add onions and green peppers; cook until tender. Pour off fat. Add beans, macaroni, juice, and salt. Pour into 1-quart casserole. Bake at 400° for 25 minutes. Top with cheese; bake 5 minutes more until cheese melts. Makes 4 cups.   —Evelyn Altizer

Potato Puff Casserole

1 pound ground beef
⅓ cup chopped onion
⅓ cup chopped green pepper
1 tablespoon chili sauce or catsup

1 10¾-ounce can cream of
    mushroom soup
¼ cup water
1 10-ounce package frozen potato
    puffs

In skillet combine ground beef, onions, and green pepper. Cook over medium heat, breaking up meat with fork, until meat is browned and onions and peppers are tender. Add chili sauce, undiluted soup, and water. Turn into 1½-quart casserole. Cover top with frozen potato puffs. Bake uncovered at 375° for 35 minutes or until potato puffs are golden brown. Makes 4 servings.   —Gladys Joyce

Hamburger Casserole

1 pound ground beef
1 medium onion, finely chopped
1 green pepper, chopped
½ cup celery, chopped
1½ cups cooked macaroni
1 8-ounce can Mexican corn

1 10¾-ounce can tomato soup
1 8-ounce can tomato sauce
Salt and black pepper to taste
Red pepper to taste (optional)
Cheese

Brown first four ingredients and cook until tender. Add remaining ingredients. Put into casserole; grate cheese on top. Bake in 350° oven until cheese is melted and casserole is hot throughout.
                    —Gladys Joyce

This is a handy method for freezing casseroles: Line a casserole dish with heavy-duty aluminum foil, put the food in it, seal, and freeze. When the casserole is frozen, lift out the package, and mold foil to surface of food. Seal securely with freezer tape, label, and return to the freezer.

Beef Rice Bake

½ pound ground beef
1 tablespoon fat
½ cup uncooked rice
1 10¾-ounce can cream of chicken
  soup

½ cup water
1 teaspoon salt
½ cup chopped celery
¼ cup chopped green pepper
½ cup cornflakes

Brown beef in hot fat. Add rice, soup, water, salt, celery, and green pepper; mix thoroughly. Pour into 1½-quart casserole. Cover. Bake in 325°-350° oven for 1½ hours. At the end of 1 hour, uncover; stir with fork, and top with cornflakes. —Essie Combs

Hot Chicken Salad Casserole

2 cups chicken, cooked and cubed
2 cups celery, chopped
½ cup slivered blanched almonds
1 cup mayonnaise
2 tablespoons onions, minced

½ teaspoon salt
½ teaspoon pepper
Small amount lemon juice
1 cup bread crumbs
½ cup sharp cheese, grated

Mix first eight ingredients together as for chicken salad. Put in casserole and cover with bread crumbs and cheese. Bake in preheated 450° oven for 10 or 15 minutes. —Evelyn Wyatt

Chicken and Dressing Casserole

6 chicken breasts, cooked and
  deboned
1 10¾-ounce can cream of chicken
  soup

1 8-ounce package chicken dressing
  with herbs

Place chicken in casserole dish; cover with undiluted chicken soup. Cover with the dry crumbs from package of chicken dressing. Mix the chicken herbs according to package directions; pour over all. Bake at 350° for 30 minutes. —Wilma Matney

Tuna Casserole 1

2 small onions, chopped
1 cup celery, chopped
2 cups water
2 10¾-ounce cans cream of chicken
  soup, undiluted
2 7-ounce cans tuna, flaked

1 teaspoon salt
½ teaspoon pepper
1 12-ounce package egg noodles,
  cooked
6 slices American cheese

Add onion and celery to 2 cups of water in large saucepan. Cook over medium heat until celery is tender. Add soup, tuna, salt, and pepper; simmer. Combine cooked noodles and tuna mixture in a 4-quart casserole bowl. Top with cheese; bake at 350° until cheese melts. Serves 6-8.

—Teresa Adkins

Tuna Casserole II

1 6-ounce can tuna
1 10¾-ounce can cream of
  mushroom soup
½ cup milk
1 cup cooked rice
2 tablespoons butter

¼ cup chopped green pepper
  (optional)
½ cup chopped onion
2 1-ounce packages potato sticks
  or chips

Sauté onion and green pepper in butter. Add soup and milk. Stir well. Grease casserole dish. Add layer of tuna, rice, and soup mixture; repeat. Add crushed chips. Bake at 350° for 20 minutes.　　　—Wilma Matney

Brown Rice Casserole

½ cup margarine
1 large onion, chopped
1 cup raw brown rice

2 10¾-ounce cans beef broth or
  consommé
⅓ cup water

Melt margarine in 2-quart casserole; add onion and rice. Stir, then pour in undiluted beef broth or consomme. Cook in 350°-375° oven about 1 hour. After first 20 minutes, stir. After first 30 minutes, add ⅓ cup water and stir. When rice is tender remove from oven.

Cooked ham, chicken, or shrimp can be added before removing from oven.　　　—Jamie Overbay

Kidney Bean and Meat Ball Casserole

2 pounds ground beef
½ cup milk
1 cup soft bread crumbs
⅛ teaspoon pepper
½ teaspoon chili powder
1 teaspoon salt
5 tablespoons oil

1 medium green pepper, sliced in
  rings
2 cups sliced onion
2 8-ounce cans tomato sauce
½ pound Cheddar cheese, cut into
  small cubes
3 16-ounce cans kidney beans

Combine milk, bread crumbs, salt, pepper, chili powder, and meat; mix thoroughly and shape into balls 1½" in diameter. Heat oil in skillet; brown meat balls. Remove meat balls; lightly brown onion in same fat. Add tomato sauce and cheese; stir gently until mixed. Drain liquid from kidney beans and pour beans in well greased oblong dish. Pour the sauce from the skillet over the beans, and arrange meat balls over top. Then add pepper rings. Place on oven rack in first set of glides from bottom. Bake in preheated 350° oven for 50 minutes.　　　—Jamie Overbay

When peeling onions, you will shed fewer tears if you
hold the onion in a bowl of cold water as you peel and slice it.

Beef Noodle Casserole

2 pounds ground beef
1 8-ounce package noodles, cooked
1 green pepper, chopped
1 medium onion, chopped
1 16½-ounce can creamed corn
1 8-ounce can ripe olives
1 2-ounce can pimientos
1 4-ounce can mushrooms

1 10¾-ounce can tomato soup
1 8-ounce can tomato sauce
⅛ teaspoon mustard
½ teaspoon salt
½ teaspoon chili powder
⅛ teaspoon pepper
1 cup Cheddar cheese

Mix all ingredients except cheese. Leave covered 24 hours in refrigerator. When ready to bake, sprinkle with cheese. Bake in 9"x13"x2" pan at 350° for 30-45 minutes. —Judy Patton

Hamburger Bean Bake

1 large onion
2 teaspoons mustard
1 cup catsup

1 pound ground beef
1 teaspoon vinegar
1 large can pork and beans

Brown the chopped onion in a little margarine; add ground beef. Season with salt and pepper; then brown. Add spices and catsup. Mix well. Add beans and stir to mix. Pour into a baking dish and bake at 350° for 30 minutes. Serves 6. —Janette Newhouse

Hamburger-Corn Pie

1 pound hamburger
1 small onion, chopped
1 16-ounce can whole tomatoes
1 16-ounce can corn, drained
1½-3 teaspoons chili powder

1½ teaspoons salt
1 cup self-rising cornmeal
1 cup milk
2 eggs
1 cup Cheddar cheese, shredded

Cook hamburger and onion until meat is brown; drain. Stir in tomatoes, corn, chili powder, and salt. Heat to boiling. Pour into 2-quart casserole. Mix cornmeal, milk, and eggs; pour over meat mixture. Sprinkle with cheese. Cook in 350° oven until golden brown, 40-50 minutes.
—Jennie Tatum

Quick Beef Pie

2 14-ounce cans chunky beef soup
Pastry for 2-crust pie

Empty soup into pie shell; top with pastry. Make slits in top crust. Bake at 400° for 35-40 minutes or until pastry is done. —Wilma Matney

APPALACHIAN

Hot Tamale Pie

2 pounds hamburger
1 large onion, chopped
2 15½-ounce cans tomato sauce
1 teaspoon salt
Pepper to taste
1 teaspoon chili powder

Few drops Tabasco sauce
1 32-ounce can pork 'n' beans
1 large bag corn chips
1 pound longhorn cheese, shredded
1 8-ounce can corn (optional)
catsup

Brown hamburger and onion; dip off fat. Cook slowly with tomato sauce, salt, chili powder, and Tabasco sauce. In casserole put layer of meat, layer of beans, layer of corn, and layer of corn chips. Sprinkle on cheese. Dot with catsup, cover, and bake until heated through. Serves 10-15 people.

—Carol Cook

Mincemeat Beans

1 9-ounce package mincemeat,
    crumbled
2 16-ounce cans pork and beans

⅓ cup chopped onions
1 tablespoon vinegar
1 teaspoon dry mustard

Preheat oven to 350°. Combine ingredients; pour into 1½-quart casserole. Bake 45-50 minutes or until hot.

—Wilma Matney

Oven-Steamed Rice

1½ cups raw converted white rice
1½ teaspoons salt
Dash of pepper

2 tablespoons butter or margarine
3½ cups boiling water

Preheat oven to 350°. In a 1½-quart ungreased casserole with tight-fitting lid, combine rice, salt, and pepper. Dot top with butter. Pour boiling water over all; stir to melt butter. Cover and bake for 45 minutes. Don't peek; don't stir. To serve, fluff up lightly with fork. Makes 6-8 servings.

—Gladys Joyce

Packaged meat should be rewrapped before freezing. Remove the plastic wrap and tray from meat; rewrap with freezer paper or heavy-duty aluminum foil. Seal the package securely; label and freeze at once. To ensure easy separation of individual servings of frozen meat, separate the pieces of meat with two pieces of freezer paper before overwrapping.

Chicken Pie

1 chicken, cooked and cubed
2 cups chicken broth

4-6 tablespoons flour
Salt and pepper to taste

Combine ingredients; pour into greased 9"x9" baking dish and cover with large-sized buttermilk biscuits. Bake in 425° oven until well browned.

—Donna Davis

Chicken Pot Pie I

1 chicken, 2½-3 pounds
1 10¾-ounce can cream of chicken
soup
1 cup chicken broth
Salt and pepper to taste

1 18-ounce can mixed vegetables
1 8-ounce can peas
1 cup biscuit mix
¼ cup butter, melted
1 cup milk

Cook chicken until tender; remove from bones. Add undiluted chicken soup, chicken broth, salt, and pepper. Add drained vegetables and drained peas. Place in 2-quart casserole. Top with mixture of biscuit mix, milk, and butter. Serves 6-8.

—Donda Kidd

Chicken Pot Pie II

1 10¾-ounce can cream of chicken
soup
2 cups chicken broth

1 chicken, cooked and cubed
Salt and pepper to taste

Mix all ingredients together and pour into a greased casserole dish. Pour pastry mixture over. Bake at 350° until brown.

Pastry:

½ cup margarine, softened
1 cup self-rising flour

Buttermilk

Cut margarine into flour with pastry blender or fork. Add enough milk to make pouring consistency.

—Donna Davis

Baked Chestnuts

Remove shells from chestnuts; leave in boiling water about 10 minutes to blanch. Remove skins. Place in greased baking dish. Add chicken broth to almost cover. Add 2 or more tablespoons brown sugar and dots of butter if desired. Cover and bake 3 hours.

—Teresa Adkins

Toasted Cheese Delights

3 English muffins, split and toasted
1/2 pound Cheddar cheese, cut into
  6 slices
6 1/2-inch thick slices tomato
12 slices bacon, cooked and
  crumbled

Place each muffin half, cut-side up, on a baking sheet. Top each with a cheese slice, tomato slice, and crumbled bacon. Bake at 350° for 10-15 minutes or until cheese melts. Makes 6 servings. —Jamie Overbay

Baked Cheese Grits

2 1/2 cups milk
3/4 cup uncooked regular grits
1/2 cup margarine
1/2 teaspoon salt
1/3 cup grated Parmesan cheese
1 5-ounce jar sharp processed
  cheese spread

Bring milk to a boil; add grits and cook until thickened (about 10 minutes), stirring often. Stir in margarine, salt, and cheese; spoon into a lightly greased 1-quart casserole. Bake at 325° for 20 minutes. Makes 6-8 servings. —Janette Newhouse

Broccoli Quiche

2 cups shredded natural Swiss cheese
2 tablespoons flour
1 10-ounce package frozen chopped
  broccoli, cooked, well drained
1 1/4 cups milk
3 eggs, slightly beaten
1 4-ounce can mushrooms, drained
1/4 teaspoon salt
Dash of nutmeg
Dash of pepper
1 9-inch unbaked pastry shell

Toss cheese with flour. Add broccoli, milk, eggs, mushrooms, and seasonings; mix well. Pour into pastry shell. Bake at 350° for 55 minutes to 1 hour, or until set. Yields 6 servings.
To make ahead: Cool baked quiche to room temperature. Cover; refrigerate. When ready to serve, bake covered at 350° for 50 minutes.
—Janette Newhouse

Bacon can be frozen. But did you know
it will shrink excessively if cooked in its frozen state?
For best results, thaw before using.

Virginia Chili

1 pound ground beef
1 large onion, chopped
1 medium green pepper, chopped
1 teaspoon salt
1½ tablespoons chili powder
½ teaspoon black pepper
1½ teaspoons cumin
¼ teaspoon allspice

2 16-ounce cans tomatoes
2 16-ounce cans red kidney beans or
  pinto beans
1½ tablespoons sugar
1 bay leaf (optional)
1 4-ounce can tomato sauce
1 12½-ounce can condensed beef
  consommé

Brown beef; add onions and green pepper, cooking until onions are transparent. Add chili powder, cumin, allspice, salt, and pepper. Mix well. Remove from heat. Put tomatoes, beans, sugar, bay leaf, tomato sauce, and consommé into large pot. Bring to boil. Add meat mixture; reduce heat, and simmer about 3 hours. Remove bay leaf and serve with corn bread.

—Sue Harris

Chili I

2½ pounds ground beef
3 tablespoons paprika
½ teaspoon pepper
4 cups water (more if necessary)

½ pound ground suet
3 tablespoons chili powder
Salt to taste

Put beef and water in kettle. Render suet in skillet until brown; add grease to beef and water. Cook for 1 hour; then add seasonings and cook for ½ hour longer.

—Gladys Joyce

Chili II

1 pound ground beef
1 medium onion, chopped
1 stalk celery, chopped
2 teaspoons chili powder
1 teaspoon salt

Dash pepper
1 16-ounce can stewed tomatoes
1 8-ounce can tomato sauce
1 15-ounce can kidney or pinto
  beans, undrained

In large skillet, brown ground beef with onion and celery; drain. Stir in remaining ingredients except beans. Simmer, covered, 30-45 minutes or until flavors are blended. Stir in beans; heat through. Makes 6 servings.

—Wilma Matney

Always store spices in the coolest, driest, darkest place
in the kitchen. Stove heat and bright sunlight are bad for them.

APPALACHIAN

Chili III

4 pounds ground beef	1/2 teaspoon black pepper
3 tablespoons chili powder	2 teaspoons onion powder
3 tablespoons sugar	32 ounces tomato catsup
2 teaspoons salt	1/2 cup water

Put meat in large skillet; fry, mashing meat to break it up. Remove all grease. Pour meat into large pan. Add all ingredients and cook slowly for about 2 or 3 hours, stirring often, until cooked down and thickened.

—Dora Abel

Chili IV

4 pounds hamburger	1/2 teaspoon black pepper
2 tablespoons chili powder	1 32-ounce bottle tomato catsup
3 tablespoons sugar	1 10³/₄-ounce can tomato soup
2 teaspoons salt	1 10³/₄-ounce can water
1 teaspoon onion powder	

Cook hamburger in large skillet until brown. Drain. Combine all ingredients in large saucepot. Cook slowly for about 3 hours, stirring often.

—Vera Tatum

Chili Beans I

2 pounds dry pinto beans	1 16-ounce can tomatoes
2 pounds ground beef	3-5 tablespoons chili powder
1 large onion, finely chopped	Salt to taste
1 8-ounce can tomato sauce	

Clean and wash beans; place in large pan and cover with cold water. Let soak overnight. Next day heat to boiling, reduce heat, and simmer 30 minutes. Add other ingredients and cook until beans are tender, about 1 hour and 15 minutes. Stir often to prevent sticking to pan. Makes 12-16 servings.

—Jamie Overbay

Chili Beans II

1 pound ground beef	3 8-ounce cans tomato sauce
1/2 cup chopped onion	1 teaspoon salt
1 minced clove garlic	1/4 teaspoon black pepper
2 16-ounce cans kidney beans	2 tablespoons chili powder

Brown ground beef in heavy saucepan. Add onion and garlic; cook until tender. Add beans, tomato sauce, salt, pepper, and chili powder. Simmer 20 minutes; stir occasionally. Serves 6.

—Mary Cure

Herb Stuffing

3 quarts bread cubes, slightly dry
1½ teaspoons ground sage
1½ teaspoons thyme
1½ teaspoons rosemary
1½ teaspoons salt
⅓ cup chopped parsley

⅓ cup finely chopped onion
⅓ cup butter, melted
1 cup chicken or turkey broth, or
2 bouillon cubes dissolved
in 1 cup hot water

Combine bread, seasonings, parsley, onion, and butter. Add broth and toss lightly to mix. Makes 8 cups—enough to stuff a 10-pound turkey.

—Evelyn Altizer

Poultry Stuffing

6 cups soft bread crumbs
¾ teaspoon salt
⅛ teaspoon pepper
½ teaspoon sage
¼ teaspoon thyme
1 teaspoon poultry seasoning

2 tablespoons chopped parsley
¼ cup shortening
¼ cup minced onions
2 tablespoons butter
½ cup water

Combine bread crumbs, salt, pepper, sage, thyme, poultry seasoning, and parsley. Mix thoroughly. Melt shortening in large skillet; add onions. Sauté for 2 minutes. Add bread crumb mixture. Turn heat to low and sauté until lightly browned. Stir constantly. Melt butter in boiling water. Pour over browned crumbs; toss lightly. Makes 3-4 cups of stuffing.

—Evelyn Altizer

Lelia's Chicken Dressing

2 20-ounce loaves bread
1 large onion, chopped fine
4 stalks celery, chopped fine
½ cup butter

Poultry seasoning
Sage
2 10¾-ounce cans cream of chicken
soup

Crumble bread. Sauté celery and onions in butter. Combine with bread. Mix soup with 2 cans water; add to bread mixture. Season to taste with poultry seasoning and sage. Bake at 350° until brown. Serves 8-10.

—Opal Honaker

Freeze extra parsley in plastic bags;
just snip off springs of frozen parsley as needed.

Cornbread Dressing

Southern Corn Bread
1 cup chopped celery with leaves
1 cup chopped onion
2 cups chicken broth

2 beaten eggs
1 teaspoon poultry seasoning
¼ teaspoon salt

Prepare Southern Corn Bread; cool. Crumble enough corn bread to make 6 cups. Cook celery and onion in broth for 5 minutes; cool. Mix eggs, poultry seasoning, salt, vegetables with broth, and corn bread. Use to stuff an 8-pound turkey, or bake in 1½-quart casserole at 325° for 30-35 minutes. Makes 6 cups of dressing.

Southern Corn Bread:
1½ cups yellow corn meal
½ cup flour
1 teaspoon baking soda
½ teaspoon salt

1½ cups buttermilk
2 tablespoons melted lard
1 beaten egg

In mixing bowl thoroughly stir together first four ingredients. Stir in rest of ingredients; mix well. Pour batter into greased 9"x9"x2" baking pan. Bake at 400° about 20 minutes.   —Donna Davis

Turkey or Chicken Dressing Bake

1 8-ounce package herb-seasoned
  stuffing
1 10¾-ounce can condensed cream
  of celery soup
2 cups chicken broth

2 well beaten eggs
2½ cups diced chicken or turkey
½ cup milk
2 tablespoons chopped pimiento
  (optional)

Toss stuffing with ½ can soup, broth and eggs. Add diced chicken. Spread in 11½"x7½" baking dish. Combine remaining soup with milk and pimiento. Pour over ingredients. Cover with foil. Bake at 350° for 45 minutes or till set. Makes 6 servings.   —Margaret Matney

E·G·G D·I·S·H·E·S

Scrambled Eggs Supreme

6 slices bacon, cut into small pieces
8 eggs
¼ cup sour cream
¼ cup pasteurized process cheese spread

¾ teaspoon seasoned salt
Dash of pepper

Fry bacon in a large skillet; drain off all but 3 tablespoons of drippings. Combine remaining ingredients in container of electric blender; process on low speed until light and fluffy. Pour into skillet with bacon and hot drippings. Cook over low heat, stirring gently until done. Serve immediately. Makes about 6 servings.   —Jamie Overbay

Special Breakfast Eggs

4 slices bacon
1/2 cup chopped green pepper
1/4 cup chopped onion

1 10¾-ounce can cream of chicken
  soup
8 eggs, slightly beaten
Dash pepper

In 10-inch skillet, cook bacon until crisp; remove and crumble. Pour off all but two tablespoons' drippings. Cook green pepper and onion in drippings until tender. In bowl stir soup until smooth. Gradually blend in eggs and pepper. Pour into skillet. Cook over low heat. Do not stir. As mixture begins to set around edges, gently lift around edges and tilt pan so uncooked portion can flow to the bottom. Continue gently lifting cooked portions until eggs are completely set, but still moist. Garnish with bacon. Makes 4 servings.
—Wilma Matney

Beefy Quiche

Two favorites, ground beef and tomato soup, add special flavor to this main dish. Kids will like this one!

1 9-inch pie shell
6 eggs, beaten
1/2 pound ground beef
1/2 cup chopped onion or 2 tablespoons instant minced onion

1 11-ounce can condensed tomato
  bisque soup or
1 10¾-ounce can condensed
  cream of tomato soup, undiluted

Brush pie shell with small amount of the beaten eggs. Prick bottom and sides with fork. If using metal pie pan, bake shell in preheated 450° oven until golden brown, about 5 minutes. If using pie plate, bake shell at 425°. Cool on wire rack. Reduce oven temperature to 375° for metal pan or 350° for pie plate.

In large fry pan over medium heat cook ground beef and onion together until beef is lightly browned. Drain well and sprinkle into pie shell. Beat together eggs and soup until well blended. Pour over beef mixture.

Bake in preheated oven until knife inserted near center comes out clean, 30-35 minutes. Let stand 5 minutes before serving. Makes 6 servings.
—Janette Newhouse

At today's prices, paper towels cost as much as steak did in the good old days. But there is at least one way to economize. Instead of using several thicknesses of paper toweling to drain bacon or other fried food, use only one towel layer placed on top of several layers of newspaper. This works well.

APPALACHIAN

Meadow Lane Game Bird

Place pieces of bird in baking dish. Cover with 1 10¾-ounce can of cream of chicken soup and ½ can of water. Cover with foil and bake until bird is tender. Bake at 350° for 2 hours. One can of soup does four quail.

—Margaret Matney

Chicken-Fried Venison

Venison	1 egg
Flour	2 tablespoons water
Salt and Pepper	4 tablespoons margarine

Add salt and pepper to flour; mix egg and water. Dip venison into seasoned flour and into egg and water mixture. Dip into flour again. Brown on both sides in margarine. Cover and cook slowly for 20-30 minutes. Gravy may be made from drippings.

—Thelma Joyce

H·A·M·B·U·R·G·E·R &
G·R·O·U·N·D B·E·E·F

Meat-Stuffed Peppers

8 green peppers	4 medium tomatoes, chopped
1 small onion, chopped	1½ cups fresh corn
1 pound ground beef	Salt and pepper
1 tablespoon fat	Buttered crumbs

Remove top and seeds from green peppers. Parboil for 5 minutes; drain. Brown onion and meat in hot fat. Add tomatoes, corn, and seasonings. Stuff peppers; top with crumbs. Stand in greased 11"x7"x1½" casserole. Add small amount of water. Bake covered at 350° for one hour.

—Thelma Joyce

Macaroni and Hamburger

1 pound hamburger	2 cups macaroni
1 large onion, chopped	2 8-ounce cans tomato sauce

Cook hamburger and chopped onion in skillet until brown. Pour off grease. Cook macaroni in boiling water until tender, then strain and put in skillet with hamburger and onion. Add tomato sauce. Simmer for 15 or 20 minutes. Season with salt and pepper to taste.

—Donna Davis

Barbecue

1 pound ground beef
3/4 cup chopped onions
1/2 teaspoon salt
1/8 teaspoon pepper

1 10 1/2-ounce can chicken gumbo
  soup
1/4 cup water
1 tablespoon catsup
1 tablespoon mustard

Cook meat and onions until brown; add remaining ingredients. Cook on low heat until thick, about 30 minutes. Serve on buns.

—Evelyn Altizer

Cornburgers

1 pound ground beef
1/4 cup finely chopped onion
1/4 cup finely chopped green pepper
1 tablespoon flour
1 teaspoon salt

1/8 teaspoon pepper
1/2 cup catsup
1/2 cup milk
1 16-ounce can whole kernel corn
8 sandwich buns

Cook beef, onion, and green pepper in skillet until brown. Sprinkle on flour, salt, and pepper; stir to blend. Add remaining ingredients. Cook over low heat 5-10 minutes to blend flavors. Serve between buns.

—Gladys Joyce

Bar B Q

1 pound hamburger
1/2 cup celery
1/2 cup chopped onion
1 tablespoon vinegar

2 tablespoons sugar
1 tablespoon mustard
1 tablespoon Worcestershire sauce
1 cup catsup

Fry hamburger, celery, and onions until brown. Add remaining ingredients and simmer for 15-20 minutes. Serve on buns.

—Evelyn Wyatt

Campfire Hash

1 cup diced green pepper
1 1/4 cups diced onion
4 slices chopped bacon
3 tablespoons butter
1 1/2 pounds ground beef

1/3 cup catsup
3/4 cup water
1 1/2 teaspoons salt
1/4 teaspoon pepper
3 cups chopped cooked potatoes

Sauté green pepper, onions, and bacon in butter. Brown meat and drain off excess fat. Add first mixture to meat. Combine catsup, water, and seasonings and add to meat, pepper, onion, and bacon mixture. Then add potatoes and cook until liquid is nearly evaporated, about 15 minutes, turning occasionally. Makes 4 hearty servings.   —Janette Newhouse

Cornbread Pie

1 pound ground beef
1 10½-ounce can tomato soup
2 15-ounce cans red kidney beans
1 16-ounce can whole kernel corn
1 teaspoon salt
1 tablespoon chili powder

1 large onion
2 cups water
1 green pepper, diced
⅓ teaspoon pepper
1 cup self-rising cornmeal
1 cup milk

Brown meat and onion; add other ingredients. Cook for 15 minutes on top of stove. Pour into 2-quart baking dish. Top with 1 cup self-rising cornmeal and 1 cup milk (or add salt and baking powder to plain meal). Bake for 1 hour at 350°.　　　　　　　　　　　—Janette Newhouse

Meat Loaf I

2 pounds ground beef
⅔ cup onions, chopped
⅔ cup sweet pickles, chopped
⅔ cup sweet peppers, chopped

½ cup cracker crumbs
2 eggs
⅔ bottle tomato catsup

Mix together and put into loaf pan. Bake in 350° oven about 1 hour or until done.　　　　　　　　　　　—Dora Abel

Meat Loaf II

1 pound ground beef
1 cup soft bread crumbs
½ cup milk
⅓ cup onions, chopped
1 teaspoon salt

¼ teaspoon black pepper
½ teaspoon dry mustard
2 tablespoons catsup
1 egg
1 8-ounce can tomato sauce

Preheat oven to 375°. Grease 9"x5"x3" loaf pan. Thoroughly combine all ingredients but use only half of the tomato sauce. Turn meat mixture into loaf pan. Smooth surface and top with remaining tomato sauce. Bake 1 hour and 30 minutes.　　　　　　　　　　　—Teresa Adkins

Meat Loaf III

1½ pounds ground beef
1 cup tomato juice
¼ cup oats, uncooked
1 egg, beaten

¼ cup onion, chopped
1½ teaspoons salt
¼ teaspoon pepper

Combine all ingredients and mix well. Press firmly into ungreased 8½"x 4½"x2½" loaf pan. Bake in preheated 350° oven about 1 hour. Let stand 5 minutes before serving. Makes 8 servings. May be made without onions. For hamburgers, omit egg and reduce tomato juice to ½ cup. Shape to form eight patties. Broil or pan fry to desired doneness.　　　　　—Gladys Joyce

Salisbury Steak

2 pounds ground beef
2 or 3 slices bread soaked in milk
2 eggs

1 10³/₄-ounce can diluted
mushroom soup

A few hours before serving, combine ground beef, bread, and eggs; season to taste. Pat out onto flat baking sheet; cover with wax paper and refrigerate. Cut into squares, roll in flour, and brown well. Place in a baking dish. Pour soup over top. Bake at 350° for one hour and 15 minutes.

—Thelma Joyce

Barbecued Meat Loaf

1¹/₂ pounds ground beef
1 cup bread crumbs
1 egg
2 tablespoons horseradish

¹/₂ 8-ounce can tomato sauce
1 teaspoon dill seed
1 teaspoon salt
1¹/₂ cups grated Cheddar cheese

Mix together all ingredients except cheese. Roll out between waxed paper sheets to a thickness of ¹/₄". Remove top sheet; sprinkle with cheese. Remove waxed paper and roll like a jelly roll. Turn ends in to keep cheese inside. Bake at 350° for 45 minutes. Top with sauce; bake 15 minutes more.

Sauce:
¹/₂ 8-ounce can tomato sauce
¹/₄ cup catsup
¹/₄ cup vinegar

2 tablespoons brown sugar
2 tablespoons prepared mustard

Combine all ingredients and cook together until thick.

—Opal Honaker

Manhattan Meatballs

2 pounds ground beef
2 cups soft bread crumbs
¹/₂ cup chopped onion
2 eggs
2 tablespoons chopped parsley

2 teaspoons salt
2 tablespoons margarine
1 10-ounce jar orange marmalade
¹/₂ cup barbecue sauce

Combine meat, crumbs, onion, eggs, parsley, and salt; mix lightly. Shape into 1-inch meatballs. Brown in margarine; drain. Place in 2-quart casserole. Combine marmalade and barbecue sauce; pour over meatballs. Bake at 350° for 30 minutes, stirring occasionally. Makes approximately 4¹/₂ dozen meatballs.

To make ahead: Prepare recipe as directed, except for baking. Cover; seal securely. Freeze. When ready to serve, place in refrigerator 6-8 hours. Uncover; bake at 350° for 1 hour, stirring occasionally.

—Janette Newhouse

APPALACHIAN

Stuffed Cabbage Leaves

12 large cabbage leaves
2 teaspoons salt
1 cup cooked rice
1 egg
1¼ pounds ground beef
½ teaspoon pepper
1 small onion, chopped

½ teaspoon poultry seasoning or thyme
2 tablespoons oil
2 8-ounce cans tomato sauce
1 tablespoon lemon juice or vinegar
1 tablespoon brown sugar
¼ cup water

Cover cabbage leaves with boiling water and let stand for 5 minutes until limp; drain. Combine the next seven ingredients. Place equal portions of meat mixture in center of each leaf. Fold sides of each leaf over meat; roll up and fasten with toothpicks if necessary. Brown in hot oil in large skillet. Pour in tomato sauce. Simmer, covered, 1 hour, basting occasionally.

—Wilma Matney

Cabbage Rolls

1 large head cabbage
½ cup rice
1 small onion, chopped
1 egg

1 pound ground beef
½ teaspoon salt
¼ teaspoon pepper
Tomato sauce

Cook rice in boiling water until partly done. Mix all ingredients, except cabbage. Separate cabbage leaves; then parboil in salty water until wilted. Cool cabbage leaves. Take big spoonful of meat mixture, put in center of cabbage leaf, and roll. Place in baking dish and roast until done. Tomato sauce may be poured over for added taste.

—Donna Davis

Stuffed Cabbage Rolls

8 large cabbage leaves
1 10¾-ounce can tomato soup, undiluted
1 pound ground beef
1 cup cooked rice

¼ cup chopped onion
1 egg, slightly beaten
1 teaspoon salt
¼ teaspoon pepper

Cook cabbage leaves in salted water a few minutes to soften; drain. Combine 2 tablespoons soup with remaining ingredients. Divide meat mixture into 8 balls and place one in each cabbage leaf. Fold in sides of leaves and roll up, securing with toothpick if necessary. Place cabbage rolls seam-side down in skillet; pour remaining soup over rolls. Cover; cook over low heat for 40 minutes. Stir occasionally; spoon sauce over rolls. Makes 4 servings.

—Evelyn Altizer

To laugh is a right of man more ancient even than death . . .
—"You Will Laugh" by Preston Newman

Easy Skillet Dinner

1 pound ground beef
½ cup uncooked rice
1 cup water
1 teaspoon salt

3 or 4 medium potatoes
1 10¾-ounce can cream of chicken soup
¼ teaspoon pepper

Brown ground beef in skillet; drain. In small saucepan cook ½ cup rice in 1 cup water. Bring to boil, lower heat, and simmer for 15 minutes. Fluff rice with fork when done. Peel potatoes and slice. Cover with water and boil in large pan for 15 minutes; drain when done. Combine all ingredients and simmer for 15 minutes. Garnish with parsley flakes if desired.

—Wilma Matney

Meat Whirl

1½ pounds ground beef
1 cup soft bread crumbs
1 egg
2 teaspoons prepared horseradish

1 8-ounce can tomato sauce
1½ cups shredded Cheddar cheese
1 teaspoon dill seed

In a bowl lightly mix meat, crumbs, egg, horseradish, and ½ cup tomato sauce. On waxed paper pat meat into a 10"x14" rectangle; sprinkle with cheese. Roll from shorter side, as for jelly roll; press ends to seal. Carefully transfer to baking pan, seam-side down. Bake at 350° for 45 minutes. Pour remaining tomato sauce over meat; sprinkle with dill seed. Bake 15 additional minutes; let stand 5-10 minutes. Remove to warm platter. Makes 6-8 servings.

—Janette Newhouse

Party Meat Balls

1 pound ground beef
1 medium onion, chopped
2 slices bread, broken
1 teaspoon salt
¼ teaspoon pepper

½ teaspoon thyme
1 tablespoon parsley
¼ cup milk over bread
1 egg, beaten

Mix all ingredients and make small balls. Fry until brown all over. Drop into sauce and simmer 30 minutes.

Meat Ball Sauce:
1 tablespoon flour
2 tablespoons brown sugar
1 tablespoon prepared mustard

2 tablespoons vinegar
½ cup catsup
¾ cup water

Mix flour, sugar, and mustard. Add vinegar, catsup, and water. Simmer 30 minutes before adding meat balls.

—Margaret Matney

Italian Spaghetti I

½ cup onion slices	1 3-ounce can broiled sliced
2 tablespoons olive or salad oil	mushrooms
1 pound ground beef	¼ cup chopped parsley
2 cloves garlic, minced	1½ teaspoons oregano
2 1-pound cans tomatoes	1 teaspoon salt
2 8-ounce cans seasoned tomato	½ teaspoon monosodium glutamate
sauce	¼ teaspoon thyme
1 cup water	1 bay leaf
Grated Parmesan or Romano cheese	Long spaghetti, cooked

Cook onion in hot oil until golden. Add meat and garlic; brown lightly. Add remaining ingredients; simmer uncovered 2-2½ hours or till thick. Remove bay leaf. Serve sauce on hot cooked spaghetti. Pass bowl of grated Parmesan or Romano cheese. Makes 6 servings.　　—Janette Newhouse

Italian Spaghetti II

1 pound ground beef	2 8-ounce cans tomato puree
¼ cup cooking oil	2 6-ounce cans tomato paste
2 tablespoons parsley, minced	2 teaspoons Worcestershire sauce
2 medium onions, chopped	Salt and pepper to taste
2 cloves garlic, minced	1 8-ounce package long spaghetti

Brown meat in hot oil. Add parsley, onions, and garlic; cook until yellow. Add tomato purée, paste, Worcestershire sauce, salt, and pepper. Simmer over low heat two hours. Serve over hot spaghetti that has been cooked as directed and drained. Serves 6.　　—Opal Honaker

Mike's Favorite Vermicelli

2 tablespoons shortening	1 cup whole kernel corn
1 16-ounce package vermicelli	2 teaspoons salt
noodles, broken in pieces	½ teaspoon pepper
1 pound ground beef	2 teaspoons chili powder
2 cloves garlic, minced	1 28-ounce can tomatoes
2 small onions, thinly sliced	¾ cup water
1 green pepper, finely chopped	1 8-ounce package processed
4 stalks celery, thinly sliced	American cheese slices

Melt shortening in frying pan at medium heat. Sauté dry vermicelli until lightly browned, stirring occasionally. Add beef and cook, stirring, until meat loses its red color. Stir in next eight ingredients. Add tomatoes and water. Stir gently. Simmer, covered, for 25 minutes. Place cheese slices on top of mixture. Heat just until cheese melts.　　—Wilma Matney

Saucy Pork Chops

6 pork chops
Salt and pepper to taste
1 medium onion, thinly sliced

1 10½-ounce can condensed cream
  of chicken soup
¼ cup catsup
2 or 3 teaspoons Worcestershire sauce

In skillet brown chops on both sides. Season with salt and pepper. Cover chops with onion slices. Combine remaining ingredients and pour over chops. Cover and simmer 45-60 minutes, or until done. Remove from skillet and spoon sauce over chops. Serves 6.   —Opal Honaker

Pork Chop and Potato Bake

6 pork chops
2 teaspoons salt, divided
2 tablespoons oil
1 cup chopped onions
1 cup chopped green peppers

1 15-ounce can tomato sauce
1 tablespoon Worcestershire sauce
4 medium potatoes, sliced (about
  6 cups)

Sprinkle both sides of pork chops with 1 teaspoon salt. In large skillet heat oil until hot; add chops; brown on both sides. Remove and set aside. Add onions and green peppers; sauté 5 minutes. Stir in tomato sauce, Worcestershire sauce, and remaining teaspoon salt; bring to boiling point. Reduce heat; simmer 2 minutes uncovered. Arrange potatoes in a layer in bottom of greased 13"x9"x2" casserole. Pour half of the sauce over potatoes; top with pork chops; pour remaining sauce over pork chops. Cover. Bake in 350° oven for 50 minutes; uncover and bake until pork chops are tender, about 25 minutes longer. Serve with salad and French bread if desired. Makes 6 portions.   —Vera Tatum

Pork Chop Casserole

7 pork chops, center cut
1 large onion
1 large green pepper

7 teaspoons quick-cooking rice
1 15-ounce can tomatoes
1 16-ounce can tomato juice

Place pork chops in skillet with a small amount of cooking oil and brown on both sides. Place browned chops in baking dish. Top each chop with slice of onion and one ring of pepper. In each pepper ring place one teaspoon of rice. Pour tomatoes and tomato juice over chops and bake in 350° oven for 45-60 minutes.   —Thelma Joyce
                                                              Vera Tatum

Pork Chops with Rice

4 lean pork chops, $\frac{1}{2}''$ thick
$\frac{1}{4}$ teaspoon salt
$\frac{1}{4}$ teaspoon pepper or paprika
1 tablespoon shortening
$\frac{3}{4}$ cup water
$\frac{1}{2}$ cup finely cut celery
1 $1\frac{3}{8}$-ounce dried soup mix

3 cups cooked rice
1 4-ounce can mushroom stems and pieces
$\frac{1}{4}$ cup flour
1 tablespoon dried parsley flakes
$\frac{2}{3}$ cup evaporated milk

Sprinkle pork chops with salt and pepper. Heat in a 10-inch skillet with shortening until brown. Drain off drippings. Stir in water, celery, and soup mix; cover. Cook over low heat for 30 minutes, or until chops are tender. Remove chops. Mix mushroom pieces and flour; stir into liquid in skillet. Add parsley flakes and the evaporated milk. Stir over low heat until steaming. Do not boil. Pour gravy over pork chops. Serve with hot rice.

—Wilma Matney

Herbed Pork Steaks

1 egg
3 tablespoons milk
$\frac{1}{3}$ cup grated Parmesan cheese
$1\frac{1}{4}$ cups herb-seasoned stuffing mix, finely crushed

4 $\frac{1}{2}''$-$\frac{3}{4}''$ thick pork steaks
2-4 tablespoons shortening
1 1-ounce package mushroom gravy mix (optional)

Combine egg and milk in a shallow dish, beating with fork until well blended. Combine cheese and stuffing mix in a shallow dish. Dip steak into egg mixture; then dredge in stuffing mixture, coating well. Heat shortening to 350° in an electric skillet; cook steaks until browned on both sides. Cover and reduce heat to 250°; cook 30 minutes or until steaks are done. If desired, prepare mushroom gravy according to package directions. Serve with steaks. Makes 4 servings.

—Dorothy Tatum

Corn Dogs

1 cup self-rising corn meal
1 cup self-rising flour
2 tablespoons sugar (if desired)
1 egg, beaten

1 cup milk
2 tablespoons fat, melted
1 pound weiners

Combine first three ingredients. Beat egg slightly, add milk, and stir into the dry ingredients. Add melted fat. Heat oil to 375°. Dip the weiners in the batter, drain, and drop into the hot oil. Let brown. Use wire basket for deep-fat frying if available.

—Thelma Joyce

Grease from frying meat won't spatter
if you shake a little flour in the pan.

Sweet-and-Sour Pork

1 egg, beaten
¼ cup flour
1 teaspoon salt
¼ cup cornstarch
¼ cup chicken broth, divided
1½ pounds boneless pork, trimmed
    of fat and cut into ¾-" cubes
Vegetable oil
1 medium green pepper, cut into
    thin strips

1 15¼-ounce can pineapple chunks
1 clove garlic, minced
2-3 medium carrots, cut into 2" strips
¼ cup sugar
¼ cup red wine vinegar
1 teaspoon soy sauce
2 tablespoons cold water
1 tablespoon cornstarch
Hot cooked rice

Combine egg, flour, salt, ¼ cup cornstarch, and ¼ cup chicken broth; beat until smooth. Dip pork cubes in batter, coating well. Deep fry in 375° oil for 5-6 minutes or until golden brown. Drain and set aside. Drain pineapple, reserving juice. Heat 2 tablespoons oil in a large skillet; add green pepper, garlic, carrots, and pineapple. Cook 2-3 minutes, stirring occasionally. Stir in pineapple juice, remaining chicken broth, sugar, vinegar, and soy sauce; boil 1 minute. Slowly add 2 tablespoons cold water to 1 tablespoon cornstarch, stirring until smooth. Stir into vegetable mixture, and cook until thickened. Stir in pork, and serve over rice. Makes 4-6 servings.

—Dorothy Tatum

Marinated Pork Roast

2 tablespoons dry mustard
2 teaspoons whole thyme leaves
½ cup dry sherry
½ cup soy sauce
2 cloves garlic, minced
1 teaspoon ground ginger

1 4- to 5-pound pork loin roast,
    boned, rolled, and tied
1 10-ounce jar apricot preserves or
    jelly
1 tablespoon soy sauce
2 tablespoons dry sherry

Combine first six ingredients in a shallow dish, stirring well. Place roast in dish. Cover and marinate 3 or 4 hours in refrigerator, turning occasionally. Remove roast from marinade and place on rack in a shallow roasting pan. Insert meat thermometer at an angle into thickest part of roast. Bake uncovered at 325° until thermometer registers 170° (2½-3 hours total cooking time).

Combine preserves, 1 tablespoon soy sauce, and 2 tablespoons sherry in a small saucepan; cook over low heat, stirring occasionally, until preserves melt. Serve with sliced roast. Garnish as desired. Makes 12-14 servings.

—Dorothy Tatum

After a roast is done,
use the leftover heat in your turned-off oven
to warm plates, serving bowls, and platters.

Tenderloin Platter

2 tablespoons butter or margarine
8 ¼-pound pork tenderloins
1 10¾-ounce can condensed cream
  of asparagus soup, undiluted
¼ cup milk

½ cup onion, chopped
1 3-ounce can sliced mushrooms,
  undrained
¼ teaspoon curry powder

Melt butter in skillet; add pork and brown on all sides. Remove pork, reserving drippings in skillet. Combine soup and milk and add to drippings in skillet. Add remaining ingredients, stirring well. Return pork to skillet; cover and simmer mixture for 40-45 minutes. Serve sauce over pork. Makes 8 servings.   —Jamie Overbay

Country Ham with Red-Eye Gravy

6 ¼"-thick slices country ham
¼ cup margarine

¼ cup brown sugar
½ cup strong black coffee

Cut gashes in fat to keep ham from curling. Sauté ham in margarine in a heavy skillet over low heat until light brown, turning several times. Remove ham from skillet and keep warm. Stir sugar into pan drippings. Cook over low heat until sugar dissolves, stirring constantly. Add coffee to pan drippings, stirring well. Simmer gravy 5 minutes and keep warm. Serve gravy over ham. Makes 6 servings.   —Jamie Overbay

Homemade Sausage

25 pounds fresh pork, about 22 lbs.
  lean meat and 3 lbs. fat
½ cup salt
½ cup firmly packed brown sugar

3 tablespoons sage
3 tablespoons ground black pepper
2 tablespoons ground red pepper

Trim off any excess fat from pork. Cut pork into 2-inch cubes and spread out on waxed paper. Combine salt, brown sugar, sage, and peppers. Sprinkle over meat. Grind meat with seasonings in meat grinder two times. Mix ground mixture well with hands. Sausage can be canned or frozen. Makes 25 pounds.   —Evelyn Altizer

Fried Apples

Use the early, thin-skinned green apples. Cut into quarters and remove core, but do not peel. Place apples in heavy skillet with a little bacon grease and start cooking on low heat. Cover and cook until tender. Add sugar to taste, stirring thoroughly and being careful not to let burn after sugar is added. Serve hot. Good for breakfast with sausage.

—Thelma Joyce

Batter for Frying
Old-Fashioned Chicken or Fish

1 cup flour
1 teaspoon baking powder
½ teaspoon salt

1 egg
½ cup milk

Mix and sift dry ingredients. Beat egg. Add milk and dry mixture. Dip each piece of chicken or fish in batter and fry in about an inch of hot fat. Turn each piece so that it will brown evenly. This makes sufficient batter for about 2½ pounds of chicken or fish. —Margaret Matney

Perfect Fried Chicken

⅓ cup flour
1 teaspoon paprika
1 teaspoon salt
¼ teaspoon pepper

1 2½- to 3-pound ready-to-cook
  broiler-fryer chicken, cut up
Shortening for frying

Combine flour, paprika, 1 teaspoon salt, and ¼ teaspoon pepper in paper or plastic bag. Add 2 or 3 pieces of chicken at a time and shake. Heat shortening (¼″ deep in skillet) until a drop of water sizzles. Brown meaty pieces first, then add remaining pieces (don't crowd). Brown one side, then turn with tongs. When lightly browned, about 15-20 minutes, reduce heat and cover tightly. If cover isn't tight, add 1 tablespoon water. Cook until tender, 30-40 minutes. Uncover last 10 minutes. Makes 4 servings.
—Jamie Overbay

Macaroni Chicken Bake

1 7-ounce package elbow macaroni
  (1¾ cups)
2 cups diced cooked chicken
½ cup thinly sliced celery
2 tablespoons chopped green pepper
2 tablespoons chopped pimientos

1 tablespoon finely chopped onions
1 teaspoon salt
⅛ teaspoon pepper
1 cup salad dressing
2 tablespoons butter
½ cup bread crumbs

Cook macaroni in boiling salted water only until tender, about 7 minutes. Drain, rinse, and drain again. Combine macaroni, chicken, celery, green pepper, pimiento, onions, salt, pepper, and salad dressing; mix lightly until well combined. Spread in greased 1½-quart shallow baking dish. Combine bread crumbs with butter and sprinkle over salad. Bake in 400° oven for 20 minutes. Makes 6 servings. Tuna may be substituted for chicken.
—Evelyn Altizer

APPALACHIAN

Candlelight Chicken

4 cups cooked rice
1 2½-ounce jar sliced dried beef, rinsed and drained
4 whole chicken breasts, split, skinned and boned

1 10¾-ounce can cream of chicken soup
1 10¾-ounce can cream of mushroom soup
1 cup sour cream
6 slices bacon, cut in half

In 2½-quart baking dish (13"x9"x2") arrange a single layer of beef. Top with chicken. Blend soup and sour cream; pour over all. Top with bacon. Bake at 400° for 1 hour or until done. Serve with rice. Serves 6.

—Vonda Kidd

Chicken Divan

2 10-ounce packages frozen broccoli
¼ cup butter
6 tablespoons flour
2 cups chicken broth or 1 10¾-ounce can cream of mushroom soup plus ½ cup water

½ cup evaporated milk
3 tablespoons lemon juice
3 cups chicken, cooked and boned
¼ cup grated cheese

Cook broccoli using package directions; drain. Melt butter; blend in flour. Add chicken broth or soup and water. Cook until thick and bubbly. Stir in cream and lemon juice. Place broccoli crosswise in baking dish. Pour ½ sauce over; top with chicken. Add cheese to remaining sauce; pour over chicken. Bake at 350° for 20 minutes. Broil until sauce is golden brown.

—Opal Honaker

Chicken Loaf

2-4 pounds chicken, cooked tender, skinned and boned, cut fine
2 cups crumbled light bread
1 cup cooked rice

1½ teaspoons salt
⅛ cup pimiento, chopped
3 cups chicken broth
4 eggs, well beaten

Mix chicken, bread crumbs, rice, salt, pimiento, and chicken broth. Add eggs last. Bake at 325° for 1 hour.

Topping:

¼ cup butter
¼ cup flour
2 cups chicken broth
¼ cup milk

⅛ teaspoon paprika
2 teaspoons parsley
1 teaspoon lemon juice
Salt to taste

Melt butter; stir in flour. Add broth, milk, and seasonings. Simmer a few minutes.

—Vernelle Herrin

Chicken Breasts Romano

3 whole chicken breasts, split in half
3 tablespoons seasoned flour
1/4 cup shortening
1/4 cup onion, finely minced
2 cups tomato juice
2 tablespoons Romano cheese
1 tablespoon sugar
1/2 teaspoon salt

1/2 teaspoon garlic salt
1/2 teaspoon oregano
1/4 teaspoon basil
1 teaspoon vinegar
1 3-ounce can sliced mushrooms
1 tablespoon fresh parsley, minced
1 cup shredded American or
   Cheddar cheese

Shake chicken breasts in a bag with salt-and-pepper-seasoned flour to coat evenly. In large skillet, brown the chicken in the shortening. Remove chicken from skillet. Discard all but 1 tablespoon shortening. Add onions and lightly brown. Add tomato juice which has been combined with Romano cheese, sugar, salt, garlic salt, oregano, basil, vinegar, mushrooms, and parsley. Add chicken, cover, and simmer 45 minutes or until chicken is tender and sauce is the consistency of gravy. Sprinkle with shredded cheese before serving. Makes 6 servings.   —Janette Newhouse

Chicken Imperial

6 split chicken breasts
2/3 cup margarine, melted
1 1/2 cups snack cracker crumbs
1/2 cup Parmesan cheese

2 tablespoons parsley
1 teaspoon paprika
Salt and pepper

Mix dry ingredients. Coat breasts with margarine; then with dry ingredients. Bake at 350° for 1 hour.   —Margaret Matney

Smothered Chicken

1/3 cup flour
1 teaspoon salt
1/2 teaspoon paprika
1 cut-up chicken, 2 1/2-3 pounds
1/2 cup shortening
1 1 3/8-ounce envelope dried chicken
   noodle soup mix

1 medium onion, sliced
1 cup evaporated milk
1/2 teaspoon poultry seasoning
2 teaspoons dried parsley flakes

Mix in paper bag: the flour, salt, and paprika. Shake chicken, a few pieces at a time, in flour mixture. Heat shortening in 10-inch skillet. Add chicken and brown over medium heat. Drain off drippings. Stir in the soup mix, water, and sliced onion. Cover. Cook over low heat 30-35 minutes, or until tender. Place chicken in deep serving dish. Add to skillet the milk, poultry seasoning, and parsley flakes. Cook and stir until thickened. Do not boil. Pour over chicken.   —Wilma Matney

Party Chicken

8 large chicken breasts, boned
   and skinned
8 slices bacon
1 4-ounce package dried beef

1 10³/₄-ounce can cream of
   mushroom soup
1 cup sour cream

Wrap each chicken breast with a slice of bacon. Arrange dried beef in ungreased 13"x9"x2" baking pan; place chicken on dried beef. Combine soup and sour cream; pour over chicken. Bake uncovered at 275° for 3 hours. Makes 8 servings.

—Wilma Matney
Jamie Overbay

Chicken with Rice

6 chicken breasts, boned and halved
¹/₂ teaspoon pepper
12 slices bacon
1 4-ounce package dried beef
1¹/₂ cups sour cream

2 10³/₄-ounce cans cream of chicken
   soup
1 3-ounce package cream cheese
4 cups hot rice

Pepper but do not salt chicken. Wrap slice of bacon around each chicken breast. Place layer of dried beef in bottom of baking dish. Arrange bacon-wrapped chicken on beef slices. Cover with mixture of chicken soup, sour cream, and cream cheese. Cover dish tightly with foil. Bake at 325° for 2 hours. When tender remove foil and let brown slightly. Serve on bed of rice. 12 servings.

—Vernelle Herrin

Chicken and Ham Supreme

6 whole chicken breasts, boned and
   halved
¹/₄ cup margarine
2 cups chopped onions
¹/₄ cup cornstarch
¹/₂ teaspoon salt
¹/₄ teaspoon pepper

1 cup dry sherry
4 cups milk
12 chicken-flavored bouillon cubes
1 pound egg noodles, cooked
   8 minutes and drained
12 slices Swiss cheese
12 slices boiled ham

In Dutch oven, brown chicken, a few pieces at a time, in margarine over medium heat 15 minutes or until tender. Remove chicken. Add onions; cook 5 minutes. Mix cornstarch, salt, and pepper; gradually stir in sherry until smooth. Add to onions with next three ingredients, stirring constantly. Bring to boil over medium heat. Grease 6-quart shallow baking pan. Add noodles; pour on sauce; toss. Roll cheese inside ham; arrange with chicken over noodles. Bake tightly covered in 325° oven for 45-60 minutes or until hot. Makes 12 servings.

—Thelma Joyce

Chicken Chips

1 medium hen
2 cups celery
3 tablespoons grated onion
2 tablespoons lemon juice
1 cup mayonnaise (you may use less)

1 10¾-ounce can cream of chicken
soup
1 cup grated American cheese
1 cup crushed potato chips

Cook hen with a bay leaf until tender. Combine chicken, celery, and onion. Dribble lemon juice over and mix. Blend chicken soup and mayonnaise; add to chicken mixture. Put in ungreased casserole dish. Top with grated cheese and potato chips. Bake at 350° for 30 minutes.

—Teresa Adkins

Hawaiian Chicken

12 boneless chicken breasts, skinned
1 cup Thousand Island salad dressing
1 10-ounce jar apricot preserves

1 1⅜-ounce package dried onion
soup mix

Arrange chicken in a baking dish. Mix the dressing, preserves, and dried soup together. Pour over chicken. Bake at 325° for 45 minutes covered, 30 minutes uncovered.

—Teresa Adkins

Brown-Bag-It Turkey

1 12-pound turkey, thawed
2 tablespoons water
⅔ teaspoon paprika

1 cup oil
Salt
1 brown grocery bag

Rub thawed turkey with salt inside and out. Combine water, paprika, and oil; mix well. Again rub turkey. Pour remainder of mixture in the bag and rub over the inside of bag. Tie ends of drumsticks loosely together so as to hold dressing in. Place turkey in bag, breast up, and tie bag tightly with string. Cook in preheated 325° oven for 14 minutes per pound. Remove from oven promptly; do not overcook.

—Margaret Matney

The moon rolls its white nub
in a packet of clouds,
eating Bogota and Shreveport,
rising up from Tennessee
like a baby face laughing
at the fence wire pushed into silence
like prayers of thanks.

—"Deals" by Clyde Kessler

Raisin Sauce for Ham

2 cups water
1 cup raisins
2 tablespoons cold water
2 tablespoons cornstarch

2 tablespoons sugar
1/8 teaspoon salt
2 tablespoons lemon juice
1 tablespoon butter

Simmer raisins in 2 cups water for 15 minutes. Make a paste of cornstarch, sugar, salt, and 2 tablespoons water. Add to raisins; heat until thick. Remove from heat; add butter and lemon juice. Serve over ham, ham loaf, or pork.
—Evelyn Altizer

Spaghetti Sauce

1 pound hamburger
4 8-ounce cans tomato sauce
1 large onion, chopped

1/2 teaspoon salt
1/4 teaspoon black pepper
1/4 teaspoon red pepper

Place hamburger and onion in skillet and cook until done—not brown. Drain. In medium saucepan, put all ingredients. Simmer for 1 hour.
—Donna Davis

Fried Fillet Fish

1 1/2 pounds fillet fish (bass)
1/4 cup buttermilk
3 tablespoons flour

3 tablespoons meal
1/2 teaspoon seafood seasoning
Salt and pepper to taste

Drain and dry fish well. Put in bowl and pour buttermilk over fish, coating all. Mix flour, meal, and seasonings in plastic bag. Coat fish and fry in about 1/4" oil at medium heat. Do not overcook.
—Margaret Matney

Baked Trout

Trout
1 egg, slightly beaten
Cornmeal

Salt and pepper to taste
1/2 lemon, squeezed
Butter

Dip trout in egg, then roll in meal. Dot with butter and squeeze lemon juice over. Salt and pepper to taste. Place in a pan and bake at 350° for 25 minutes or until flaky. Baste twice with pan juices.
—Thelma Joyce

Fish Bake

1 cup chopped onions	⅛ teaspoon pepper
½ cup chopped celery and tops	¼ cup vegetable oil
½ cup chopped parsley, fresh or dried	¾ teaspoon paprika
2 pounds fish fillets	2 8-ounce cans tomato sauce
1 teaspoon salt	

Combine onion, celery, and parsley. Arrange in large shallow greased 2-quart baking dish. Place fish in overlapping layers over vegetables. Season with salt and pepper. Drizzle oil over top. Sprinkle with paprika. Bake in 375° oven for 10 minutes. Pour tomato sauce over. Bake 30-35 minutes; baste frequently. Makes 6 servings.   —Evelyn Altizer

Salmon Cakes

1 15½-ounce can pink salmon	1 cup meal
2 eggs	Milk, small amount
1 large potato, chopped fine	Salt
1 cup flour	Pepper

Mix ingredients in bowl. Make into small patties and fry in deep hot fat until golden brown.   —Thelma Joyce

Seadogs

2 6-ounce cans chunk light meat tuna	2 tablespoons pimientos, chopped
⅔ cup crushed potato chips	Salt and pepper to taste
⅓ cup mayonnaise	6 hot dog buns
3 tablespoons sweet pickle relish	6 olives

Mix first six ingredients to spread. Split and butter hot dog buns. Spread tuna mixture on bottom halves and hold together with an olive on a toothpick.   —Thelma Joyce

Broiled Shrimp

16 ounces boiled shrimp	Dash red pepper
¼ cup butter	Salt to taste
Juice of ½ lemon	Garlic salt (optional)
½ clove garlic, chopped	

Melt butter in skillet; add garlic and cook for a few minutes. Add shrimp, lemon juice, and seasonings. Stir until shrimp is well coated with butter. Place skillet under broiler for 3 or 4 minutes. Stir occasionally to lightly brown all shrimp. Overcooking will toughen shrimp.
—Thelma Joyce

Salmon Patties

1 15- to 16-ounce can pink salmon
1 egg
⅓ cup onion

½ cup flour
1½ teaspoons baking powder
1½ cups shortening

Drain salmon; set aside 2 tablespoons of the juice. In a mixing bowl mix salmon, egg, and onion until sticky. Stir in flour. Add baking powder to salmon juice; stir into salmon mixture. Form into small patties and fry until golden brown, about 5 minutes, in hot shortening.   —Wilma Matney

---

S·O·U·P·S & S·T·E·W·S

Clam Chowder

3 slices bacon
1 large potato, peeled and cubed
1 medium stalk celery, chopped
1 small onion, chopped
¾ teaspoon salt
⅛ teaspoon pepper

⅛ teaspoon thyme
2 6½-ounce cans minced clams,
     drained, reserving liquid
¼ cup flour
3 cups milk

In large saucepan, fry bacon until crisp; drain on paper towel. Add to drippings in pan potato, celery, onion, salt, pepper, thyme, and liquid from clams. Heat to boiling and cook covered, about 10 minutes or until vegetables are tender. Combine flour and milk; add to vegetable mixture. Heat over medium heat until thick, stirring occasionally. Stir in clams. Heat through, but do not boil. Garnish with bacon. Makes 5-6 servings.
                                        —Wilma Matney

Old-Fashioned Beef Stew

2 pounds beef chuck, cubed
3 tablespoons flour
3 tablespoons fat
2 teaspoons salt
¼ teaspoon pepper
6 cups water
12 small white onions, peeled

2 cups yellow turnips, peeled and
     diced
6 carrots, peeled and cut into chunks
4 medium potatoes, peeled and cut
     into quarters
¼ cup cooked peas

Dredge meat with flour and brown on all sides in fat in kettle. Add salt, pepper, and water. Bring to a boil; cover and simmer 1½ hours or until meat is almost tender. Add remaining ingredients except peas; simmer 45 minutes or until vegetables are tender. Season and sprinkle with peas. Makes 6 servings.   —Evelyn Altizer

Ham-It-Up Soup

1 pound dried beans, navy or great
   northern
2½ quarts water
2 ham hocks
1 carrot, chopped

2 8-ounce cans tomato sauce
½ teaspoon salt
1 teaspoon Worcestershire sauce
½ teaspoon seasoned salt
¼ teaspoon pepper

In Dutch oven or kettle combine all ingredients; bring to a boil. Simmer, covered, for 2 hours, stirring occasionally. Remove skin and bone from ham; skim off excess fat from broth. Return meat to soup. Makes 6-8 servings.
—Donna Davis

Cream of Potato Soup

2 cups potatoes, diced and cooked
3 cups Thin White Sauce
Salt and pepper to taste

Mix ingredients in a 1½- to 2-quart saucepan. Heat through. Makes 6 servings.

Thin White Sauce (makes 1½ cups):

1 tablespoon butter or margarine
1 tablespoon flour

¼ teaspoon salt
1½ cups milk

Melt butter or margarine in saucepan over low heat. Blend in flour, salt, and white pepper (optional). Add milk all at once. Cook quickly, stirring constantly, until mixture thickens and bubbles. Remove sauce from heat when it bubbles.
—Donna Davis

Old Virginia Stew

1 pound beef, cut into 1-inch cubes
2½ cups boiling water (approx.)
1 chopped onion
½ teaspoon lemon juice
1½ teaspoons salt
½ teaspoon Worcestershire sauce
¼ teaspoon pepper

¼ teaspoon paprika
Dash of allspice
1 teaspoon sugar
¼ cup tomato juice
1 cup sliced carrots
1 cup cubed potatoes
1 cup diced celery

Brown meat in hot fat. Add hot water, onion, lemon juice, seasonings, and tomato juice; simmer for 2 hours. Add more water if needed. Add vegetables and cook until done.
—Donna Davis

Grate a raw potato and add it to your soup
when you put too much salt in it.
The potato absorbs the salt.

Hamburger Soup

1 pound hamburger	2 cups tomato juice
4 tablespoons margarine	1 teaspoon salt
1 cup chopped onion	1/4 teaspoon pepper
1 cup diced carrots	4 cups milk
1 cup diced potatoes	6 tablespoons flour

Cook onion in margarine until tender. Add hamburger. Cook until well browned. Add tomato juice, carrots, and seasonings. Cover and cook slowly until carrots are partly tender. Then add potatoes and cook until potatoes and carrots are well done. Mix a little milk with flour to make a thin paste. Add to milk and cook until thick. Add to soup mixture. If soup becomes too thick, thin with water or milk. Makes 8 servings.

—Janette Newhouse

Cabbage Soup

6 slices fatback	2 16-ounce cans tomatoes
1/2 head cabbage	Flour and water paste

Fry grease out of fatback. Remove fatback and do not use. Lower heat on grease and add bite-sized pieces of cabbage. Cook a few minutes until cabbage is limp. Blend tomatoes in blender. Add to frying pan. Cover and cook on low heat for 1/2 hour. Mix a little flour and cold water. Add to soup to thicken. Salt and pepper to taste.

—Donna Davis

Weight Watcher's Vegetable Soup

4 10¾-ounce cans tomato soup	1 cup chopped celery
4 cans water	1 10-ounce package frozen French-
1/2 head shredded cabbage	style green beans
4 beef bouillon cubes	1 pound carrots, shredded or
2 teaspoons salt	chopped

Simmer the first six ingredients for 30 minutes. Then add beans and carrots and simmer for 30 minutes more.

—Donna Davis

When adding vegetables to homemade soup, remember that all vegetables should not be added at the same time. Vegetables that take the longest cooking time should be added first. These include green beans, potatoes (unless diced very thinly), and corn. Canned vegetables need only to be heated, so add them last.

— HINTS FROM OUR COOKS —

If time allows, the best method for removing fat is to refrigerate soups or stews until the fat congeals on the top. But if you're in a hurry, drop ice cubes into the pot. As you stir, the fat will cling to the cubes. Discard the cubes before they melt. Or, wrap ice cubes in a piece of cheesecloth or paper towel and skim over the top.

To make successful white sauce, follow this procedure: Melt butter in a saucepan; then remove from heat to blend in flour. Use cold milk; add it gradually, stirring constantly. Return to heat; cook, stirring constantly, until mixture thickens and bubbles. Add seasonings; cook at least 5 minutes, stirring occasionally.

To reheat cooked pasta or rice, place it in a strainer over a pan of boiling water. Cover and steam 10-15 minutes.

When grating a small amount of cheese, use your vegetable peeler. It is easier to clean than the grater.

This is one of the best secrets for making fluffy rice. When the rice is done, remove the lid and cover the pot with two layers of paper toweling. Then cover with a tight-fitting lid and let stand from 5-30 minutes until you are ready to serve it. The excess moisture from the rice will be absorbed by the towels. The end result is light, dry, fluffy rice.

When you need just a few drops of onion juice for flavor, sprinkle a little salt on a slice of onion; scrape the salted surface with a knife or spoon to obtain the juice.

— TIPS ON GROUND BEEF —

Lowest price ground beef is 70-75% lean—some shrinkage.

Medium price (lean ground beef) is 75-80% lean—less shrinkage.

Highest price (extra lean ground beef) is 80-85% lean—little shrinkage.

THE HOUSE BIRD

The house bird has held the sunlight upon a seed
it waves itself like a mirror of an outside
to my aunt who has not seen anything
her hands could not know: there is one bird
made from the whistle in a room
and there is something else that moves the moment
across her back: a family made
into one creature, and the walking
of memory upon tile: she says
that where the mynah works its voice
is where her husband and children rest
like a whisper leafing through a magazine.

—Clyde Kessler

Pies

P·I·E C·R·U·S·T·S

Never Fail Pie Crust I

One Crust:
    1⅓ cups sifted flour
    1 teaspoon salt

    3 tablespoons cold milk
    ⅓ cup vegetable oil

Double Crust:
    2 cups flour
    1½ teaspoons salt

    ¼ cup cold milk
    ½ cup vegetable oil

Mix flour and salt in bowl. Put oil and milk together and pour into flour. Stir until well mixed. Put ball of dough between two pieces of wax paper and roll thin. This will make an 8-inch or 9-inch pie shell.

—Wilma Matney

Never Fail Pie Crust II

1 cup sifted cake flour
2 cups sifted bread flour
1 tablespoon sugar
1 teaspoon salt

1 cup shortening
1 egg, slightly beaten
Milk

Rub fat, cut into the size of peas, into combined dry ingredients. Add enough milk to the slightly beaten egg to make ½ cup. Add all liquid to the shortening and flour mixture. Stir with fork until mixture sticks together. Roll out on slightly floured board or pastry canvas. This makes three single crusts. Bake single crusts for 8-10 minutes in 425° oven.

—Gladys Joyce

Fool Proof Pie Crust

4 cups flour
1¾ cups shortening
1 tablespoon sugar
2 teaspoons salt

1 tablespoon vinegar
1 egg
½ cup ice water

With a fork mix together the first four ingredients. In a separate bowl beat remaining ingredients. Combine the two mixtures, stirring with a fork until all ingredients are moistened. Then, with hand, mold dough into a ball. Chill at least 15 minutes before rolling it into desired shape. Dough can be left in refrigerator up to three days, or it can be frozen until ready to use. Dough will remain soft in the refrigerator and can be taken out and rolled at once. Makes two 9-inch double crust pies and one 9-inch single shell.

—Thelma Joyce

Vinegar Pie Crust

4 cups flour
1 tablespoon sugar
2 teaspoons salt
1¾ cups shortening

½ cup water
2 tablespoons cider vinegar
1 egg

In large bowl combine flour, sugar, and salt with shortening until mixture resembles coarse crumbs. Combine water, vinegar, and egg. Beat with fork and add to flour mixture. Mix until it holds together (dough will be sticky). Cover and chill at least two hours. Divide dough into four or five balls. Wrap tightly. May refrigerate up to two weeks or freeze up to two months. If frozen, thaw, wrapped, in refrigerator about 2 hours. Roll out for pies. Makes 4 or 5 single crusts. —Opal Honaker

Graham Cracker Crust

1½ cups graham cracker crumbs
  (about 18 graham crackers)

⅓ cup sugar
½ cup butter, melted

Mix crumbs, sugar, and melted butter. Press firmly in greased 9-inch pie pan. Chill until set, about 45 minutes. —Marilyn Wells

Pastry Pie Crust

⅔ cup lard
  (add 1 tablespoon if using
  shortening)

2 cups flour
1 teaspoon salt
4-5 tablespoons cold water

Cut lard into flour and salt until crumbly. Sprinkle in water, 1 tablespoon at a time; mix with fork until all flour is moistened. Shape into two balls; flatten on lightly floured pastry cloth. Roll pastry 2 inches larger than inverted pie plate with floured stockinette-covered rolling pin. Fold pastry into quarters; lay into pie plate and unfold. Makes two 9-inch crusts.
  —Donna Davis

— PIE CRUST HINTS —

To prevent a soggy crust in custard pies, brush egg white on the uncooked pie shell; bake at 425° for 5-10 minutes. Add filling, and bake according to recipe directions.

To help a pastry shell keep its shape while baking, line it with fitted waxed paper and fill with dried peas or rice. Bake about 5 minutes or until shell sets; remove paper and dried peas or rice.

Bob Andy Pie

4 eggs	1/2 cup butter or margarine
2 cups sugar	1 teaspoon vanilla
1/4 cup flour	2 9-inch pie crusts, unbaked
1 cup cream	

Beat together the first three ingredients. Add cream, butter, and vanilla. Pour into pie crusts. Bake at 300° for about 45 minutes or until set. This is good for picnics and bake sales.

—Dora Abel

Brown Sugar Pie I

4 cups brown sugar	3 eggs
5 tablespoons flour	2 teaspoons vanilla
6 tablespoons butter	2 9-inch pie shells, unbaked
2 cups evaporated milk	

Mix together the first six ingredients and pour into pie shells. Bake at 400° for 30 minutes; reduce heat to 300° and bake 30 minutes more.

—Evelyn Altizer

Brown Sugar Pie II

2 tablespoons flour	4 eggs, beaten
1 pound light brown sugar	1 tablespoon vanilla
1/2 cup butter, melted	2 8-inch pie shells, unbaked
1 cup milk, hot	

Mix first six ingredients and pour into pie shells. Bake in a 350° oven for 30 minutes.

—Opal Honaker

Butterscotch Pie

1 9-inch crust, baked	2 egg yolks, beaten
3/4 cup brown sugar	2 cups milk
1/3 cup flour	4 tablespoons butter
1/2 teaspoon salt	1 teaspoon vanilla

Mix dry ingredients; add egg yolks and milk. Cook until thick. Cool; add vanilla. Pour in baked pie crust. Cover with meringue.

—Opal Honaker

Add a tablespoon of cornstarch to the sugar
when making meringue for a pie. It will not weep.

Buttermilk Pie

2 cups sugar
¼ cup flour
1 teaspoon vanilla
3 eggs, slightly beaten

½ cup margarine
¾ cup buttermilk
1 9- or 10-inch pie shell, unbaked

Mix all ingredients together, beating well, and pour into unbaked pie shell. Bake at 325° for about 45 minutes, until set and well browned.

—Marilyn Wells

Chess Pie 1

1½ cups sugar
3 eggs
½ cup butter, melted

1 tablespoon vinegar
1 tablespoon cornmeal
1 9-inch pie shell, unbaked

Add eggs to sugar one at a time, beating well after each addition. Add melted butter slowly. Add cornmeal and vinegar. Mix well. Pour into pie shell. Bake at 325° about 45 minutes.

—Evelyn Wyatt

Chess Pie II

1 pound brown sugar
4 tablespoons cornstarch
1 13-ounce can evaporated milk
4 eggs, slightly beaten

2 teaspoons vanilla
¾ cup margarine
2 9-inch pie crusts, unbaked

Mix sugar and cornstarch together. Add margarine and milk. Heat until margarine is melted. Stir continually. Remove from heat and let cool. Add beaten eggs and vanilla. Put in pie crusts and bake at 350° for 35 minutes.

—Margaret Matney

Eggnog Pie 1

2 3¾-ounce packages vanilla pie
    filling
2 cups eggnog
1¼ cups milk

1 tablespoon light rum
⅛ teaspoon nutmeg
1 9-inch pie shell, baked and cooled

Combine pudding mix, eggnog, milk, and nutmeg in a saucepan. Cook and stir over medium heat until mixture comes to a full boil. Remove from heat. Add rum and cool 5 minutes, stirring twice. Pour into pie shell; cover with plastic wrap.

—Gladys Joyce

When separating the yolk from the white of an egg,
break it into a funnel over a glass. The white will pass
through and the yolk will remain in the funnel.

Eggnog Pie II

3 eggs
1/3 cup sugar
1/4 teaspoon salt
1 3/4 cups milk
1 envelope gelatin

3 tablespoons water
6 teaspoons sugar
1 1/2 teaspoons rum flavoring
1 teaspoon nutmeg
1 9-inch pie shell, baked

Beat egg yolks slightly. Blend in 1/3 cup sugar and salt; add milk. Cook in double boiler until just thick enough to coat spoon. Sprinkle gelatin on top of water and allow to soften. Add to custard and stir until dissolved. Chill until slightly thickened. Beat egg whites until frothy. Add 6 teaspoons sugar gradually, beating until meringue stands in peaks. Fold into custard together with flavoring and nutmeg. Fill baked pie shell. Refrigerate.

—Margaret Matney

Oatmeal Pie I

6 tablespoons margarine, softened
3/4 cup sugar
2 eggs
2/3 cup dark corn syrup

2/3 cup regular oatmeal, uncooked
1 teaspoon vanilla
1 9-inch pie shell, unbaked

Cream together sugar and margarine. Add eggs and beat well. Stir in corn syrup, oatmeal, and vanilla. Pour into pie shell and bake at 325° about 40-45 minutes or until done.

—Gladys Joyce

Oatmeal Pie II

2/3 cup sugar
2 eggs
2/3 cup pancake syrup
2/3 cup 1-minute oatmeal
2/3 cup butter, melted

1/2 teaspoon salt
1/2 teaspoon vanilla
1/2 cup nuts
1 9-inch pie shell, unbaked

Mix first nine ingredients well in blender. Spoon into pie shell. Bake at 350° for 45 minutes.

—Thelma Joyce

Peanut Butter Pie

1 3-ounce package cream cheese
1 9-ounce carton whipped topping
1 cup confectioners' sugar

1/3 cup crunchy peanut butter
1 9-inch chocolate crumb pie crust

Mix together first four ingredients until well blended. Pour into crust. Chill well. This is great when frozen.

—Teresa Adkins

Frozen Fluffy
Peanut Butter Pie

1 4-ounce package cream cheese,
   softened
1 cup confectioners' sugar
1/3 cup creamy peanut butter

6 tablespoons milk
1 9-ounce carton whipped topping
1/4 cup finely chopped peanuts
1 9-inch graham cracker crust

Whip cream cheese until fluffy. Add sugar and peanut butter. Slowly add milk and blend. Fold whipped topping into above mixture. Pour into pie crust and sprinkle nuts over pie. Freeze. Wrap after it is frozen. Serve frozen and keep frozen at all times.   —Margaret Matney

Sweet Potato Pie

1 cup cooked, mashed sweet potatoes
1/3 cup butter, melted
2 eggs, beaten
1/3 cup milk or half-and-half
1/2 teaspoon baking powder

Pinch salt
1 teaspoon nutmeg
1 teaspoon vanilla
1 cup sugar, or less if desired
1 9-inch pie shell, unbaked

Combine sweet potatoes with all ingredients except pie shell, blending well with electric mixer (or hand mix using a wooden spoon). Pour into pie shell. Bake in preheated 400° oven about 30 minutes, or until golden and puffy. Serve alone or topped with whipped cream.   —Gladys Joyce

Sweet Potato Meringue Pie

1 30-ounce can sweet potatoes,
   drained and mashed
1 cup sugar
1 tablespoon flour
1/4 cup butter or margarine, melted
1/3 cup evaporated milk
1/2 cup milk

Dash of salt
1/8 teaspoon lemon extract
3 eggs, separated
1 10-inch pie crust, unbaked
1/4 teaspoon cream of tartar
1/2 teaspoon vanilla
1/3 cup sugar

Combine first nine ingredients and egg yolks; beat until combined. Pour mixture into crust and bake at 400° for 10 minutes. Reduce heat to 350° and bake for 30 additional minutes or until set. Beat egg whites with cream of tartar and vanilla until soft peaks form. Gradually add 1/3 cup sugar, one tablespoon at a time, beating until stiff peaks form. Spread meringue over filling, sealing to edge of pastry. Bake at 350° for 10-12 minutes or until golden. Cool completely before serving.   —Jamie Overbay

From mountains
she sprang as clean as dogwood.
—"The Alleghany Woman" by Preston Newman

Chocolate Pie
Baked In Crust

4 tablespoons margarine
1½ cups sugar
2 tablespoons cornstarch
½ cup cocoa
2 whole eggs

½ cup evaporated milk
½ cup water
1 teaspoon vanilla
1 unbaked crust

Cream margarine, sugar, and cornstarch well. Add cocoa and eggs. Mix milk with water to make one cup. Add with vanilla to mixture. Bake at 350° about 35 minutes or until done, but still soft in center of top. Do not overcook. —Margaret Matney

Almond Fudge Pie

1 cup slivered almonds
1 3¾-ounce package chocolate
    fudge pudding and pie filling
¾ cup light corn syrup

¾ cup evaporated milk
1 egg, slightly beaten
½ cup chocolate chips, melted
1 8-inch pie shell, unbaked

Chop almonds; toast at 350° for 3-5 minutes. Set aside. Blend together until smooth: pie filling mix, corn syrup, milk, eggs, and chocolate chips. Add almonds and pour into pie shell. Bake at 375° about 45 minutes, or until top is firm and begins to crack. Garnish with whipped topping if desired. —Gladys Joyce

Chocolate Cream Pie

1 9-inch pie crust, baked
1 cup sugar
3 tablespoons cocoa
⅓ cup flour

⅛ teaspoon salt
2 egg yolks, slightly beaten
2 cups milk
1 teaspoon vanilla

Mix dry ingredients; add egg yolks and milk. Cook until thick; add vanilla. Cool. Put in previously baked crust; top with meringue. —Opal Honaker

... The rain I once knew was soft on the ground;
    The raindrops then were warm and light.
    But now I ache; and they, too, sound
        Alone tonight.
                    —"Homesick" by Cecil Mullins

Cocoa Cream Pie

1/4 cup cocoa
3/4 cup sugar
3 tablespoons cornstarch
1/4 teaspoon salt
2 cups milk
2 egg yolks
1 tablespoon butter

1 teaspoon vanilla
1 8-inch pie shell, baked
2 egg whites
1/4 teaspoon cream of tartar
3 tablespoons sugar
1/2 teaspoon vanilla

Mix together cocoa, 3/4 cup sugar, cornstarch, and salt in a saucepan. Gradually stir in milk, mixing well until smooth. Cook over medium heat until filling thickens, stirring constantly. Boil 1 minute and remove from heat. Slowly stir about half the chocolate mixture into slightly beaten egg yolks, then blend into hot mixture in saucepan. Boil 1 minute more, stirring constantly. Remove from heat and stir in butter and vanilla. Pour into baked pie shell and cover with meringue. Brown in 400° oven for 8-10 minutes.

Meringue: Beat the egg whites with cream of tartar until foamy; add 3 tablespoons sugar gradually and beat until stiff peaks hold. Flavor with 1/2 teaspoon vanilla. Pile onto pie, seal edges to crust.

—Dorothy Tatum

C·O·C·O·N·U·T

Coconut Pie

2 9-inch unbaked pie shells
4 eggs
2 cups sugar
1/2 cup evaporated milk

1/2 cup butter, melted
Pinch salt
1 7-ounce can flaked coconut
1 teaspoon vanilla

Beat eggs with sugar; add other ingredients. Pour into pie shells. Bake at 375° for 35-45 minutes.

—Opal Honaker
Vera Tatum

Impossible Coconut Pie

4 eggs
1 1/2 cups sugar
1/2 cup self-rising flour
1/4 cup butter or margarine, melted

2 cups milk
1 teaspoon vanilla
1-1 1/2 cups coconut

Combine all ingredients. Mix well; pour into two 9-inch pie plates. Bake at 350° for 30-35 minutes or until brown. This pie makes its own crust, so easy to make.

—Evelyn Wyatt

Coconut Pie
makes Its Own Crust

2 cups milk
3/4 cup sugar
1/2 cup biscuit mix
4 eggs

1/4 cup butter or margarine
1 1/2 teaspoons vanilla
1 cup flaked coconut

Combine milk, sugar, biscuit mix, eggs, butter, and vanilla in electric blender container. Cover and blend on low speed for 3 minutes. Pour into greased 9-inch pie pan. Let stand about 5 minutes, then sprinkle with coconut. Bake at 350° for 40 minutes. Serve warm or cool.

—Gladys Joyce

Coconut Cream Pie

2/3 cup sugar
5 tablespoons flour
1/4 teaspoon salt
2 cups milk

2 egg yolks, slightly beaten
2/3 cup moist shredded coconut
1 teaspoon vanilla
1 9-inch pie shell, baked and cooled

Combine sugar, flour, and salt in a 2-quart saucepan; stir in milk gradually. Cook on high heat until mixture starts to steam; turn heat to medium and cook until thick, stirring constantly. Turn heat to low. Stir a little of the hot mixture into slightly beaten egg yolks; slowly stir into remaining hot mixture. Cook 2 minutes more, stirring constantly. Cool and chill in refrigerator. Then add coconut and vanilla. Mix well and pour into baked pie shell.

Meringue for Pie:
2 egg whites
1/4 cup sugar

1/3 cup shredded coconut

Beat egg whites until foamy. Add sugar gradually; beat until stiff. Spread evenly on pie, carefully sealing at edge of pastry. Sprinkle coconut over meringue.

—Evelyn Altizer

Coconut Dream Pie

2 1 1/2-ounce envelopes whipped
   topping mix
2 3/4 cups cold milk
1 teaspoon vanilla

2 3 3/4-ounce packages coconut cream
   flavor pudding and pie filling or
   instant pudding and pie filling
1 1/3 cups flaked coconut
1 9-inch pie shell, baked and cooled

Prepare whipped topping mix with 1 cup of the milk and vanilla as directed on package, using large mixer bowl. Add remaining 1 3/4 cups milk and the pie filling mix. Blend, then beat at high speed for 2 minutes, scraping bowl occasionally. Stir in coconut. Spoon into pie shell. Chill at least 4 hours. Garnish if desired.

—Gladys Joyce

Ambrosia Pie

2 9-inch pie shells
2 cups sugar
1 cup coconut
1 cup white raisins
1 cup chopped pecans

Pinch salt
1/2 cup melted butter
6 eggs
1 teaspoon vanilla
1 tablespoon vinegar

Combine all ingredients and pour into pie crusts. Bake at 350° for 35 minutes or until golden brown. 　　　　　　　　　　—Evelyn Altizer

Impossible Pie

2 cups milk
4 eggs
1/2 cup sugar
2 tablespoons vanilla

1 cup flaked coconut
1/2 cup butter or margarine, cubed
1/2 cup biscuit mix

In blender, combine milk and egg. Blend. Add remaining ingredients and blend 1 minute. Pour batter into greased 9-inch pie pan. Bake for 35-40 minutes or until knife inserted in center comes out clean.
　　　　　　　　　　—Gladys Joyce

C·R·E·A·M

Blueberry Cream Pie

Crust:

1 1/2 cups sifted flour
1/2 teaspoon salt

1/2 cup shortening
3 tablespoons cold water

Follow directions for mixing Pastry Pie Crust (page 177). Fit pastry into 9-inch pie pan, prick with fork. Bake at 425° until brown. Cool.

Filling:

1 cup blueberries
1 1/2 cups milk
1 8-ounce package cream cheese
1 3 3/4-ounce package cream vanilla
　instant pudding mix

1/4 cup apple jelly
1 tablespoon water
2 teaspoons lemon juice

Wash blueberries and stem. Blend milk into cream cheese until smooth. Add instant pudding. Mix and beat slowly one minute. Pour into cooled shell. Arrange blueberries on top.

Combine apple jelly, water, and lemon juice in saucepan. Heat slowly, stirring constantly, just until jelly melts. Cool slightly. Spoon over blueberries. Chill until firm. 　　　　　　　　　　—Ruth Bales

Strawberry Cream Pie

1 cup sugar
2 tablespoons flour
2 eggs, separated
1½ cups milk

1 tablespoon butter
1 quart strawberries
1 9-inch pie crust, baked
6 tablespoons sugar

Mix sugar and flour well. Beat egg yolks until light lemon color; then add flour and sugar gradually, alternately with the milk. Cook until thick and smooth; add butter; cool. Put 1 quart berries into crust. Pour the cooled, cooked mixture over berries. Cover with meringue prepared with the 2 egg whites and 6 tablespoons sugar. Bake at 350° until meringue is brown.

—Dora Abel

Vanilla Cream Pie

¾ cup sugar
⅓ cup flour or 3 tablespoons
   cornstarch
¼ teaspoon salt
2 cups milk

3 egg yolks, slightly beaten
2 tablespoons butter or margarine
1 teaspoon vanilla
1 9-inch pastry shell, baked
1 recipe meringue

In saucepan combine sugar, flour, and salt; gradually stir in milk. Cook and stir over medium heat until mixture boils and thickens. Add some of hot mixture to eggs, stirring until smooth. Then add warm eggs to mixture in saucepan. Cook 2 minutes longer, stirring constantly. Remove from heat; add butter and vanilla. Cool to room temperature. To prevent a crust from forming, put clear plastic wrap or waxed paper directly on top, touching surface of the hot pudding clear to sides of bowl. Pour into baked pastry shell.

Chocolate Cream Pie:

In vanilla cream pie filling, increase sugar to 1 cup. Chop two 1-ounce squares unsweetened chocolate; add with milk.

Coconut Cream Pie:

Add 1 cup flaked coconut to vanilla cream pie filling. Sprinkle ⅓ cup coconut over meringue before browning.

Meringue:

3 egg whites
¼ teaspoon cream of tartar

½ teaspoon vanilla
6 tablespoons sugar

Beat egg whites with cream of tartar and vanilla till soft peaks form. Gradually add sugar, beating till stiff peaks form and all sugar is dissolved. Spread on top of pie, sealing to pastry. Bake in 350° oven about 12-15 minutes, or until meringue is golden.

—Gladys Joyce

Velvet Custard Pie

4 eggs
²/₃ cup sugar
¹/₂ teaspoon salt

¹/₂ teaspoon nutmeg
2²/₃ cups milk
1 teaspoon vanilla

Beat eggs; add sugar, salt, nutmeg, milk, and vanilla and stir until smooth. Pour into lined 9-inch pie shell. Bake at 425° for 15 minutes; reduce temperature to 350° and bake 30 minutes longer.

—Jennie Tatum

Old-Fashioned Custard Pie

3 large eggs
¹/₂ cup sugar
¹/₂ teaspoon salt

¹/₂ teaspoon nutmeg
2²/₃ cups milk
1 9-inch unbaked pie shell

Beat eggs lightly; add sugar, salt, nutmeg, and milk. Beat well together and pour into unbaked pie shell. Bake in 350° oven for 40 minutes. Sprinkle with more nutmeg.

—Jamie Overbay

Custard Pie

4 slightly beaten eggs
¹/₂ cup sugar
¹/₄ teaspoon salt
¹/₂ teaspoon vanilla

2¹/₂ cups scalded milk
1 9-inch unbaked pastry shell
Nutmeg

Blend eggs, sugar, salt, and vanilla. Gradually stir in scalded milk. Pour into unbaked pastry shell; sprinkle with nutmeg. Bake at 350° for 35-40 minutes or until knife inserted in center comes out clean. Cool on rack.

—Opal Honaker
Hazel Whitt

Egg Custard Pie

6 egg yolks
6 tablespoons sugar
4 cups milk
2 teaspoons flour

1 teaspoon vanilla
Nutmeg
2 9-inch unbaked pie crusts

Beat together and pour into two 9-inch unbaked pie crusts. Sprinkle with nutmeg. Bake in 300-350° oven until custard is set.   —Dora Abel

Custard Pie
Makes Its Own Crust

4 eggs
1/2 cup margarine, softened
2 cups milk

1/2 cup self-rising flour
1 cup sugar
1 teaspoon vanilla

Blend together and pour into a 9-inch pie pan. Sprinkle with nutmeg. Bake at 350° for 25-30 minutes.
—Opal Honaker

Rhubarb Custard Pie

2 tablespoons flour
2 eggs
1 cup sugar
2 tablespoons butter

1/2 teaspoon salt
1 cup rhubarb
1 uncooked pastry shell

To make custard, mix first five ingredients together. Put rhubarb in bottom of pie crust; pour custard over it. Bake at 400° for 10 minutes, then at 325° for 30 minutes.
—Thelma Joyce
Vera Tatum

F·R·U·I·T

Apple Pie

1 cup sugar
1/2 cup plus 2 tablespoons flour
1/2 teaspoon nutmeg
1/2 teaspoon cinnamon
1/4 teaspoon allspice

4 or 5 large apples, sliced
Pastry for one 9-inch double-
crust pie
2 tablespoons lemon juice
1/2 cup butter

Combine ½ cup sugar, 2 tablespoons flour, nutmeg, cinnamon, and allspice in cup. Sprinkle over apples; toss to coat apples well, spoon into pie shell, and drizzle with lemon juice. Combine remaining sugar and flour, cut in butter; sprinkle over apples. Top with crust, slide into brown paper bag; fold over twice and fasten with paper clip. Place on cookie sheet. Bake at 425° for 15 minutes, then reduce heat to 350° and bake an additional 45 minutes.
—Thelma Joyce

When soft custard separates on removal from the stove,
beat it hard for 5 minutes with an egg beater.

APPALACHIAN

Real Apple Pie

Pastry for one 9-inch double-
    crust pie
6 cups tart apples, sliced
3/4-1 cup sugar
2 teaspoons butter
2 tablespoons flour

1/4 teaspoon nutmeg
1/4 teaspoon cloves
1/2 teaspoon cinnamon
1/4 teaspoon salt
Juice and rind of 1/2 large lemon

Toss apples with flour, spices, salt, and lemon until well coated. Fill lightly floured bottom crust with apples; dot with butter; cover with top pastry. Place on baking sheet. Bake in 450° oven for 10 minutes. Reduce heat to 350° and continue baking for 40 minutes. Serve warm with good chunks of cheddar cheese, or with vanilla ice cream, or just plain.

—Gladys Joyce
Donna Davis

Crustless Apple Pie

1/2 cup sugar
1 teaspoon cinnamon

1 cup water
6 medium-sized cooking apples

Blend sugar and cinnamon in heavy saucepan. Stir in water and apples; cook 10 minutes. Turn apples and syrup into greased baking dish. Cover with topping. Bake at 350° for about 35 minutes. Serve with whipped cream.

Topping:
1 cup flour
1 teaspoon baking powder
1/4 teaspoon salt

6 tablespoons shortening
1/2 cup brown sugar

Sift flour, baking powder, and salt together. Cream shortening and brown sugar. Add flour mixture.   —Thelma Joyce

Blueberry Pie

2 3-ounce boxes concord grape
    gelatin
2 cups boiling water

1 21-ounce can blueberry pie filling
1 9-inch pie crust, baked, or 1
    9-inch crumb crust

Mix together gelatin, boiling water, and pie filling. Pour into crust and let congeal.

Topping:
1 8-ounce package cream cheese
1 cup sour cream

1 teaspoon vanilla
1/2 cup chopped nuts

Mix together and spread over congealed mixture.

—Evelyn Altizer

Cherry Cheese Pie

1 8-ounce package cream cheese,
  softened
1 14-ounce can sweetened
  condensed milk
1/3 cup lemon juice

1 teaspoon vanilla extract
1 ready-prepared graham cracker
  pie crust
1 21-ounce can cherry pie filling,
  chilled

In medium bowl, beat cheese until light and fluffy. Add sweetened condensed milk; blend thoroughly. Stir in lemon juice and vanilla. Pour into crust. Chill 3 hours or until set. Top with desired amount of pie filling before serving. Refrigerate leftovers. —Evelyn Altizer

Citrus Chiffon Pie

1 envelope unflavored gelatin
1/2 cup sugar
Dash salt
4 egg yolks
1/2 cup lemon juice
1/2 cup orange juice
1/4 cup water

1/2 teaspoon grated lemon peel
1/2 teaspoon grated orange peel
4 egg whites
1/3 cup sugar
1 9-inch coconut crust or 1 9-inch
  baked pastry shell

Mix together gelatin, sugar, and salt in saucepan. In a bowl beat egg yolks with juices and water. Add to dry ingredients. Cook until mixture comes to a boil. Add peels. Chill until slightly thickened. Beat egg whites and remaining 1/3 cup sugar until stiff. Fold into gelatin mixture. Pour into crust. Chill.

Coconut Crust:
  1 teaspoon butter or margarine
  1 3 1/2-ounce can flaked coconut (1 1/3 cups)

Butter a 9-inch pie plate. Press coconut against bottom and sides. Bake in 325° oven about 10 minutes, or till edges are golden.
—Marilyn Wells

Japanese Fruit Pie 1

1 cup sugar
1/2 cup raisins or chopped dates
1/2 cup coconut
1 tablespoon vinegar

2 beaten eggs
6 tablespoons butter, melted
1 9-inch pie shell, unbaked

Mix first six ingredients and pour into pie shell. Bake at 325° for 45 minutes.
—Opal Honaker

Japanese Fruit Pie II

½ cup margarine, melted
2 eggs
½ cup raisins
½ cup pecans

½ cup sugar
1 tablespoon vinegar
½ cup coconut
1 9-inch pie shell, unbaked

Mix first seven ingredients together well. Pour into pie shell. Bake in 300° oven until golden brown, about 40 minutes. —Evelyn Wyatt

Lemon Pie

1 8-inch crumb or baked pastry
  pie shell
1 14-ounce can sweetened
  condensed milk
½ cup lemon juice

1 teaspoon grated lemon rind or
  ¼ teaspoon lemon extract
2 eggs, separated
¼ teaspoon cream of tartar, if desired
4 tablespoons sugar

Put sweetened condensed milk, lemon juice, lemon rind or extract, and egg yolks into mixing bowl; stir until mixture thickens. Pour into chilled crumb crust or cooled pastry shell. Add cream of tartar to egg whites; beat until frothy. Add sugar gradually; beat until stiff. Pile lightly on pie filling. Bake in 325° oven until lightly browned. Cool. —Gladys Joyce

Frozen Lemon Pie

3 eggs, separated
½ cup sugar
5-7 tablespoons lemon juice

½ cup sugar
½ cup cream, whipped
Vanilla wafer crumbs

Cook egg yolks, ½ cup sugar, and juice in double boiler until thick. Fold into egg whites beaten stiff with ½ cup sugar. Fold this mixture into cream which has been whipped (chilled evaporated milk may be used). Line ice cube tray with vanilla wafer crumbs. Add lemon mixture and put crumbs on top. Freeze 24 hours at low temperature. Serves 12-15.
  —Jamie Overbay

Lemon Supreme Pie

1 cup sugar
2 eggs, separated
3 tablespoons butter
3 tablespoons flour

1 cup milk
Juice and rind of 1 lemon
1 9-inch pie shell, unbaked

Beat sugar, egg yolks, and butter together. Add juice, grated rind, and flour; mix. Add the milk and stiffly beaten egg whites. Pour into pie shell. Bake in 325° oven for 45 minutes. —Donna Davis

Lemonade Pie

2 9-inch pie crusts, baked and
cooled
1 14-ounce can sweetened
condensed milk
1 6-ounce can frozen lemonade
concentrate
1 9-ounce carton frozen whipped
topping

Mix condensed milk with lemonade concentrate. Add whipped topping; mix well. Pour into pie shells and chill.　　　　—Judy Fogleman

Orange Pie

1 9-inch pie shell, baked
1/2 cup undiluted frozen orange juice
1 envelope unflavored gelatin
   (1 tablespoon)
3 eggs, separated
1 cup sugar
1/4 teaspoon cream of tartar
1 teaspoon vanilla
1/4 teaspoon salt
1 8-ounce package cream cheese
1 cup whipping cream

Combine 1/4 cup orange juice and gelatin in top of double boiler. Add egg whites, 1/2 cup sugar, and cream of tartar. Cook over boiling water, beating constantly with electric mixer or rotary beater until stiff peaks form. Set aside. In medium saucepan combine 1/4 cup undiluted orange juice, egg yolks, 1/2 cup sugar, vanilla, and salt. Beat with electric mixer until light. Cook, stirring constantly, until smooth and thick. Remove from heat. Add cream cheese; beat until smooth. Fold into gelatin-egg white mixture. Chill until thickened but not set, about 30 minutes. Beat 1 cup whipping cream until thick; fold into gelatin mixture. Spoon into pie shell; chill.
—Wilma Matney

Fresh Peach Pie

3 cups peach slices
1 tablespoon lemon juice
3/4 cup sugar
3 tablespoons cornstarch
2 tablespoons butter
Dash of salt
1/4 teaspoon almond extract
1 9-inch pie shell, baked

Combine peaches, sugar, and lemon juice; let stand one hour, drain. Measure one cup syrup (add water to make cup if necessary); add cornstarch, and blend. Cook over low heat, stirring until thick. Remove from heat; add butter, salt, and flavoring. Cool. Place peaches in shell. Chill. Serve plain or with ice cream.　　　　—Gladys Joyce

Save lemon and orange rinds. Store in the freezer and
grate as needed for pies, cakes, breads, and cookies.
Or the rinds can be candied for holiday uses.

Million Dollar Pie

1 9-ounce package whipped topping
mix
1 14-ounce can sweetened
condensed milk
1 17-ounce can crushed pineapple

$^{1}/_{2}$ cup chopped pecans
1 4-ounce package flaked coconut
$^{1}/_{4}$ cup lime juice
2 9-inch baked pie crusts

Mix all ingredients as listed. Pour into two pie crusts. Chill about 4 hours.

—Margaret Matney

Sea Breeze Pineapple Pie

Pastry for 1 9-inch double crust pie
$^{1}/_{2}$ cup sugar
3 tablespoons cornstarch
$^{1}/_{2}$ teaspoon salt
1 20-ounce can crushed pineapple

$^{1}/_{2}$ cup canned pineapple juice
2 tablespoons butter or margarine
2 tablespons lemon juice
1 teaspoon grated lemon peel
$^{2}/_{3}$ cup flaked coconut

Preheat oven to 425°. Blend together sugar, cornstarch, and salt. Stir in undrained pineapple and pineapple juice. Cook over moderate heat, stirring constantly, until mixture boils and thickens. Remove from heat; add butter, lemon juice, peel, and coconut. Cool about 5 minutes. Pour into pie crust. Cover with pastry strips arranged lattice fashion. Lay ½"-wide pastry strips across filled pie about 1" apart. Weave with remaining strips to make lattice effect. Fold bottom crust up over edges of pastry strips. Press to seal; flute edges. Bake for 30-35 minutes. Cool before serving.   —Helen Steele

Rhubarb Pie

2 cups rhubarb, uncooked
1 cup sugar
2 eggs

2 tablespoons butter
1 tablespoon flour
1 9-inch pie crust, unbaked

Mix rhubarb, sugar, eggs, butter, and flour. Pour into pie crust and bake at 350° for 25-30 minutes.   —Opal Honaker

Rhubarb Strawberry Pie

Pastry for 1 9-inch double-crust pie
1 pint strawberries, sliced
2 cups rhubarb, sliced
$^{3}/_{4}$ cup light brown sugar

$^{1}/_{2}$ cup sugar
2 tablespoons flour
1 teaspoon grated lemon rind

Combine sugars, flour, and rind; toss lightly with fruit. Pour into pie shell; cover with top crust. Bake in 375° oven for 50 minutes.

—Gladys Joyce

Strawberry Pie I

3 tablespoons cornstarch
1 cup sugar
1 cup crushed strawberries

Whole strawberries
1 9-inch pie crust, baked and cooled

Cook first three ingredients until thick, about 5-10 minutes. Cover bottom of pie crust with whole berries, then pour in cooked mixture which has cooled some. Put more whole berries on top. Served with whipped cream or non-dairy whipped topping, or serve plain.   —Gladys Joyce

Strawberry Pie II

1¹/₂ cups sugar
1¹/₂ cups water
3 tablespoons cornstarch

1 3-ounce box strawberry gelatin
2 cups sliced strawberries
1 9-inch pie shell, baked

Mix sugar, water, and cornstarch. Cook until thick and clear. Remove from heat. Add gelatin; mix well and cool. Place sliced strawberries in pie shell. Pour gelatin mixture over berries. Refrigerate until ready to serve.
—Margaret Matney

Fresh Strawberry Pie I

2 1¹/₂-ounce packages whipped
   topping mix
1 cup milk
1 8-ounce package cream cheese
1 teaspoon vanilla
1 cup sugar
2¹/₂ cups water

1 cup sugar
2 tablespoons cornstarch
1 3-ounce package strawberry
   gelatin
4 cups strawberries
2 9-inch pie shells, baked

Mix topping mix as directed. Add sugar, vanilla, and cream cheese. Pour into baked pie shells. Make a glaze by combining water, sugar and cornstarch, and bringing to a boil. Cook two minutes. Add gelatin to cooked mixture and let thicken in refrigerator. When it starts to thicken, fold in the berries and pour into the pie shells on top of the first mixture. Return to refrigerator to chill.
—Thelma Joyce

Fresh Strawberry Pie II

3 tablespoons flour
3 tablespoons strawberry gelatin
1 cup sugar
1 cup boiling water

Few drops red food coloring
Fresh strawberries
1 9-inch pie crust, baked

Boil first five ingredients until thick and clear. Cool. Pour over fresh strawberries in crust and chill.
—Teresa Adkins

Derby Pie

2 eggs, slightly beaten
1 cup sugar
1/2 cup flour
1/2 cup butter

1 cup pecans, chopped
1/2 cup chocolate chips
1 teaspoon vanilla
1 9-inch pie shell, baked

Combine ingredients in order given. Spread in pie shell; bake in 350° oven for 30 minutes. The filling puffs up, but will settle after it is cooked.

—Peggy Whitt

Southern Pecan Pie

3 eggs
2/3 cup sugar
1 cup dark corn syrup
1/3 cup margarine, melted

1 cup pecans
Dash of salt
1 9-inch pie crust, unbaked

Beat eggs thoroughly with sugar; add salt, syrup, and melted butter. Add pecans. Pour in pastry shell. Bake at 350° for 50 minutes or until knife inserted in center comes out clean.

—Donda Kidd

Pudding Pecan Pie

1 3³/₄-ounce package vanilla pudding
1 cup corn syrup
3/4 cup evaporated milk

1 egg, slightly beaten
1 cup pecans, chopped
1 9-inch pie shell, unbaked

Blend pudding mix with corn syrup. Gradually add evaporated milk and egg, stirring to blend. Then add pecans. Pour into pie shell. Bake at 375° until firm and just beginning to crack, about 40 minutes.

—Margaret Matney

Mincemeat Pecan Pie

1 9-ounce package condensed
  mincemeat, broken up
1/2 cup light or dark corn syrup
1/4 cup margarine
3 eggs, slightly beaten

1/2 cup pecans, coarsely chopped
1 tablespoon orange peel, grated
1 9-inch pastry shell, unbaked
1/4 cup dry sherry

In small saucepan, combine mincemeat, syrup, and margarine. Heat, stirring constantly, until boiling. Gradually stir mixture into eggs. Add pecans and orange peel. Pour into pastry shell. Bake in 350° oven for 45 minutes or until top springs back when lightly pressed with finger. Pour dry sherry over top of pie. Cool.

—Gladys Joyce

Old-Fashioned Pecan Pie

1/4 cup butter
1 1/4 cups sugar
1/2 cup corn syrup

3 eggs, beaten
1 cup pecans .
1 9-inch pie crust, unbaked

Combine first three ingredients and bring to a boil; cool. Add eggs slowly; add pecans. Pour into pie crust and bake at 350° for 30 minutes.

—Teresa Adkins

Pecan Pie

1 9-inch pastry shell, unbaked
1/2 cup butter
1 cup sugar
3 eggs, slightly beaten

3/4 cup dark corn syrup
1/4 teaspoon salt
1 teaspoon vanilla
1 cup chopped pecans

Cream butter; add sugar gradually and cream together until light and fluffy. Add remaining ingredients and blend well. Pour into pastry shell. Bake on lower shelf in a 375° oven for 40-45 minutes.

—Jamie Overbay

Tea Time Tasseys

1 3-ounce package cream cheese
1/2 cup margarine
1 cup flour
1 egg

2 tablespoons butter, softened
3/4 cup brown sugar
1 teaspoon vanilla
1 1/2 cups broken pecans

Cream butter and cheese together; work in flour. Pinch off and roll into balls about the size of a walnut. Press into tea time tassey pans for crust. Beat egg, butter, sugar, and vanilla together; add crushed pecans. Pour into crusts and bake at 350° for 30 minutes.

—Donda Kidd

P·U·M·P·K·I·N

Perfect Pumpkin Pie

1 cup brown sugar
1 tablespoon flour
1/2 teaspoon salt
1 1/4 teaspoons cinnamon
1/2 teaspoon nutmeg
1/2 teaspoon ginger

1/4 teaspoon cloves
2 cups pumpkin
1 13-ounce can evaporated milk
 (1 2/3 cups)
1 egg, slightly beaten
2 9-inch pie crusts, unbaked

Mix sugar, flour, salt, and spices. Add, and stir until smooth: pumpkin, milk, and egg. Pour into pie crust. Bake in 375° oven for 50-55 minutes. Serves 12.

—Margaret Matney

Pumpkin Cheese Pie

1 8-ounce package cream cheese,
   softened
¾ cup brown sugar
1 teaspoon cinnamon
1 teaspoon nutmeg
½ teaspoon ginger
½ teaspoon salt

3 eggs
1 cup canned or mashed cooked
   pumpkin
1 cup milk
1 teaspoon vanilla
1 9-inch pie shell, unbaked

Beat together cream cheese, brown sugar, spices, and salt. Add eggs one at a time, beating well after each. Stir in pumpkin, milk, and vanilla. Pour into pie shell. Bake at 375° for 45-50 minutes, or until knife inserted in center of pie comes out clean. Chill thoroughly before serving. Serve with whipped cream. —Wilma Matney

The I-Can't-Bake-A-Pie Pumpkin Pie

1 16-ounce can pumpkin
1 14-ounce can sweetened
   condensed milk
1 egg

1 teaspoon cinnamon
1 teaspoon pumpkin pie spice
1 9-inch pie shell, unbaked

Preheat oven to 375°. In large bowl, blend together all ingredients. Turn into pie shell. Bake 50-55 minutes or until knife inserted near center comes out clean. Cool before cutting. —Hazel Whitt

Pumpkin Pie Topped with Peanuts

¾ cup roasted salted peanuts
1 9-inch pastry shell, unbaked
2 cups mashed pumpkin
1⅓ cups sweetened condensed
   milk, undiluted
¾ cup water

1 egg
½ teaspoon cinnamon
¼ teaspoon nutmeg
¼ teaspoon ginger
½ cup light brown sugar

Combine pumpkin, sweetened condensed milk, water, egg, cinnamon, nutmeg, and ginger. Beat slowly until almost well blended. Spoon into pastry shell. Bake at 400° for about 50 minutes. Remove from oven. Sprinkle with ¼ cup peanuts, then with brown sugar. Cover pie edges with aluminum foil. Broil 3 inches from heat about 1 minute, or until sugar bubbles. Cool. Gently crack topping with tip of knife before cutting to serve. —Gladys Joyce

A small pumpkin can become an attractive vase for flowers.
Cut out top and insides, fill with water, and arrange flowers.

Pumpkin Pie

1 9-inch pie shell, unbaked
2 eggs
¾ cup sugar
1 teaspoon cinnamon
½ teaspoon salt
½ teaspoon ginger

¼ teaspoon cloves
1 16-ounce can pumpkin or 2 cups
cooked pumpkin
1 13-ounce can evaporated milk
(1⅔ cup)

Heat oven to 425°. In large bowl beat eggs slightly. Add remaining ingredients; blend well. Pour into pie shell. Bake at 425° for 15 minutes; reduce oven temperature to 350° and continue baking for 45 minutes or until knife inserted near center comes out clean. —Wilma Matney

Instant Dream Pumpkin Pie

1 2⅛-ounce package dessert topping
mix
½ cup cold milk
½ teaspoon vanilla
1 3¾-ounce package vanilla instant
pudding

1 cup mashed cooked pumpkin
⅔ cup milk
½ teaspoon nutmeg
½ teaspoon ginger
½ teaspoon cinnamon
1 8-inch gingersnap pie crust

Prepare topping mix with ½ cup milk and vanilla according to package directions. Combine 1 cup of prepared topping mix with remaining ingredients. Beat slowly with a rotary beater until mixed. Spoon into pie shell. Chill until set. Garnish with remaining topping mix.

Gingersnap Pie Shell:
1 cup gingersnap cookie crumbs
2½ tablespoons sugar
3 tablespoons melted butter or margarine

Combine ingredients and mix well. Press firmly on bottom of an 8-inch pie pan. Bake at 350° for 8-10 minutes. —Donna Davis

A GOOD NEIGHBOR RECIPE

1 tongue that does not slander
1 mind full of tolerance
2 ears closed to gossip
2 eyes overlooking others' faults
1 heart generous and kind
2 hands extended to help others
1 dash wit
1 dash smiles
1 dash sunny disposition
1 dash cheerfulness

Blend together above ingredients. Form into one being.
Serve generous portions to everyone you meet daily.

Preserving

Cured Ham

1 fresh ham	2 tablespoons black pepper
1 quart non-iodized salt	1 tablespoon red pepper
2 tablespoons brown sugar	

Mix salt, sugar, and peppers thoroughly. Pour ¼ of this mixture onto a large piece of brown paper (grocery bags split open work well for this). Paper must be large enough to completely wrap ham. Lay ham skin-side down on the paper. Pour the remaining ¾ of the mixture over the entire ham. Be sure to put plenty of salt in the hole above the bone in the center of the ham. Wrap tightly with brown paper. Secure with some type of strong tape. Place in a white cloth sack. Tie tightly; be sure there are no holes for bugs to get through. Hang with butt-end up, shank-end down, so it will drain. Leave for 6-12 months. Ham needs cool weather for first part of cure. This also works with pork shoulders. —Ernest Tatum

Dandelion Wine

3 pounds brown sugar	1 quart of dandelion blossoms
1 8-ounce box seedless raisins	3 sliced lemons
1 yeast cake	

Boil blossoms in a gallon of water; add 3 sliced lemons and let cool. Strain and add sugar, raisins, and yeast. Let stand for ten days. Strain off and bottle. —Thelma Joyce

Sandwich Spread

9 sweet green peppers	6 tablespoons flour
9 sweet red peppers	2 tablespoons prepared mustard
6 green tomatoes	3 tablespoons salt
1½ cups vinegar	1 16-ounce jar mayonnaise
1½ cups water	1 small jar olives, chopped,
2½ cups brown sugar	undrained
1 tablespoon ground mustard	2 or 3 pickles, chopped

Put peppers and tomatoes through food chopper; drain. Combine with vinegar, water, and brown sugar; cook 5 minutes. Mix ground mustard, flour, prepared mustard, and salt with a small amount of cold water and add with the mayonnaise, pickles, and olives with juice. Bring to a boil and seal in hot jars. —Gladys Joyce

Sausage Seasoning

20 pounds ground pork, fat and
   lean mixed
1 tablespoon red pepper
⅓ cup salt

⅓ cup sage
¼ cup black pepper
½ cup brown sugar

—Opal Honaker

Tomato Paste

Your own tomato paste can be better and more versatile than commercial varieties because you govern what goes into it. This paste can be used as a color booster for otherwise pallid dishes and for sauces, as well as in Italian-style dishes, as might be expected.

Peel, trim, and chop tomatoes (4-4½ pounds of tomatoes will make about 4 half-pint jars). Measure and add ¾ teaspoon salt for every pint of chopped tomatoes. Simmer in an enameled kettle over very low heat for 1 hour, stirring so it doesn't stick. Remove from heat; put it through a fine sieve. Then continue cooking very slowly, stirring occasionally until the paste holds shape on the spoon—about 2 hours more. Pack hot into half-pint jars, leaving one-half inch of headroom. Process in a boiling water bath for 35 minutes. —Marilyn Wells

C·A·B·B·A·G·E

Homemade Kraut

Kraut must be made when the sign in the almanac is in the heart or the head. Salt used must be pickling salt—no iodine. Use large solid heads of cabbage. Chop cabbage very finely in large pan. Do not chop stalk.

In the bottom of a large crock or jar, put ½ cup salt. On top of this firmly pack a pan of finely chopped cabbage. Sprinkle a little more salt over the cabbage. Continue layers of cabbage and salt. Pack firmly until you have the amount of kraut you want to make. Do not add any water. Weight top with plate, rock, or board. Leave at room temperature. It will take at least two weeks in a warm place for the kraut to ferment. Taste to check. When the kraut is seasoned to your taste, it can be heated to the boiling point and sealed in hot sterile jars. —Thelma Joyce

Tomato Kraut

Salt (plain)
Cabbage
Green tomatoes

Sweet green peppers
Hot peppers

Chop all ingredients and pack in jars. Add 1 tablespoon salt to each half-gallon jar. Fill jars with boiling water and seal. —Opal Honaker

APPALACHIAN

Apple Butter 1

6 cups apple sauce
6 cups sugar

2 tablespoons vinegar
1 cup cinnamon drops

Cook apples, sugar, and vinegar 20 minutes. Add cinnamon drops. Cook to melt. Put in jars and seal. —margaret matney

Apple Butter 11

5¼ cups applesauce
1 1¾-ounce box powdered fruit pectin
5½ cups sugar

Heat applesauce and pectin to boiling. Add sugar. Bring to a boil. Put in jars and seal. —margaret matney

Apple Butter 111

1 gallon sweet apple cider
7 pounds tart cooking apples (about
   3 dozen medium) cored, peeled,
   and quartered

1 tablespoon ground cinnamon
2 teaspoons ground nutmeg
¾ teaspoon ground cloves
4 cups sugar (to taste)

Bring cider to a boil in a large saucepan or Dutch oven; boil until reduced by half; add apples. Allow mixture to return to a boil; reduce heat. Simmer, stirring frequently, 4-5 hours or until mixture is dark brown and has the consistency of marmalade. Stir in remaining ingredients. Pour hot mixture into sterilized jars, leaving ¼" headspace; cover at once with metal lids and screw metal bands tight. Process in boiling water bath for 10 minutes. Yields 4 pints. —Jamie Overbay

20-minute Apple Butter

8 cups cooked apples that have been
   put through colander
5½ cups sugar

½ cup white vinegar
½ cup cinnamon candies
5 drops oil of cinnamon

Mix together all ingredients; cook 20 minutes after mixture starts to boil. Pour into hot jars and seal. —Evelyn Altizer

Put marbles in the bottom of a double boiler.
When the water boils down, the marbles will make enough racket to call you from the farthest corner of the house.

Spiced Preserved Cantaloupe

3 pounds firm ripe cantaloupe
1 tablespoon whole allspice
1 tablespoon crystallized ginger,
   chopped
1 lemon, thinly sliced and seeded

$3^1/_2$ cups sugar
1 cup light corn syrup
$^1/_2$ cup water
$^1/_2$ cup dry white wine
$^1/_4$ teaspoon non-iodized salt

Halve cantaloupe from stem end to blossom end; discard seed and stringy pulp. Cut each half into quarters. Remove skin. Cut melon pieces crosswise into slices about $3/_4$" thick. Measure 6 cups. Tie allspice and ginger in cheesecloth bag to make spicebag.

In 5-quart saucepot place spicebag, lemon, 2 cups of the sugar, corn syrup, water, wine and salt. Stirring occasionally, bring to a boil over medium-high heat. Reduce heat; add cantaloupe. Stirring occasionally, bring to a boil and boil for about 20 minutes. Remove from heat; place plate on fruit to hold below syrup level. Let stand overnight.

Remove plate; stir in remaining $1^1/_2$ cups sugar. Stirring occasionally, bring to a boil and boil gently about 20 minutes until fruit is transparent and syrup is thick. Skim surface; remove spicebag. Immediately pack cantaloupes into clean hot $^1/_2$-pint jars. Pour boiling syrup into jars, completely covering cantaloupe. Seal. Process in boiling water bath for 5 minutes. Makes 4 half-pint jars.
        —Donna Davis

Peach & Pineapple Jam

4 cups prepared freestone peaches
1 $8^1/_2$-ounce can crushed pineapple

1 $1^3/_4$-ounce box powdered fruit
   pectin
$5^1/_2$ cups sugar

Peel, pit and finely chop peaches. Measure 4 cups. Combine peaches and pineapple in large saucepan. Stir in pectin. Measure sugar and set aside. Over high heat, bring fruit mixture to full rolling boil, stirring constantly. Stir in sugar at once. Bring to boil again. Boil hard 1 minute, stirring constantly. Remove from heat. Lay a piece of wax paper on top of jam just long enough to pick up skim; throw away. Ladle into clean, hot canning jars to within $^1/_8$" of tops. Wipe jar rims and threads clean. Adjust caps securely. Invert jars on towel until sealed. Store in a cool dark place. Makes 3 pints.
        —Donna Davis

Rhubarb Jelly

10 cups cut-up rhubarb
10 cups sugar

2 ounces strawberry or cherry gelatin

Mix rhubarb and sugar; cook over low heat for 30 minutes. Remove from heat and add gelatin. Stir and cook 5 minutes more. Can in hot jars. Yields 5 pints.
        —Evelyn Altizer

Pear Butter

5 cups finely chopped or ground
  pears
3 cups sugar

1 cup crushed pineapple
Grated peel and juice of one lime
1 tablespoon ground ginger

Core pears and chop finely, or put through a food grinder. Measure 5 cups. Put pears in large saucepan and add sugar, pineapple, lime peel, juice, and ginger. Bring to a boil. Reduce heat and simmer 35-40 minutes, stirring occasionally, until fruit is clear and thick. Pour into clean, hot canning jars. Invert on towel until sealed. Store in a cool, dark place. Makes 5 pints.

—Donna Davis

Deep Purple Conserve

4 cups prepared purple prune plums
Shredded peel of one orange
Shredded peel of one lemon

1 1¾-ounce package powdered fruit
  pectin
6½ cups sugar
1 cup chopped walnuts

Wash, pit, and chop very finely or grind plums. Measure 4 cups. Mix plums with shredded peels and pectin in deep kettle. Bring to full rolling boil and boil hard 1 minute, stirring constantly. Ladle into clean, hot canning jars to within ⅛″ of tops. Invert jars on a towel until sealed. Store in a cool, dark place. Makes 9½ pints.

Freezer Strawberry Preserves

2 pints strawberries
2 pints sugar
1 tablespoon lemon juice

Crush 1 pint strawberries in blender. Mix with 1 pint whole berries and 1 pint sugar. Add lemon juice; boil for 3 minutes. Set off stove and cool 5 minutes. Add other pint of sugar; boil 8-10 minutes. Skim. Let set in pot overnight, shaking occasionally to keep berries from floating. Put in jars. Store in freezer.

—Margaret Matney

Rhubarb-Strawberry Jelly

10 cups fresh rhubarb
8 cups sugar
3 3-ounce boxes strawberry gelatin

Cut rhubarb into small pieces. Add sugar and cool 10 minutes. Add gelatin; bring to a full rolling boil. Pour into jars and seal.

—Thelma Joyce

P·I·C·K·L·E·S

— COMMON CAUSES OF POOR-QUALITY PICKLES —

Hollow Pickles—Hollowness in pickles usually results from:
— Poorly developed cucumbers;
— Holding cucumbers too long before pickling;
— Too rapid fermentation;
— Too strong or too weak a brine during fermentation.

Shriveled Pickles—Shriveling may result from using too strong a vinegar, sugar, or salt solution at the start of the pickling process. In making the very sweet or very sour pickles, it is best to start with a dilute solution and increase gradually to the desired strength.

Soft Pickles—Soft pickles usually result from:
— Too little salt;
— Cucumbers not covered with brine during fermentation;
— Scum scattered throughout the brine fermentation period;
— Blossoms, if not entirely removed from the cucumbers before fermentation, may contain fungi or yeasts responsible for enzymatic softening of pickles.

Pickled Beans I

Put in a large pot 4 gallons green beans which have been broken and washed thoroughly. Add water to just cover beans; cook for 10 minutes. Let cool. Pour beans, 1 gallon at a time, into a 5-gallon jar (stone churn is best). Add 1 tablespoon plain salt to each gallon of beans. Pour the water in which the beans were cooked over all. Cover with clean cloth weighted down with a clean washed fruit jar that has been filled with water, or use a flat clean rock. Cover and put in a cool place for three weeks. Watch beans and take off skim as it forms while pickling. Keep cloth and weight clean.

—Gladys Joyce

Pickled Beans II

Check the almanac and only make pickled beans when the signs are in the heart or head.

8 quarts beans	1 cup vinegar	1 cup plain salt

String, break, and wash beans. Cook beans until tender in plain water. Drain and cool. Add vinegar and salt to one gallon warm water. Dissolve salt. Put beans in quart jars. Pour water, vinegar, and salt solution over beans. Finish filling jars with warm water if needed. Seal jars tight with zinc tops and jar rubbers.

—Thelma Joyce

Bread-and-Butter Pickles

4 quarts sliced cucumbers	3 cups vinegar
6 large onions, sliced thin	½ teaspoon turmeric
2 sweet peppers, cut in rings	½ teaspoon celery seed
5 cups sugar	2 tablespoons mustard seed

Cover cucumbers, onions, and peppers in ice water and let stand 3 or 4 hours; drain well. Combine sugar, vinegar, turmeric, celery, and mustard seed. Pour over cucumbers, onions, and peppers. Bring to a boil; simmer 5 minutes. Pack in jars and cover with boiling syrup. Seal jars. Makes about 6 pints.

—Opal Honaker

Crystal Pickles

25 cucumbers	2 quarts sugar
4 tablespoons alum	2 sticks cinnamon (or less)
1 quart vinegar	1 teaspoon whole cloves

Wash cucumbers. Put in cold water with enough salt added to float an egg. Let stand one week in this brine. Drain and wash cucumbers thoroughly. Slice any way you desire. Place cucumbers in water and 4 tablespoons of alum. Let stand for three days. Wash cucumbers again thoroughly. Combine vinegar, sugar, cinnamon, and cloves. Bring to a boil; pour over pickles in jars.

—Gladys Joyce
Vera Tatum

Crystal Cucumber Pickles

1 cup salt	8 cups sugar
1 gallon cucumbers	2 sticks cinnamon
1 tablespoon alum	1 teaspoon whole cloves
4 cups vinegar	

Mix salt in 2 gallons of cold water. Place 1 gallon of cucumbers in stone jar and pour brine over cucumbers. Let stand two weeks. Drain brine and wash cucumbers well. Slice thin and return to jar. Cover with cold water and add 1 tablespoon alum. Let stand 24 hours. Remove cucumbers and wash well. Also wash jar well. Place cucumbers back in jar and cover with hot syrup made from sugar, vinegar, and spices. Let stand 24 hours. Drain syrup and heat to boiling for three mornings and pour over cucumbers. On fourth morning, drain syrup and heat to boiling again. Pack cucumbers in jars. Cover cucumbers with boiling syrup and seal jars.

—Opal Honaker

... But the phrasemakers are always with us.
Be wary, learn to read between their lines.
—"The Phrasemakers" by Preston Newman

Dill Pickles

2 gallons sliced cucumbers
1 gallon sliced onions
4 cups sugar
4 cups vinegar

2 cups water
1/2 cup salt
1 head of dill for each quart

Pack cucumbers and onions in jars. Heat sugar, salt, vinegar, and water to boiling. Put 1 head dill in each jar. Pour boiling syrup over pickles and seal jars.
—Opal Honaker
Vera Tatum

Kosher Dill Pickles

20-25 four-inch cucumbers
1/8 teaspoon alum
1 clove garlic
2 heads fresh dill
1 hot red pepper

1 cup coarse medium salt
3 quarts water
1 quart cider vinegar
Grape leaves

Wash cucumbers; let stand in cold water overnight. Pack in hot, sterilized jars. To each quart add above amount of alum, garlic, dill and red pepper. Combine salt, water and vinegar; heat to boiling and fill jars. Put grape leaf in each jar; seal. Makes 6-8 quarts.
—Donna Davis

Sweet-Sour Dill Pickles

2 gallons cucumbers
2 or 3 hot peppers
8 medium onions
6 sweet peppers
8 heads fresh dill

4 cups sugar
1/2 cup salt
4 cups vinegar
2 cups water

Wash freshly picked cucumbers and cut into 1" chunks or into quarters. Pack in jars. Add sliced onion, peppers, and dill. Dissolve sugar and salt in vinegar and water. Bring to a boil; pour while still hot over cucumbers, peppers, and onions to cover. Seal jars at once. Do not open for 30 days. Makes 4 quarts.
—Opal Honaker

Dill Bean Sticks

1 peck green beans (8 quarts)
1/4 teaspoon crushed red pepper
1 teaspoon dill seed
1 clove garlic

8 cups water
8 cups vinegar
1 cup salt
1 cup sugar

String beans and leave whole. Cook for 12 minutes. Drain and chill in ice water; drain. Put beans in pint jars with pepper, dill seed, and garlic. Boil water, vinegar, salt, and sugar for 5 minutes. Pour over beans and seal. Turn jars upside down for a few minutes. Yields 15 pints.
—Evelyn Altizer

Sweet Dill Pickles I

2 gallons cucumbers	2 cups vinegar
2 cups salt	1/4 teaspoon oil of cloves
2 tablespoons alum	1/4 teaspoon oil of cinnamon
6 cups sugar	6 or 8 heads of dill

Cut cucumbers in strips and put in stone jar. Add salt to one gallon of water. Bring to a boil and pour over cucumbers. Let stand one week; drain well. Cover with boiling water and alum. Let stand 24 hours; drain well. Pour one gallon of boiling water over cucumbers. Let stand 24 hours; drain. Combine sugar, vinegar, cloves and cinnamon; bring to a boil. Pour over cucumbers; let stand 24 hours. Reheat three mornings. The third morning, heat and add one head dill to each jar. Pack in jars and seal.

—Opal Honaker

Sweet Dill Pickles II

2 gallons cucumbers	12 cups sugar
2 cups salt	3/4 teaspoon oil of cloves
2 tablespoons alum	3/4 teaspoon oil of cinnamon
2 pints vinegar	1 head of dill

Wash cucumbers and cut in strips. Add salt dissolved in 1 gallon of boiling water. Let stand one week. Drain off brine. Add alum dissolved in 1 gallon of boiling water. Let stand 24 hours. Drain and cover with fresh boiling water. Let stand 24 hours. Drain well.

Bring vinegar, sugar, and flavorings to a boil; pour over pickles. Let stand 24 hours. Each day for three days, reheat solution, adding 1 cup of sugar each day. The third day, put in jar and add 1 head of dill.

—Eunice Rector

Dilly Beans

2 pounds green beans	2 1/2 cups water
1 teaspoon cayenne pepper	2 1/2 cups vinegar
1 teaspoon granulated garlic	1/4 cup salt
4 teaspoons dill seed	

Pack beans lengthwise into hot jars, leaving 1/4" head space. Add 1/4 teaspoon granulated garlic and 1 teaspoon dill seed to each jar. Combine remaining ingredients and bring to boiling. Pour, boiling hot, over beans, leaving 1/4" head space. Adjust caps. Process pints 10 minutes in boiling water bath. Makes about 4 pints. Let stand at least two weeks to develop flavor.

Dilly Beans and Carrots:

Follow recipe as for Dilly Beans, only pack jars with a mixture of whole green beans and baby carrots.

—Gladys Joyce

Lime Cucumber Pickles

1½ gallons large cucumbers
1 gallon water
½ cup pickling lime
1½ quarts vinegar
5 pounds sugar

1 teaspoon turmeric
1 tablespoon celery seed
2 tablespoons pickling spices
Green or red food coloring as desired

Peel cucumbers and cut out seeds; cut in strips or chunks. Soak in the lime and water for 24 hours; then drain and wash four times. Mix together vinegar, sugar, turmeric, celery seed, pickling spices, and food coloring; boil 5 minutes. Pour over cucumbers and let stand 24 hours. Then bring to boil for 35 minutes and can. Yields 8-9 pints.   —Evelyn Altizer

Lime Pickles

3 gallons cucumbers, sliced
2 cups lime
3 gallons water
8 cups vinegar

12 cups sugar
2 tablespoons salt
Pickling spices

Mix water and lime and let cucumbers stand in mixture 12-14 hours. Wash well through four waters. Mix and heat vinegar, sugar, salt, and spices. Pour over cucumbers. Let stand 2 hours, then cook 25-30 minutes. Place in jars and seal.   —Edna Scott

Pickle Slices

4 quarts sliced cucumbers
6-10 sliced onions
2 cloves garlic or ½ teaspoon garlic
    powder
⅓ cup salt
1 tray ice cubes

4 cups sugar
1½ teaspoons turmeric
1½ teaspoons celery seed
2 tablespoons mustard seed
2½ cups white vinegar

Mix cucumbers, onions, garlic or garlic powder, and salt in large container. Place ice cubes on top. Let stand 2½-3 hours. Drain thoroughly. Combine sugar, turmeric, celery seed, mustard seed, and vinegar. Heat just to boiling. Add cucumber slices and heat about 5 minutes. Stir two or three times. Pack into hot jars and seal.   —Helen Smith

Pickled Beets — Sliced or Whole

2 cups sugar
2 cups water
2 cups vinegar

1 tablespoon cinnamon
1 teaspoon cloves
1 teaspoon allspice

Cover beets with mixture and simmer 15 minutes. Seal in clean hot jars.
                              —Vera Tatum

Plastic Pickles

7 pounds sliced cucumbers	2 quarts vinegar
1 quart lime	6 pounds sugar + 1 cup
3 pounds salt	½ box pickling spice
1 box alum	

Soak cucumbers in lime water 12 hours. Rinse. Drain and soak in salt water four hours. Wash, drain, and soak in clear water two hours. Bring to boil in alum water; drain and wash well in hot water. Boil cucumbers in vinegar, sugar, and spices 30 minutes; let stand overnight. Add 1 cup sugar to pickles before canning. Heat to boiling. Pour in jars and seal.

—Opal Honaker

Pickled Okra

2 pounds young okra pods	4 cups white vinegar
3 small hot peppers	2 cups water
3 medium cloves garlic	5 tablespoons non-iodized salt
2 teaspoons dill seeds	

Wash and drain okra; do not cut off caps. Into each of 6 clean pint canning jars put half a pepper, half a clove of garlic, and ⅓ teaspoon dill seeds. Pack the okra into the jars, standing the pods upright and alternating stem ends and tips. Bring the vinegar, water, and salt to a boil; fill the jars to within ½" of the rims; seal. Process in boiling water bath for 5 minutes. Let mellow 6 weeks before using.   —Marilyn Wells

Sweet Cauliflower Pickles

2 medium heads cauliflower	½ cup light corn syrup
2 sweet red peppers, cut into strips	1 tablespoon each mustard and
2 green peppers, cut into strips	celery seed
1 quart onions, cut into wedges	1 teaspoon whole cloves
1 quart white vinegar	¼ teaspoon turmeric
2 cups sugar	2 tablespoons pure granulated salt

Break cauliflower into pieces—there should be about two quarts. Cook in a small amount of unsalted water for 5 minutes; drain. Combine remaining ingredients and bring to a boil. Add cauliflower and simmer 2 minutes. Pack in 6 hot sterilized pint jars and seal. Process 5 minutes in boiling water bath. Makes 6 pints.   —Evelyn Altizer

Prevent a crust from forming inside the lids and around the rims of jars of mustard, chili sauce, pickles, olives, honey and such, by covering the top of the jar with plastic wrap before screwing on the lid.

Squash Pickles

½ gallon squash (about 10 very small)
6 large onions
2 tablespoons salt
4 cups sugar

2 teaspoons celery seed
2 cups vinegar '
½ teaspoon turmeric

Slice squash and onions very thin. Soak in ice water with 2 tablespoons of salt added. Drain thoroughly. Mix sugar, vinegar, celery seed, and turmeric; pour over squash and onions. Seal in jars. Process in boiling water bath 5 minutes. Makes 3 pints.   —Opal Honaker

Salad Dressing Pickles

12 large cucumbers
½ cup salt
12 onions
2 sweet red peppers
3-4 cups sugar
1 tablespoon celery seed

½ teaspoon red pepper, or 3-4
  banana peppers
1 tablespoon turmeric
½ cup flour
1 quart vinegar

Peel and chop cucumbers. Let stand overnight in brine, using salt dissolved in 3 quarts water. In the morning, drain cucumbers. Chop onions and pepper fine. Mix sugar, spices, flour, and vinegar; add to cucumbers, onions, and peppers. Cook 10 minutes. Pack in jars and seal. Process 5-10 minutes at 5 pounds pressure. Makes 5 or 6 pints.   —Opal Honaker

Watermelon Pickles

1 watermelon (5½ pounds rind)
4 tablespoons salt
3 tablespoons powdered alum
5½ pounds sugar (11 cups)

2 cups white vinegar
1½ tablespoons whole cloves
6 blades mace
3 sticks cinnamon

Remove most of the pink fruit from watermelon rind; a little rim of pink makes your pickles prettier. Cut all outer green skin from rind. Water should cover rind; add more if needed. Add sugar and cook until rind looks transparent, about 45 minutes. Now add vinegar and cook 25 minutes more. Toss in all spices and cook 5 minutes only—longer cooking darkens the syrup. Pack into 6 sterilized pint jars along with spices and syrup; seal. Store two weeks before using.   —Vera Tatum

In the East, time has been divorced
From things. No clocks hem the hours
In, and time, not being firmly forced,
Slops around. ...

"Form and Substance" by Cecil Mullins

Relish 1

½ gallon cucumbers, chopped	1 hot red pepper (optional)
1 large head of cabbage, chopped	1 quart onions, chopped
4 large green peppers, chopped	1 gallon water
1 quart tomatoes, chopped	1 cup salt

Make a brine of the water and salt; pour over the chopped vegetables. Let stand overnight, then bring to a boil and drain.

Dressing:

1 cup flour	6 tablespoons prepared mustard
6 cups brown sugar	1 quart vinegar

Mix ingredients and boil until thick. Mix with vegetables. Heat, and put into pint jars. Seal. —Dorothy Tatum

Relish 11

8 cups green tomatoes, chopped	Black pepper and salt to taste
4 cups cabbage, chopped	2 cups vinegar
6 pods sweet pepper, chopped	1 cup flour
9 onions, chopped	3 cups sugar
1 cup prepared mustard	

Cook vegetables in salt water until tender; drain. Mix sugar and flour together; stir in vinegar and mustard; cook until thick. Add vegetables and mix well. Pour into hot jars and seal. —Evelyn Altizer

Ripe Cucumber Relish

8 large ripe cucumbers	1 teaspoon celery seed
2 cups chopped onion	1 teaspoon mustard seed
½ cup salt	1 tablespoon dry mustard
2 tablespoons flour	2 teaspoons turmeric
2 cups sugar	1 pint vinegar

Pare cucumbers, remove seeds, and cut into 1" squares. Add onion. Sprinkle with salt and let stand overnight. Drain. Rinse well.

To make sauce:

Combine remaining ingredients. Heat to boiling, stirring frequently to make a smooth sauce.

Add vegetables to the sauce. Cook on low heat for 1 hour or until vegetables are transparent.

Ladle into hot, sterilized jars. Seal at once. Process in boiling water bath for 5 minutes. Makes 4 pints. —Eunice Rector

Uncooked Relish I

1 pint sweet red peppers	1 quart white vinegar
1 pint sweet green peppers	4 cups sugar .
1 quart cabbage, chopped	2 tablespoons salt
1 hot medium pepper	4 tablespoons white mustard
1 pint onions, chopped	2 teaspoons celery seed

Chop all vegetables. Mix and allow to set at least 12-24 hours. Pour in hot jars and seal. —Gladys Joyce

Uncooked Relish II

1 hot red pepper	4 cups sugar
1 pint onions	2 tablespoons salt
1 pint sweet red pepper	4 tablespoons white mustard seed
1 quart cabbage	2 teaspoons celery seed
1 quart white vinegar	

Chop peppers, onions, and cabbage finely. Mix all together; let set 12-24 hours. Pour in jars and seal. Makes 4 pints. —Opal Honaker

Pepper Relish

12 red peppers	3 cups vinegar
12 green peppers	2 cups sugar
3 large onions	2 tablespoons salt

Chop peppers and onions. Cover with boiling water; let stand 10 minutes, then drain. Cover again with boiling water and let come to a boil. Let stand 10 minutes, drain, then add remaining ingredients. Cook 15 minutes. Seal while hot. —Vera Tatum

Green Pepper Relish

6 large green peppers	6 cups sugar
1 1/2 cups vinegar	1/2 teaspoon salt
1 teaspoon crushed red pepper	1 bottle liquid pectin

Chop peppers finely and blend with vinegar, or complete this step with a blender. Bring to a boil. Add red pepper, sugar, and salt. Add pectin and cook until it gels. —Eunice Rector

Whenever you buy fruit or vegetables in nylon mesh bags, save the bags because they make great scouring pads. Cut and fold them to fit your hand and then stitch them around the edges with nylon thread. They are wonderful to use when you wash dishes, pots, or pans, and they last a lot longer than ordinary dishcloths.

Cranberry Blender Relish

2 envelopes unflavored gelatin
3/4 cup cold water
2 cups cranberries
1 medium navel orange, seeded and
  cut into eighths

1 medium apple, cored and cut into
  eighths
3/4 cup sugar
1/4 cup chopped walnuts

Soften gelatin in cold water in saucepan for 5 minutes. Warm over low heat until gelatin is dissolved. Place cranberries, orange, apple, sugar, and gelatin mixture in blender. Cover and blend until orange peel is finely chopped. Fold in walnuts. Pour into serving bowl. Cover and refrigerate until well chilled. Garnish with halved orange slices. Makes about 4 cups. This relish will keep well for about two weeks and is very good with poultry or ham.
—Margaret Matney
Gladys Joyce

Corn Salad

18 medium ears corn
1 medium head cabbage
4 medium onions
3 medium green peppers
1 1/2 teaspoons black pepper

1 1/4 pounds brown sugar
1/4 cup salt
1/4 cup white mustard
2 quarts vinegar

Chop all vegetables and add the remaining ingredients. Cook 15 minutes. Can hot and seal.
—Evelyn Altizer

Chow-Chow

1 quart chopped cabbage
2 cups chopped onions
2 cups chopped green tomatoes
2 cups corn
1 cup chopped sweet red pepper
2 cups carrots
3 tablespoons salt

2 1/2 cups vinegar
2 1/2 cups sugar
2 teaspoons dry mustard
1 teaspoon turmeric
1 teaspoon ground ginger
2 teaspoons celery seed
1 teaspoon mustard seed

Combine chopped vegetables; sprinkle with salt. Let stand 4-6 hours. Drain well. Combine vinegar, sugar, and spices; simmer 10 minutes. Add vegetables and simmer 10 minutes more (bring to a boiling point). Pack in hot sterilized jars, leaving 1/2" space at top; seal. Chopped cucumbers or cauliflower may be added.
—Evelyn Altizer

Be present at our table, Lord.
Be here, as everywhere, adored.
These creatures bless, and grant that we
May feast in fellowship with Thee! Amen.

Hints From Our Cooks IV

— HOUSEHOLD AIDS —

Salt sprinkled along baseboards and corners
will help keep ants out of the kitchen.

A fork makes an excellent recipe-card holder.
Stand it, tines up, in a glass and put the card between the tines.
The card stays clean and is easy to read.

It is said that you will not be troubled with many flies
if you keep geraniums growing in the house.
Why not have more flowers and fewer flies?

Pouring a strong solution of salt and hot water down the sink
will help eliminate odors and remove grease from drains.

If you haven't thrown away last year's phone book, don't!
Save it for the car. It will have some information
you need while driving or shopping. Put it
under the front seat, out of the way but handy.

Does your door lock stick? You can easily oil it in a hurry
by dipping the key in oil, inserting it in the lock,
and turning it several times.

When shoestrings lose their plastic tips,
dip the ends in clear fingernail polish.

An inexpensive shoe bag hung on the garage wall
or gardening area can serve as an excellent organizer.
Pockets hold hand tools, nozzles, gloves, and other small items.

Use an old toothbrush and toothpaste to polish your jewelry.

When a cedar chest loses its aroma,
the fragrance can be restored
by lightly sanding the interior with fine sandpaper.

To shine copper pots and pans,
pour a little catsup on the surface, gently rub in,
let set for a few minutes, and wash.

Hints From Our Cooks V

GLOSSARY

Baste To moisten foods during cooking with pan drippings, water, or special sauce.

Blanch To pour boiling water over a food to loosen skin, to remove color, or to set color.

Blend To combine ingredients until smooth.

Braise To brown food in a small amount of hot fat, then adding a small amount of liquid and cooking slowly.

Broil To cook food by exposing it to a direct source of heat.

Caramelize To melt sugar slowly over low heat until it becomes brown in color.

Cream To make soft, smooth, or creamy by pressure with a spoon or by beating with a beater.

Dice To cut into very small cubes— about ¼″ in size.

Fold To combine ingredients by cutting down through mixture with spoon or whip, then turning spoon across bottom of bowl and bringing it up and over the top, turning bowl a bit after each fold.

Knead To work and press dough with the palms of the hands, turning a small amount after each push.

Marinate To allow a food to stand in a liquid, to soften the food or add to the flavor.

Mince To cut with knife or scissors into very fine pieces (less than ¼″).

Pan-broil To cook uncovered in a hot frying pan, pouring off fat as it accumulates.

Parboil To boil for a few minutes without completely cooking the food.

Roast To cook by dry heat, usually in an oven.

Sauté To cook in a small amount of hot fat.

Simmer To cook slowly over very low heat, at a temperature of about 185°.

Steam To cook by steam in a pressure cooker, double boiler, or a steamer made by fitting a rack in a kettle fitted with a tight cover. A small amount of boiling water is used.

EQUIVALENT MEASURES

Dash	less than ⅛ teaspoon
3 teaspoons	1 tablespoon
2 tablespoons	⅛ cup or 1 ounce
4 tablespoons	¼ cup
5 tablespoons + 1 teaspoon	⅓ cup
8 tablespoons	½ cup
12 tablespoons	¾ cup
16 tablespoons	1 cup
2 cups	1 pint
4 cups	1 quart
2 pints	1 quart
4 quarts	1 gallon
8 quarts	1 peck
4 pecks	1 bushel
16 ounces	1 pound

HOW MUCH TO BUY
FOR 25

Beef, Veal or Pork Roasts	10 pounds
Ham (to bake)	10 pounds
Ground Beef (for burgers)	6 pounds
Poultry (to roast)	15 pounds
Baked Beans	6 16-ounce cans
Cabbage (to shred)	4 pounds
Carrots	6 pounds
Corn, canned	6 16-ounce cans
Corn, frozen	6 10-ounce packages
Green Beans, canned	6 16-ounce cans
Green Beans, fresh	5-6 pounds
Green Beans, frozen	6 10-ounce packages
Peas, canned	6 16-ounce cans
Peas, frozen	6 10-ounce packages
Potatoes	6½-7½ pounds
Tomato Juice	2 46-ounce cans

Salads

Dill Salad Dressing for Cole Slaw

¼ cup vegetable oil
½ cup evaporated milk
2 tablespoons vinegar
½ teaspoon dill seeds

¼ teaspoon dry mustard
¼ teaspoon salt
Few grains pepper
1 teaspoon sugar

Mix all ingredients into a jar with a tight-fitting cover. Screw lid on securely, then shake vigorously until dressing is creamy and smooth. Chill until ready to use. Use with 2 cups shredded cabbage. Makes about 1 cup.

—Margaret Matney

Blender Cole Slaw Dressing

1 egg, well beaten
½ cup milk
½ cup vinegar

1 cup sugar
1 teaspoon mustard
1 tablespoon butter

Combine egg and milk in blender; add vinegar. Mix sugar and mustard thoroughly. Add butter; blend well. Makes 1½ cups.

—Wilma Matney

Cole Slaw Dressing

2 eggs, well beaten
½ cup cold water
¾ cup sugar

¼ teaspoon salt
½ cup vinegar
2 tablespoons butter

Combine all ingredients. Boil in double boiler until thick; leave until cold. Add to 6 cups shredded cabbage. This is also good to add to potatoes for potato salad.

—Dora Abel

Celery-Seed Dressing

⅓ cup sugar
1 teaspoon salt
1 teaspoon dry mustard
1 teaspoon grated onion

¼ cup vinegar
1 cup vegetable oil
1 teaspoon celery seed

Mix dry ingredients; add onion and vinegar. Add oil, one tablespoon at a time, beating constantly with rotary or electric beater. Stir in celery seed. Makes 1½ cups. Good with fruit salads as well as with tossed green salads.

—Marilyn Wells

Blender Mayonnaise

1 cup vegetable oil, divided
2 eggs
2 tablespoons vinegar or lemon juice
1 teaspoon sugar

1 teaspoon dry mustard
1/2 teaspoon salt
Dash red pepper

Put 1/4 cup oil, plus all remaining ingredients, in blender. Mix on high speed for 5 seconds. Turn off blender; then re-blend at high speed, adding remaining 3/4 cup oil very slowly until thick and smooth. Turn off blender and clean sides with rubber spatula. Chill. Makes about 1 cup.

—Margaret Matney

Salad Dressing Without Oil

2 eggs
1/2 teaspoon dry mustard
1 teaspoon salt
2 tablespoons butter

3 tablespoons vinegar
3 tablespoons sugar, or to taste
1 cup whipping cream, whipped

Beat eggs; add mixed seasonings and beat a little more. Add melted butter and vinegar. Set over boiling water and stir constantly until thick and smooth. Use cold. Add one cup cream, whipped very stiff, before serving. If not sweet enough to taste good, add sugar to dressing when you add cream. Makes about 3 cups.

—Thelma Joyce

F·R·U·I·T S·A·L·A·D·S

Apricot Gelatin Salad

1 6-ounce package apricot gelatin
1 cup crushed pineapple, drained—
   reserve juice

2 bananas, sliced
1 cup marshmallows

Make gelatin as directed on package. Add pineapple, bananas, and marshmallows; let congeal in a 2-quart glass dish.

Topping:

1/2 cup sugar
1/2 cup pineapple juice
2 tablespoons flour
1 teaspoon butter

1 egg
1 3-ounce package cream cheese
1 9-ounce carton whipped topping

Mix sugar and flour with pineapple juice. Add beaten egg and butter; cook until thick. Add cream cheese; beat until smooth, and add whipped topping. Spread on congealed salad. Makes 12 servings.

—Opal Honaker

Apricot Salad I

1 29-ounce can crushed pineapple
½ cup sugar
2 3-ounce boxes apricot gelatin
1 cup chopped celery

1 cup chopped nuts
1 13-ounce can evaporated milk,
  well chilled
1 8-ounce package cream cheese

Combine sugar and pineapple; bring to a boil. Add apricot gelatin and mix well. Cool a little, then add cheese at room temperature; mix well with the beater. Add nuts and celery; pour into a 2-quart glass baking dish. Refrigerate. When mixture begins to thicken, add stiffly beaten milk. Makes 12 servings. —Teresa Adkins

Apricot Salad II

2 3-ounce boxes lemon gelatin
4 cups apricot nectar
1 8-ounce package cream cheese
½ cup mayonnaise

1 cup nuts
¾ cup chopped celery
1 8½-ounce can crushed pineapple

Boil apricot nectar, dissolve gelatin; cool, and add pineapple. Pour half of the mixture in pan; let set. Cream cheese; add mayonnaise, nuts, celery, and ½ cup gelatin mixture. Pour over first layer; let set. Pour in the rest of the gelatin mixture; let set. —Vera Tatum

Apricot Congealed Salad

1 17-ounce can apricots
1 3-ounce box lemon gelatin
½ cup finely chopped celery

½ cup chopped pecans
½ cup miniature marshmallows
1 cup frozen whipped topping,
  thawed

Drain apricots, reserving syrup. Add water to syrup to make 1 cup liquid. Heat to boiling; add gelatin; stir until dissolved. Cool. Chop apricots and combine with remaining ingredients; stir into gelatin. Pour into a 2-quart mold and refrigerate. Makes 8 servings. —Margaret Matney

Apricot Gelatin and
Ice Cream Salad

1 6-ounce box apricot gelatin
2 cups boiling water
1 10-ounce can mandarin oranges,
  cut up

2 16-ounce cans apricots or peaches,
  cut up
2 cups juice from fruit
1 quart vanilla ice cream

Mix gelatin in boiling water. Add ice cream, then 2 cups of juice and cut-up fruit. Chill in a 2-quart dish. Makes 12 servings.
—Wilma Matney

Blueberry Salad

2 3-ounce packages grape gelatin
2 cups boiling water
1 21-ounce can blueberry pie filling
1 15-ounce can crushed pineapple
1 8-ounce package cream cheese

1/2 cup sugar
1 teaspoon vanilla
1 8-ounce container sour cream
1 cup chopped pecans

Dissolve gelatin in boiling water; add pineapple and blueberry filling. Chill in a 9"x13" pan. Combine cream cheese, sugar, and vanilla; add sour cream and mix well. Slowly stir in pecans. After gelatin mixture has hardened, pour cream cheese mixture over it and spread evenly. Chill. Makes 15-18 servings.   —Jamie Overbay

Cranberry Salad I

2 cups cranberries, chopped
1 cup sugar
1 orange and rind, chopped
1 apple, diced

1 cup chopped nuts
2 3-ounce packages lemon gelatin
2 cups liquid
1 cup chopped celery

Heat liquid; add gelatin. Mix all ingredients. Chill in a 2-quart baking dish. Makes 12 servings.   —Margaret Matney

Cranberry Salad II

2 cups raw cranberries
1 orange without peel
1 orange with peel
2 cups sugar

2 chopped apples
1 cup chopped nuts
2 3-ounce packages cherry gelatin
1 1/2 cups water

Grind cranberries and oranges in food chopper. Add sugar, apples, and nuts; combine with gelatin prepared by directions on package less 1/2 cup water. Serve on lettuce with or without dressing. Makes 12 servings.
                              —Opal Honaker

Cranberry Relish Mold

2 1/2 cups crushed pineapple
1 3-ounce package cherry gelatin
3/4 cup sugar
2 cups hot water
1/2 cup cold water
1-2 tablespoons lemon juice

1 1/2 cups ground raw cranberries
  (1 pound)
1 small orange, ground (1/2 cup)
1 cup chopped celery
1/2 cup broken walnuts

Drain pineapple, reserving syrup. Combine gelatin and sugar; dissolve in hot water. Add cold water, lemon juice, and reserved pineapple syrup; chill till partially set. Add pineapple and remaining ingredients; turn into 2-quart mold. Chill until firm. Makes 12 servings.   —Evelyn Altizer

Frozen Banana Salad

2 3-ounce packages cream cheese
½ teaspoon salt
⅓ cup sugar
½ cup mayonnaise
Juice of 1 lemon

½ cup crushed pineapple
2 medium bananas, diced
½ cup nuts
½ cup maraschino cherries
1 cup whipping cream, whipped

Mix cream cheese with salt, sugar, mayonnaise, and lemon juice. Add pineapple, bananas, nuts, and cherries. Fold in whipped cream; pour in freezing trays. Freeze from 8 hours to overnight. Serve on crisp lettuce leaves. Makes 8 servings.   —Opal Honaker

Banana Sour Cream Salad

2 cups sour cream
¾ cup sugar
2 tablespoons lemon juice
1 small can crushed pineapple

2 tablespoons chopped maraschino
  cherries
½ cup miniature marhsmallows
2 bananas, crushed
¼-½ cup finely chopped pecans

Combine all ingredients in order given; mix well. Pour into 12 baking cups and freeze. Serve on lettuce. Makes 12 servings.
                                                                —Teresa Adkins

Sweetheart Salad

Pineapple juice drained from crushed
  pineapple
½ cup sugar
1½ teaspoons unflavored gelatin
¼ cup cold water
2 tablespoons lemon juice

2 tablespoons cherry juice
1 3-ounce package cream cheese
12 maraschino cherries, finely
  chopped
½ pint heavy cream, whipped
2 cups crushed pineapple, drained

Heat pineapple juice and sugar. Soften gelatin in water; add pineapple juice; add lemon and cherry juices. Soften cream cheese; gradually add with cherries to mixture. Chill until thickened; fold in whipped cream and pineapple. Makes 12 servings.   —Thelma Joyce

Orange Sherbet Salad

2 3-ounce packages orange gelatin
2 cups boiling water
1 pint orange sherbet
1 15-ounce can crushed pineapple

2 bananas, sliced
1 10-ounce can mandarin oranges
Nuts (optional)

Mix gelatin and water well; add sherbet. Chill till slightly firm and add drained fruits. Add nuts if desired. Makes two quart molds.
                                                                —Jamie Overbay

Cherry Salad Supreme

1 3-ounce package raspberry gelatin
2 cups boiling water, divided
1 16-ounce can cherry pie filling
1 3-ounce package lemon gelatin
1/3 cup mayonnaise
1/2 cup whipping cream

1 3-ounce package cream cheese
1 8 1/2-ounce can crushed pineapple, undrained
1 cup miniature marshmallows
2 tablespoons chopped nuts

Dissolve raspberry gelatin in 1 cup boiling water. Stir in cherry pie filling; chill until partially set. Dissolve lemon gelatin in 1 cup boiling water. Blend cream cheese and mayonnaise together; gradually add lemon gelatin. Stir in undrained pineapple. Whip cream and fold into lemon mixture with marshmallows. Spread on top of cherry layer in 2-quart baking dish and sprinkle with 2 tablespoons of chopped nuts. Makes 8 servings.

—Wilma Matney

Fruit and Cottage Cheese Salad

2 3-ounce packages peach gelatin
1 9-ounce container whipped topping
1 9 or 12-ounce carton dry curd cottage cheese

1 1/2 cups diced peaches, fresh or canned
1 cup marshmallows

Mix dry gelatin and whipped topping together. Add remaining ingredients and chill. May be left in bowl or put into 9"x12" baking dish. Makes 12 servings.

—Margaret Matney

Fruit Salad

1 29-ounce can peaches, chopped
1 17-ounce can fruit cocktail
1 6-ounce jar maraschino cherries, chopped
1 17-ounce can pineapple, cut small
5 bananas, cut small

5 oranges, cut small
5 tangerines, cut small
5 apples, cut small
1 pound grapes, cut up
1 cup chopped pecans

Drain all fruit; use peach juice for dressing.

Dressing:
2 cups sugar
1/2 cup flour

1 1/3 cups peach juice

Mix sugar and flour; add to juice, and cook until thick. Pour over all fruits. Stir to mix well. Keep in tight container in refrigerator. Makes about 20 servings.

—Margaret Matney

Frozen Fruit Salad I

4 tablespoons sugar
4 tablespoons vinegar
4 egg yolks
4 bananas

4 pineapple rings, chopped finely
1 cup pecans
1 cup maraschino cherries
1 pint whipping cream, whipped

Combine sugar, vinegar, and egg yolks. Cook over hot water until thick; cool. Combine with whipped cream and fruits. Put in freezer; let freeze about two hours. Remove from freezer and fold over and over; let freeze again for two hours. Fold over again; leave in freezer until ready to eat. Should be eaten icy. Keeps well in freezer. Makes 12 servings.

—Opal Honaker

Frozen Fruit Salad II

4 egg yolks
4 tablespoons sugar
4 tablespoons vinegar
1/4 teaspoon salt
1/4 pound marshmallows

1/4 pound nuts
4 tablespoons mayonnaise
1 15$1/2$-ounce can pineapple tidbits
1 pint whipped cream

Combine first four ingredients in saucepan and heat. Add marshmallows and let cool. Add nuts, mayonnaise, pineapple, and whipped cream; freeze.

—Jennie Tatum

Frozen Fruit Salad III

1 3-ounce package strawberry
    gelatin
1 cup boiling water
1 6-ounce can frozen lemonade or
    limeade concentrate

3 cups thawed whipped topping
1 8$1/2$-ounce can pear halves,
    drained, chopped

Dissolve gelatin in boiling water; add lemonade concentrate; stir until melted. Chill until slightly thickened. Blend in whipped topping, then fold in fruits. Pour into 9"x5" loaf pan; freeze until firm—about four hours. Unmold and slice. Makes 12 servings.

—Evelyn Altizer

Ice Cream Gelatin Salad

2 3-ounce boxes lime gelatin
1 cup hot water
1 quart vanilla ice cream

1 cup pineapple juice
1 cup pineapple
1 cup nuts, if desired

Dissolve gelatin in hot water. Add ice cream and let melt. Add pineapple, juice, and nuts; pour into 2-quart baking dish. Let congeal. Makes 12 servings.

—Opal Honaker

24-Hour Dessert Salad

2 cups chilled cooked white rice
1 16-ounce can fruit cocktail, drained
1 11-ounce can mandarin oranges, drained
1 20½-ounce can pineapple chunks, drained
1 3½-ounce can flaked coconut
1 6¼-ounce package miniature marshmallows
1 cup sour cream
Lettuce leaves

On day before serving, into large bowl combine rice, fruit cocktail, oranges, pineapple chunks, coconut, marshmallows, and sour cream. Cover and refrigerate, tossing occasionally. Serve on lettuce leaves. Makes 8 servings.
—Evelyn Altizer

Lemon-Lime Salad

1 3-ounce box lemon gelatin
1 3-ounce box lime gelatin
2 cups boiling water
1 8½-ounce can crushed pineapple
1 8-ounce package cream cheese, softened
1 14-ounce can sweetened condensed milk

Dissolve gelatin in boiling water; add remaining ingredients. Pour into 2-quart container and chill until firm. Makes 12 servings.
—Opal Honaker

Frosted Fruit Salad

2 3-ounce packages strawberry gelatin
1 10-ounce package frozen strawberries
1 15¼-ounce can crushed pineapple
2 large ripe bananas, mashed
1 cup sour cream

On the day before serving, into large bowl combine gelatin, 2 cups boiling water, and strawberries. Set aside until strawberries are thawed. Add pineapple with its juice and bananas. Pour into 8″ springform pan or 12″x8″ pan. Refrigerate until set. Spread top with sour cream. Refrigerate until serving time. Makes 12 servings.
—Evelyn Altizer
Essie Combs
Wilma Matney

Sour cream keeps best if stored in the tightly covered container in which it is purchased. If stored upside down in the refrigerator, maximum retention of texture and flavor is assured.

Pear Salad

2 3-ounce packages orange gelatin
2 cups boiling water
1 8-ounce package cream cheese
2 tablespoons mayonnaise
1 15½-ounce can crushed pineapple

1 15½-ounce can pears, mashed
1 1½-ounce package non-dairy
  whipped topping mix, prepared
  as on package

Dissolve gelatin in boiling water. Add mayonnaise, cream cheese, pears, and pineapple. Fold in whipped topping. Chill overnight.

—Vera Tatum

Gone with the Wind Salad

1 pound large marshmallows
1 cup milk
1 9-ounce carton whipped topping
1 13-ounce can crushed pineapple,
  drained

2 cups graham cracker crumbs
⅓ cup margarine, softened
⅓ cup sugar
Coconut (optional)

Melt marshmallows with milk in heavy pan; stir and cool completely. In mixing bowl combine whipped topping and pineapple; add to cooled marshmallow mixture. Mix graham cracker crumbs, sugar, and margarine. Pat into a 9"x12" buttered dish. Cool in refrigerator for one hour. Pour marshmallow mixture into crust. Sprinkle with graham cracker crumbs or coconut. Chill.

—Gladys Joyce

Pineapple Supreme Salad

1 8-ounce package cream cheese
2 cups marshmallows
1 3-ounce package lemon gelatin
1 3-ounce package lime gelatin
2 cups pineapple juice

1 29-ounce can crushed pineapple
2 cups whipped cream
½ cup maraschino cherries
½ cup pecans

Melt cream cheese and marshmallows in double boiler. Add to lemon gelatin dissolved in hot pineapple juice. Chill to jelly consistency. Add crushed pineapple, cherries, and pecans. Whip cream until stiff; fold in. Pour into 2-quart dish and chill until firm. Prepare lime gelatin according to package directions. Chill until it starts to set. Pour over salad; chill until firm.

—Margaret Matney

How to unmold a mold: Do not dip the mold in hot water because all too often the gelatin melts more than you'd like. Instead, run a thin, hot knife around the edge of the mold, rinse a kitchen towel in very hot water, and squeeze the towel as dry as possible. Wrap the hot towel around the mold. It will create just enough heat to enable you to slide the gelatin from its container without any melting.

Gelatin Fruit Salad

2 3-ounce packages orange-
 pineapple gelatin
2 cups hot water
1 15½-ounce can apricots, diced and
 drained—reserve juice

1 15½-ounce can crushed
 pineapple, drained—reserve juice
1 cup juice from fruit
1 cup miniature marshmallows

Dissolve gelatin in hot water. Add juice and chill until thickened. Stir in apricots, pineapple, and marshmallows. Chill until firm in 2-quart shallow glass casserole.

Cooked Topping:

½ cup sugar
1 egg, beaten
3 tablespoons flour
1 cup juice from fruit

2 tablespoons butter
1 cup whipping cream, whipped
Shredded cheese or nuts

Cook sugar, egg, flour, and juice until thick in double boiler. Add butter; let cool. Fold in whipped cream. Spread on gelatin layer. Top with shredded cheese or nuts.　　　　　　　　　　　　　　　　—Dorothy Tatum

Pink Frozen Salad

1 16-ounce can cherry pie filling
1 13½-ounce can crushed pineapple
1 14-ounce can sweetened
 condensed milk

1 13½-ounce carton whipped
 topping
2 cups miniature marshmallows

Mix all ingredients together in order given. Spoon into a 7"x9" baking dish. Freeze. Makes 8 servings.　　　　　　　　—Margaret Matney

Rhubarb Salad

1 pound rhubarb (about 4 cups)
1 cup water
¾ cup sugar
1 6-ounce package strawberry
 gelatin
1¼ cups cold water

1 cup diced celery
2 10-ounce cans mandarin oranges,
 drained
Sour cream
Dash of nutmeg

Bring rhubarb, 1 cup water, and sugar to a boil; simmer 4-5 minutes. Add gelatin, stirring to dissolve. Stir in cold water. Pour into a 2-quart baking dish; refrigerate until thickened but not congealed. Stir in celery and oranges. Garnish each serving with sour cream and sprinkle with nutmeg. Serves 10-12.　　　　　　　　　　　　　—Janette Newhouse

A pasture feeling blue
cannot scamper up a knoll
and taunt the woods below...
　　—"Flat Country" by Preston Newman

Overnight Salad 1

2 3-ounce packages cream cheese
1 cup chopped celery
1 4-ounce jar pimiento, drained
2 3-ounce packages lemon gelatin

1 15½-ounce can crushed pineapple,
drained—reserve liquid
1 cup chopped nuts

Mix gelatin using 1 cup of the pineapple juice in place of water; let cool. Combine cream cheese and pimiento; mix in pineapple, celery, and nuts. Add gelatin mixture. Pour into 13"x9"x1½" pan; let stand in refrigerator overnight. Makes 12 servings. —Evelyn Altizer

Quick and Easy Salad

1 9-ounce container whipped
topping
1 3-ounce package orange gelatin

1 1-pound container cottage cheese
1 8½-ounce can crushed pineapple

Stir orange gelatin into whipped topping with fork. Add cottage cheese and drained pineapple. Stir well with fork until well blended; chill. Makes 8 servings. —Opal Honaker
Wilma Matney

Pistachio Salad

1 3¾-ounce package pistachio
pudding mix, used dry
1 20-ounce can crushed pineapple
and juice

1 9-ounce carton whipped topping
½ cup chopped pecans
½ cup miniature marshmallows

Mix dry pudding mix with whipped topping. Add remaining ingredients. Makes 6-8 servings. —Donda Kidd
Margaret Matney

Saucy-Raspberry Salad

2 3-ounce packages raspberry
gelatin
1 cup boiling water

1½ cups frozen raspberries
1 cup applesauce

Mix gelatin and boiling water. Add partly frozen raspberries and applesauce. Pour into 9"x9" dish; chill till set. Makes 8 servings.
—Margaret Matney

Once pimientos have been opened, keep them in the refrigerator. Pour a little vinegar or water over them and cover tightly; they will stay fresh for days.

Chicken Salad Supreme

3 5-ounce cans boned chicken, flaked
½ cup mayonnaise
1 tablespoon lemon juice
1 tablespoon prepared mustard
1 teaspoon seasoned salt

1 cup thinly sliced celery
1 medium avocado, peeled and cubed
1 4-ounce jar diced pimiento
¼ cup minced parsley
Salad greens

Drain chicken, reserving broth; combine broth with next four ingredients, mixing well. Add chicken, celery, avocado, pimiento, and parsley; stir gently. Chill and serve on salad greens. Yields 4-6 servings.

—Jamie Overbay

Chicken Salad

1 cup chopped cooked chicken
1 tablespoon chopped onion
2 tablespoons chopped pimiento

2 or 3 dashes hot sauce
½ cup salad dressing or mayonnaise
½ cup chopped pecans

Combine all ingredients; mix well and chill. You may wish to use less salad dressing or mayonnaise. Makes 2 servings.   —Opal Honaker

Beef Supper Salad

½ cup mayonnaise or salad dressing
1 tablespoon chili sauce
1 tablespoon sweet pickle relish
¼ teaspoon salt
2 cups cubed cooked beef

1 cup drained kidney beans
1 cup sliced celery
⅓ cup chopped onion
2 hard-cooked eggs, chopped

Mix all together; add beans and beef last. Serves 6-8.

—Jennie Tatum

Corned Beef Salad

4 hard-cooked eggs, chopped
1 cup celery, chopped
1 large onion, chopped
2 10-ounce packages frozen mixed
  vegetables, cooked as directed,
  cooled, and drained

1 12-ounce can corned beef, chilled
Salt to taste

Chop corned beef into small pieces; mix with vegetables and eggs. Add enough mayonnaise to moisten; add salt to taste. Makes 8 servings.

—Wilma Matney

Ham Macaroni Salad

8 ounces shell macaroni
  (2½ cups cooked)
½ cup mayonnaise
2 tablespoons prepared mustard
1 small onion, minced

2 cups cut or diced cooked ham
2 ribs celery, chopped
⅓ cup sweet pickle relish
¼ teaspoon salt
¼ teaspoon pepper

Cook macaroni as directed on package; drain, rinse, and drain again. In a large bowl mix mayonnaise and mustard, then stir in remaining ingedients. Add macaroni and toss gently. Cover and chill several hours. Makes about 6 servings.   —Gladys Joyce

Macaroni Salad

1 7-ounce package macaroni
2 tablespoons chopped onion
½ cup chopped sweet pickles
⅓ cup chopped green pepper

1 tablespoon mustard
1 teaspoon celery seed
½ cup mayonnaise

Cook macaroni until tender; drain. Add remaining ingredients. Makes 12 servings.   —Opal Honaker

Taco Salad

1 head lettuce, shredded
1 pound ground beef
1 pound sharp Cheddar cheese,
  shredded
1 16-ounce can red kidney beans,
  rinsed with hot water and drained
1 large green pepper, diced

1 large onion, diced
1 package taco seasoning
1 tablespoon chili powder
1 medium bottle French salad
  dressing
1 package tortilla chips

Sauté ground beef until well done and crumbly. Add taco seasoning according to directions. Place in strainer when done and let excess grease drain from beef. When well drained, toss all ingredients; add dressing as desired—approximately ½-¾ bottle. Crumble tortilla chips and toss into mixture when ready to serve. Crumble more tortilla chips on top of salad. Makes 8 servings.   —Thelma Joyce

The trout lily blooms now
I hear the waterthrush singing
Uncle Crow stands full of straw
in glory weeds and beggar ticks...
    —"April: Rock Castle Creek" by Clyde Kessler

Cucumber Salad

1 3-ounce package lime gelatin	¹/₄ teaspoon salt
³/₄ cup hot water	1 cup chopped cucumber
¹/₄ cup lemon juice	1 cup sour cream
1 teaspoon onion juice	

Dissolve gelatin in water; add lemon juice, onion juice, and salt. Chill until slightly thick. Fold in cucumber and sour cream; pour in 1-quart mold. Chill until set. Makes 6 servings. —Teresa Adkins

Sour Cream Cucumber Salad

4 cucumbers	¹/₄ cup vegetable oil
1 tablespoon salt	¹/₂ teaspoon sugar
1 cup sour cream	3 tablespoons chopped fresh dill
1¹/₂ tablespoons white vinegar	Salt and pepper

Scrub cucumbers but do not peel. Cut off ends. Score with tines of a fork. Slice thinly. Sprinkle with salt and let stand at room temperature for one hour. Drain and rinse to remove salt. Squeeze dry. Combine sour cream, vinegar, oil, sugar, and dill. Pour over cucumbers. Add salt and pepper to taste. Chill before serving.

Serve in glass dish—decorate with dill sprigs. —Marilyn Wells

Cole Slaw

8 cups finely shredded cabbage
¹/₂ medium green pepper, minced
1 medium yellow onion, finely chopped

Dressing:

3 tablespoons sugar	¹/₂ teaspoon salt
3 tablespoons cider vinegar	¹/₈ teaspoon pepper
3 tablespoons hot water	¹/₄ cup vegetable oil
¹/₂ teaspoon celery seed	

Place cabbage, green pepper, and onion in large bowl; toss well to mix. For dressing, combine sugar and hot water, stirring until sugar dissolves. Stir in vinegar, celery seed, salt, and pepper. Pour over slaw and toss well. Drizzle in oil and toss well. Cover and marinate in refrigerator 2 or 3 hours before serving. Toss again before serving. —Evelyn Altizer

Refrigerator Slaw

2 or 3 stalks celery, cut small
1½ pounds cabbage, shredded
1 medium onion, diced
1 medium green pepper, diced
2 tablespoons diced pimiento
½ cup vinegar

½ cup sugar
½ cup vegetable oil
1 tablespoon salt
1½ tablespoons prepared mustard
1 teaspoon celery seeds
1 small carrot, cut up

Combine cabbage, onion, green pepper, and pimiento; set aside. Combine remaining ingredients and bring to a boil. Pour over cabbage mixture and mix thoroughly. Refrigerate overnight. Makes 8-10 servings.

—Dora Abel

Corn Relish Salad

Dressing:
⅔ cup salad oil
2½ tablespoons vinegar
2½ teaspoons salt

½ teaspoon pepper
1¼ teaspoons dry mustard

Combine all ingredients; set aside.

1 16-ounce can whole-kernel corn
½ green pepper, chopped
2½ teaspoons pimiento, diced

5 small stalks celery, diced
1 medium onion, chopped

Mix vegetables; add dressing. Refrigerate for 24 hours. Makes 8-10 servings.

—Wilma Matney

Wilted Lettuce

Pick tender lettuce, wash carefully; drain on toweling, and pat dry. Break or cut into pieces into a medium-sized bowl, filling bowl to top. Slice spring onions over top of lettuce, including the tender part of the green onion tops. Some people like a little sugar sprinkled over the lettuce and onions. Sprinkle salt over top of mixture. Mix three or four tablespoons of vinegar to ⅓ cup bacon drippings. Let come to a boil, and pour over lettuce and onions.

—Thelma Joyce

Broccoli Salad

1 package broccoli, chopped
1 small onion, chopped
3 boiled eggs, chopped
¾ cup pimiento-stuffed olives, chopped

1 package Buttermilk Dressing,
  prepared according to package
  directions

Mix all ingredients and marinate in refrigerator overnight. Also good with one small can of mushroom buttons. Makes 6 servings.

—Wilma Matney

Overnight Salad II

1 head lettuce, cut up
1 large red onion, sliced thinly

1 pound bacon, fried and crumbled
1 head cauliflower, cut in small pieces

Dressing:
2 cups salad dressing
¼ cup sugar

⅓ cup Parmesan cheese, grated
Salt and pepper to taste

Layer lettuce, onion, bacon, and cauliflower in above order. Mix dressing ingredients and pour on top of salad. Do not stir dressing into salad. Cover tightly and refrigerate overnight. Stir before serving. Makes 12 servings.　　　　　　　　　　　　　　　　　　　—Opal Honaker

Make-Ahead Layered Salad

1 head lettuce
1½ cups carrots, chopped
1½ cups cooked green peas
1½ cups chopped celery
1½ cups sliced purple onions

1½ cups parsley
2 cups sour cream
2 cups mayonnaise
1 12-ounce package bacon, fried and
　crumbled

Break lettuce into small pieces; add carrots, peas, celery, onions, and parsley. Mix mayonnaise with sour cream and pour over layered ingredients. Sprinkle with fried bacon bits. Do not stir until ready to serve. Chill at least 6 hours. Makes 15 servings.　　　　　　　　　—Opal Honaker

Pea Salad

1 8½-ounce can tiny garden peas,
　drained
1 7-ounce can shoe peg corn,
　drained
1 2-ounce can pimiento, drained;
　diced or minced

1 large green pepper, diced finely
¼ cup diced onions
1 cup diced celery (remove all strings
　from celery before dicing)

Dressing:
1 cup sugar
1 cup vegetable oil
¾ cup vinegar

½ teaspoon white pepper
1 teaspoon salt

Mix dressing ingredients together; pour over combined vegetables. Put in bowl, cover, and keep in refrigerator. Stir once or twice. Makes 8 servings.　　　　　　　　　　　　　　　　　　　—Gladys Joyce

To prevent soggy salads, place an inverted saucer in
the bottom of the salad bowl. The excess liquid drains
off under the saucer, and the salad stays fresh and crisp.

Sour Cream Potato Salad

1½ cups mayonnaise
1 8-ounce carton sour cream
1½ teaspoons prepared horseradish
1 teaspoon celery seed

8 medium potatoes, cooked, peeled
  and sliced
1 cup fresh minced parsley, divided
¾ cup chopped green onion, divided

Combine first four ingredients; set aside. Place half of sliced potatoes in a medium bowl; sprinkle with ⅓ cup parsley and ¼ cup onion. Top with half of mayonnaise mixture. Repeat layers. Use remaining parsley and onion to garnish top. Cover; chill. Makes 8-10 servings.   —Evelyn Altizer

Sour Cream Dill Potato Salad

1 cup sour cream
½ cup salad dressing
3 tablespoons vinegar
1½ teaspoons salt
¼ teaspoon pepper
1 teaspoon dill weed

4 cups sliced cooked potatoes
1 cup thinly sliced celery
¾ cup finely chopped onion
½ cup diced sweet pickles, drained
½ cup chopped green pepper
4 hard-cooked eggs, sliced

Combine first six ingredients; mix well. Combine remaining ingredients in mixing bowl; add sour cream mixture and toss lightly. Chill several hours to blend flavors. Serve on crisp salad greens.   —Evelyn Altizer

Tomato Vegetable Aspic

1 envelope unflavored gelatin
  (1 tablespoon)
2 cups tomato juice
1 tablespoon Worcestershire sauce

1 cup minced celery
¼ cup minced onion
¼ cup minced green pepper

Soften gelatin in ½ cup cold tomato juice. Heat remaining juice to boiling point. Add softened gelatin and Worcestershire sauce. Stir until gelatin is dissolved. Cool; chill until syrupy. Fold in vegetables. Pour into lightly oiled custard cups or into a 3-cup mold. Chill until firm. Unmold onto salad greens. Serve with chilled Russian Dressing.   —Ruth Bales

Sauerkraut Salad

1 quart chopped sauerkraut
1 cup chopped celery
1 cup chopped green pepper
1 2-ounce jar sliced pimientos
1 cup sugar

½ cup chopped onion
½ teaspoon dry mustard
½ cup vinegar
½ cup salad oil

Early in the day or the day before serving, mix ingredients and stir until well combined. Cover and refrigerate to blend flavors.   —Evelyn Altizer
                                                                 Gladys Joyce
                                                                 Thelma Joyce

BALANCE

I have a friend who's always had it rough.
No house belonged to him in all his life.
There often wasn't even food enough
And never baubles for his pretty wife.
I know he felt it now and then. His face
Would cloud. For just a moment you could see,
That though he stood it with uncommon grace,
Silently he may have thought, "Why me?"
Sometimes his luck would turn around a bit
And something middling good would come their way.
When it did, they made the most of it
And laughed and thanked their God for one more day.
    He puzzled me until I thought it through.
    I hope my Heaven has a thorn or two.

—Cecil Mullins

Vegetables

Asparagus and Pea Casserole

1 10-ounce package frozen green
   peas
1 10-ounce package frozen
   asparagus, or 1 14½-ounce can

Salt
1 10¾-ounce can cream of
   mushroom soup
Cracker crumbs

Place peas in bottom of casserole, then a layer of asparagus. Salt to taste.
Pour canned soup over asparagus. Cover with cracker crumbs. You can dot
with butter for extra flavor, and add shreds of red pimiento over top for
decoration. Pour a little of the asparagus broth over the casserole. Bake at
350° for 30 minutes. Makes 8 servings.　　　　　　　　—Wilma Matney

Asparagus Casserole I

4 cups cooked or canned asparagus
1 cup shredded cheese

1 tablespoon butter
½ cup soft bread crumbs

Combine white sauce with asparagus in 2-quart casserole. Sprinkle
bread crumbs and cheese over top, dot with butter. Bake at 350° for 20-25
minutes. Makes 6 servings.

Medium White Sauce:

2 tablespoons butter
2 tablespoons flour

¼ teaspoon salt
1 cup milk

Melt butter, stir in flour and salt. Gradually add milk, stirring to keep
mixture smooth. Cook until thickened.　　　　　　　　—Opal Honaker

Asparagus Casserole II

3 hard-cooked eggs, sliced
2 14½-ounce cans asparagus,
   drained
1 10¾-ounce can mushroom soup

1 cup grated Cheddar cheese
Salt and pepper
2 tablespoons butter

Line a 1½-quart casserole with sliced eggs. Top with asparagus and
soup. Sprinkle with cheese, salt, and pepper. Dot with butter. Bake uncovered at 350° for 30 minutes. Makes 6 servings.　　　　　　—Evelyn Wyatt

Baked Beans

4 slices bacon	2 tablespoons brown sugar
½ cup chopped onion	1 tablespoon Worcestershire sauce
2 1-pound cans pork and beans	1 teaspoon prepared mustard

Cook bacon until crisp; drain, reserving 2 tablespoons of drippings. Crumble bacon. Cook onion in reserved drippings till tender; add onion and bacon to remaining ingredients; mix well. Pour into 1½-quart casserole. Bake at 350° for 2 hours. Serves 6.　　　　　—Donna Davis

Lima Bean Casserole

1 pound large dry lima beans	½ cup lima bean water
½ pound hamburger	1 tablespoon brown sugar
1 medium onion, chopped fine	1½ teaspoons salt
2 8-ounce cans tomato sauce	Dash of poultry seasoning

Soak beans overnight; drain. Cover with boiling water; cook slowly 1-2 hours or until tender. Drain, saving ½ cup bean water. Lightly brown meat and onions; stir to break into bits. Add tomato sauce, bean water, salt, sugar, and poultry seasoning. Place beans in large casserole; cover with sauce. Bake at 350° for 30 minutes.　　　　　—Evelyn Altizer
　　　　　　　　　　　　　　　　　　　　　　　　　　Vera Tatum

Green Bean Casserole

1 16-ounce can green beans	1 3½-ounce can French fried onion
1 10½-ounce can cream of	rings
mushroom soup	

Place beans in a 1-quart casserole; cover with soup. Bake at 350° for 15-20 minutes. Sprinkle onion rings over top; return to the oven until golden brown. Asparagus may be substituted for beans. Makes 4-5 servings.
　　　　　　　　　　　　　　　　　　　　　　　　—Jamie Overbay

Harvard Beets

2 cups freshly cooked, drained and	⅛ teaspoon salt
diced beets	⅓ cup vinegar
½ cup sugar	⅓ cup water
1 tablespoon cornstarch	2 tablespoons butter

Mix sugar, cornstarch, salt, vinegar, and water; cook until clear. Pour over beets; let set 30 minutes. Add butter. Keep warm until ready to serve.
　　　　　　　　　　　　　　　　　　　　　　　　—Opal Honaker
　　　　　　　　　　　　　　　　　　　　　　　　Gladys Joyce

Spiced Beets

1 16-ounce can beets, diced, partly drained
¼ teaspoon ground cinnamon

⅛ teaspoon ground cloves
2 teaspoons sugar
1 tablespoon margarine

Combine all ingredients except margarine in a non-metal covered container. Let stand for 2 or 3 hours in refrigerator. Before serving, add margarine and simmer 5-8 minutes.   —Margaret Matney

B·R·O·C·C·O·L·I

Broccoli Casserole I

2 10-ounce packages chopped broccoli
1 10¾-ounce can cream of mushroom soup

2 eggs
¾ cup mayonnaise
1 cup cubed Cheddar cheese
1 cup butter cracker crumbs

Cook broccoli 15 minutes. Beat eggs well; add soup and mayonnaise, and mix well. Add cheese. Put into shallow 2-quart pan or dish; sprinkle crumbs on top. Bake at 325° for 25-30 minutes. Makes 8 servings.
—Dora Abel

Broccoli Casserole II

1 10-ounce package frozen chopped broccoli
1 medium onion, chopped
1 10¾-ounce can cream of mushroom soup

1 cup mayonnaise or salad dressing
2 eggs
1 cup grated cheese
½ cup butter
1 cup butter cracker crumbs

Cook broccoli; drain. Mix all ingredients except butter and crumbs; pour over broccoli in 9"x11"x2" casserole dish. Cut butter in pieces and arrange over mixture; sprinkle cracker crumbs over all. Bake at 350° for 30 minutes. Let stand 20 minutes before serving. Makes 8 servings.
—Essie Combs
Opal Honaker

Broccoli Casserole III

2 cups instant rice
2 cups water
½ cup chopped onion
¾ cup chopped celery
2 10-ounce packages chopped broccoli

½ cup margarine, melted
2 10¾-ounce cans cream of mushroom soup
1 8-ounce jar processed cheese spread or 1 cup grated cheese

Mix in order given. Bake in 13"x9"x2" dish. Bake at 350° for 30 minutes. Makes 12 servings.
—Vonda Kidd
Evelyn Wyatt

Broccoli Casserole IV

2 10-ounce boxes frozen chopped
   broccoli
1 10¾-ounce can cream of
   mushroom soup
1 cup mayonnaise

2 eggs, beaten
1 cup sharp cheese, grated
1 medium onion, minced
½ 8-ounce package herb stuffing
Salt and pepper to taste

Cook broccoli until tender; drain. Combine soup, mayonnaise, onions, eggs, salt, and pepper. Add to broccoli, put into greased 9"x12" casserole dish, and spread grated cheese on top. Sprinkle dressing on top and dot with butter. Makes 8 servings. —Margaret Matney

Broccoli Strata

1 10-ounce package frozen chopped
   broccoli
6 slices wheat bread
4 slices American cheese
4 slices Swiss cheese
4 eggs

2 cups milk
1 tablespoon chopped onion
1 teaspoon salt
½ teaspoon prepared mustard
2 tablespoons butter

Cook and drain broccoli. Toast 4 slices of the bread; arrange them in an ungreased 8" square pan. Top with American cheese, then broccoli, then Swiss cheese. Mix together eggs, milk, onion, salt, and mustard; pour over casserole and refrigerate for 1 hour. In blender make bread crumbs out of 2 remaining slices of bread. Top with melted butter. Sprinkle over casserole. Bake at 325° for 60-65 minutes. Let stand 10 minutes before cutting. Makes 8 servings. —Evelyn Altizer

C·A·B·B·A·G·E

Scalloped Cabbage

1 medium head cabbage, shredded
2 tablespoons flour
2 tablespoons butter
1 cup milk

Salt and pepper
½-1 cup grated cheese
Bread crumbs

Cook cabbage until tender; drain. Combine flour, butter, milk, salt, pepper, and cheese. Cook on low heat until melted. Put cabbage in 13"x9"x2" casserole. Pour sauce over cabbage. Cover with bread crumbs; brown in 350° oven. Makes 6 servings. —Opal Honaker
Hazel Whitt

Place a heel of bread on top of cabbage before putting the lid on the pot and cooking it. There will be no odor. The bread has no effect on the cabbage and should be removed after cooking. Good also for broccoli and Brussels sprouts.

Tex-Mex Cabbage

1 head cabbage	1 green pepper, sliced
1 tablespoon sugar	2 cups canned tomatoes, drained
2 tablespoons butter	Salt and pepper to taste
1 onion, sliced	¾ cup shredded Cheddar cheese

Cut cabbage into 6 slices and cook about 10 minutes or until tender but crisp. Put in buttered 2-quart casserole dish. Sauté sugar, butter, onion, and green pepper; add tomatoes, salt, and pepper. Pour the mixture over the cabbage and sprinkle with cheese. Bake at 350° until heated all the way through. Makes 8 servings. —Jennie Tatum

Sautéed Cabbage

4 pounds cabbage	¼ teaspoon black pepper
2 tablespoons butter, melted	1 teaspoon sugar (optional)
¾ teaspoon salt	

Wash and drain the cabbage. Grate cabbage with a coarse grater or shred it. Melt the butter in a skillet. Sauté the cabbage, sprinkled with the salt and pepper; cook for 10 minutes, or until tender. Mix frequently, and add a tablespoon or two of water to avoid burning. Makes 6 servings.
—Marilyn Wells

C·A·R·R·O·T·S

Copper Penny Carrots

2 pounds carrots, sliced	1 cup sugar
1 large green pepper, sliced	¾ cup vinegar
1 large onion, sliced	1 teaspoon mustard
1 10¾-ounce can tomato soup	1 teaspoon Worcestershire Sauce
½ cup vegetable oil	

Cook carrots in salted water until medium done. Arrange layers of carrots, pepper, and onion in bowl. Combine soup, oil, sugar, vinegar, and Worcestershire Sauce in pan. Bring to a boil, stirring until blended. Pour over carrot mixture and refrigerate. Serve cold. —June Harris

Marinated Carrots

2 pounds carrots, diced	1 cup tomato soup
1 cup sugar	1 bell pepper, cut into rings
½ cup vinegar	1 medium onion, cut into rings
¼ cup vegetable oil	

Cook carrots in salt water until done. Mix remaining ingredients and simmer 20 minutes. Add to drained carrots. Makes 12 servings.
—Violet Cooper,
Margaret Matney, Wilma Matney

Cauliflower Suisse

2 medium heads cauliflower	½ cup sour cream
½ cup shredded Swiss cheese	Crumbled bacon
¼ cup mayonnaise	Well-buttered bread crumbs

Divide cauliflower into flowerets; cook, and drain. Melt cheese and mayonnaise in a double boiler and stir in sour cream. Put cauliflower in casserole and pour sauce over. Top liberally with both the crumbled bacon and the bread crumbs. Bake in a 350° oven until heated through—about 30 minutes. Sauce may also be used on broccoli. Makes 6 servings.

—Donna Davis

Cheese Cauliflower Italiano

3 tablespoons flour	3 tablespoons butter, cut into small
¼ teaspoon salt	pieces
½ teaspoon garlic powder	1 cup ripe olives, sliced
½ teaspoon coarsely ground pepper	2 cups grated Mozzarella cheese
1 pound fresh cauliflower, cored,	½ cup grated Parmesan cheese
cleaned, and cut vertically into	2 tablespoons chopped parsley
thin slices (4 cups)	Paprika
1 small onion, sliced into very thin	¼ cup dry white wine
slices	¾ cup milk

Preheat oven to 350°. Combine flour, salt, garlic powder, and coarsely ground pepper. In a greased 8″ square casserole, layer half of each of the following ingredients in order: cauliflower, onion, flour mixture, butter pieces, olives, Mozzarella cheese, and Parmesan cheese. Repeat layering with second half of ingredients, adding chopped parsley between olive slices and Mozzarella cheese. Sprinkle with paprika. Combine wine and milk; pour over. Bake uncovered in preheated oven 40-45 minutes or until golden and bubbly. Makes 4-6 servings. *Variation:* For stronger cheese flavor, grated Romano cheese may be substituted for all or part of Parmesan cheese.

—Janette Newhouse

Pickled Cauliflower

½ medium cauliflower	1 tablespoon chopped green pepper
1½ tablespoons vinegar	½ teaspoon sugar
1 tablespoon melted butter	⅛ teaspoon salt
1 tablespoon diced pimiento	

Break cauliflower into flowerets. Cook in a small amount of boiling salted water about 10 minutes; drain. Combine remaining ingredients in a small saucepan; cook over low heat about 5 minutes. Pour over hot cauliflower. Serve either hot or cold. Makes 2-3 servings.

—Marilyn Wells

Boiled Fresh Corn

Fill a large kettle two-thirds full of water. Remove the husks and all the silk from fresh corn and rinse under cool running water. Add no salt to the water, but some old-timers like to add 2 tablespoons of sugar. Put in the corn and bring the water back to a boil. Boil 5-10 minutes according to the age of the corn; large kernels take longer. Do not overcook. Serve in a large dish covered with a napkin. Butter, salt, and pepper are the only seasonings.

—Gladys Joyce

Foil-Baked Corn on Cob

12 ears fresh corn	1/2 teaspoon dried whole rosemary
1/2 cup butter or margarine, softened	1/2 teaspoon dried whole marjoram
1/2 teaspoon salt	1/8 teaspoon pepper

Remove husks and silk from corn just before cooking. Combine remaining ingredients, stirring well. Spread herb butter on corn, and place each ear on a piece of aluminum foil. Wrap tightly. Bake at 450° for 25 minutes, turning several times. Makes 12 servings. —Jamie Overbay

Corn Pudding I

1 quart corn	1 1/2 cups milk
1/4 cup butter	2 tablespoons sugar
1 teaspoon salt	2 eggs

Beat eggs in mixing bowl; add milk, sugar, and salt; then add corn. Pour into buttered 2-quart baking dish; put butter on top. Bake at 350° for 45 minutes or until firm. Makes 8 servings. —Gladys Joyce

Corn Pudding II

2 cups fresh corn	3 eggs, slightly beaten
2 teaspoons sugar	2 tablespoons butter
1 1/2 teaspoons salt	2 cups milk
1/8 teaspoon pepper	

Combine corn, sugar, salt, and pepper. Add eggs and mix. Add butter to milk; heat until butter is melted. Blend the milk with the corn and eggs. Put into 1-quart baking dish; bake at 325° for 1 hour, or until knife comes out clean. —Donna Davis

Corn Pudding III

2 10-ounce packages frozen corn,
   thawed and drained
3 eggs, well beaten
¼ cup flour
1 teaspoon salt

¼ teaspoon white pepper
1 tablespoon sugar
Dash nutmeg
2 tablespoons margarine, melted
2 cups light cream

Combine corn and eggs; mix well. Combine flour, salt, pepper, sugar, and nutmeg. Stir into corn mixture. Add margarine and cream; mix well. Pour into a greased 1½-quart casserole. Bake uncovered at 325° for 1 hour and 10 minutes, or until pudding is firm. Makes 8 servings.

—Margaret Matney

Golden Corn Pudding

2 16-ounce cans whole kernel corn,
   drained
¼ cup instant minced onion
1 tablespoon parsley flakes
1 tablespoon sugar
¾ teaspoon salt

⅛ teaspoon black pepper
½ teaspoon monosodium glutamate
2 tablespoons melted butter
⅔ cup cream
4 eggs, beaten

Butter a shallow 1½-quart baking dish. Mix together corn, onion, parsley, sugar, salt, pepper, and monosodium glutamate. Blend in butter, cream, and eggs. Pour in baking dish. Bake at 300° about 40 minutes, or until a silver knife inserted in center comes out clean. Serve immediately. Makes 8 servings.

—Opal Honaker

Super Hominy

1 29-ounce can hominy, drained
1 4-ounce can green chiles, chopped
1 2-ounce jar pimientos, drained
   and chopped (optional)

1 8-ounce carton sour cream
1½ cups grated Cheddar or
   Monterey Jack cheese

Mix all ingredients; put in greased 1½-quart casserole. Bake at 350° for 30-40 minutes. Let rest 10-15 minutes before serving.

—Marilyn Wells

— HELPFUL CORN MEASUREMENTS —

16- or 17-ounce can = about 2 cups kernels

12-ounce can = about 1½ cups kernels

1 10-ounce carton frozen cut corn = about 2 cups kernels

3 medium ears fresh = 1-1½ cups kernels

6 medium ears fresh = about 1 cup grated or cream-style corn

Potato Cakes

3 cups mashed potatoes
1 egg

¼ cup flour
1 small onion, chopped (if desired)

Combine all ingredients. Mix well. With hands, pat into 2- or 3-inch patties. Fry in skillet with small amount of grease until brown. Makes 10-12 potato cakes.
—Donna Davis

Young Potatoes and Gravy

1 cup boiling water
2 cups raw potatoes, diced
1 tablespoon onion, chopped
1 teaspoon salt
1 bay leaf

⅛ teaspoon pepper
Pinch of celery salt
3 cups milk
1 tablespoon butter
3 tablespoons flour

Cook potatoes and onion in boiling water until tender. Make thickening using flour and ⅓ cup of the milk; add rest of ingredients. Simmer for 30 minutes. Makes about 4 servings.
—Thelma Joyce

Scalloped Potatoes 1

6 medium potatoes (about 2 pounds)
1 10¾-ounce can cream of potato soup
¼ cup water
1 teaspoon salt

1 tablespoon prepared mustard
½ teaspoon margarine
2 medium onions, thinly sliced
1 tablespoon grated Parmesan cheese

Pare potatoes; cut into ¼"-thick slices. Cook in boiling salted water 15 minutes; drain. Combine soup, water, salt, and mustard in a small bowl. Grease a 2-quart shallow baking dish with margarine. Arrange one-third of the potatoes in baking dish. Spread half the sliced onions over them. Pour half the soup mixture over potatoes and onions. Spread half the remaining potatoes, the remaining onions, then the remaining potatoes. Pour remaining soup mixture over all and sprinkle with cheese. Bake in 375° oven 40 minutes, or until potatoes and onions are tender. Makes 8 servings.
—Evelyn Altizer

I've reached the age I used to want to be,
And that is nice, but something bothers me.
I must have overshot, because I creak
And something purple's growing on my cheek.
But that's the way it always goes.
I'm sure it's nothing. I suppose.
—"That's The Way It Goes" by Cecil Mullins

Scalloped Potatoes II

6 medium potatoes	1 10¾-ounce can cream of chicken
4 tablespoons butter	soup
2 tablespoons flour	1 teaspoon salt
3 cups milk	½ teaspoon pepper
	1 onion, chopped

Peel potatoes and slice thinly. Make a sauce of butter, flour, and milk. Heat until sauce begins to thicken; add soup, stir, and set aside. Place half of sliced potatoes in a 2-quart casserole. Sprinkle with seasonings and onion. Pour half the sauce over potatoes. Add remaining potatoes, seasonings, and onion. Pour on remaining sauce. Cover and bake at 350° for one hour. Makes 8 servings. —Wilma Matney

Scalloped Potatoes III

8 medium potatoes, sliced	1 cup milk
¼ cup chopped green pepper	2 teaspoons salt
¼ cup minced onion	Dash of black pepper
1 10¾-ounce can cream of	1 cup grated cheese
mushroom soup	

Alternate layers of sliced potatoes, green peppers, and onion in greased 11"x7"x1½" baking dish or 2-quart casserole. Combine soup, milk, and seasonings. Pour over potatoes, sprinkle with cheese. Cover. Bake at 350° for 45 minutes. Remove cover and bake 20-30 minutes longer, or until potatoes are tender. Makes 8 servings. —Jamie Overbay

Scalloped Potatoes IV

6 medium potatoes	2 teaspoons salt
4 tablespoons butter	2½ cups milk
4 tablespoons flour	1½ cups grated processed cheese

Peel and slice potatoes. Place in 2-quart greased casserole. Make a white sauce of butter, flour, salt, and milk. Cook over low heat until thickened. Remove from range. Add cheese to sauce and stir well. Cover potatoes with hot sauce and bake uncovered for 1-1½ hours at 375°. Makes 6 servings.
—Donda Kidd

Don't have a microwave? You can still bake potatoes in only 13 minutes, without even heating the oven to do it. Wrap the potatoes in foil, place them on a rack in your pressure cooker, and add water up to the rack. Cook 10-15 minutes, depending on the size of the potatoes.

Scalloped Potatoes With Ham

1 10¾-ounce can cream of mushroom or celery soup	1 cup diced, cooked ham
¾ cup milk	1 small onion, sliced
Dash pepper	1 tablespoon margarine
4 cups sliced potatoes	Paprika

Combine soup, milk, and pepper. In greased 2-quart casserole arrange layers of potatoes, ham, onion, and soup mixture (be sure ham is covered to prevent drying). Dot top with butter; sprinkle with paprika. Cover. Bake at 375° for 1 hour. Uncover; bake 15 minutes longer, or until potatoes are done. Makes 6 servings.
—Margaret Matney

Au Gratin Potatoes

2 cups cooked potatoes, sliced

Cheese Sauce:

2 tablespoons butter	¼ teaspoon dry mustard
2 tablespoons flour	1 cup milk
¼ teaspoon salt	1 cup grated cheese

Melt butter over low heat in heavy saucepan; blend in flour, salt, and mustard. Cook over low heat, stirring until mixture is smooth and bubbly. Remove from heat, and stir in milk. Bring to a boil, stirring constantly. Boil 1 minute; add cheese and stir until melted. Place cooked potatoes in greased casserole; pour cheese sauce over top. Sprinkle with paprika. Bake at 400° for 15-20 minutes.
—Dorothy Tatum

Potato Casserole Deluxe

2 1-pound packages frozen hash brown potatoes, thawed	1 16-ounce carton sour cream
1 cup diced onion	½ cup margarine, melted
1 10¾-ounce can cream of chicken soup, undiluted	8 ounces sharp Cheddar cheese, grated
	1 cup or more crushed potato chips

Put all ingredients except potato chips in a large bowl; add salt and pepper to taste. Mix well. Put in greased 9"x13" baking dish. Sprinkle generously with the crushed potato chips. Bake at 375° for 1 hour. Serves 12-15.
—Virginia Tatum

If you put your cheese in the freezer
for 30 or 40 minutes, it will grate more easily.

To prevent mold on cheese, wrap it in a cloth
dampened with salt water before refrigerating.

Baked Potato Thins

8 large potatoes, sliced thin
1/4 cup melted butter
1/2 teaspoon salt

Place potatoes in 13"x9" pan, pour melted butter over potatoes, and sprinkle on salt. Bake at 350° for 1½ hours. Make 8 servings.

—Donna Davis

Gourmet Stuffed Potatoes

6 large baking potatoes
1 pint sour cream
1 cup plain or pimiento cheese, grated
1/4 cup chopped fresh parsley

2 tablespoons margarine
1 small onion, grated
1 teaspoon garlic salt
Paprika, salt, and pepper to taste

Bake potatoes until soft; remove from oven. Mix rest of ingredients in large bowl with electric mixer. Cut warm potatoes in half, lengthwise, and scoop potatoes from shell with spoon. Add potatoes to mixture and beat thoroughly. Spoon mixture into shells and sprinkle with paprika. (These freeze well and may be removed from freezer, warmed in oven. and served on short notice.) Bake at 350° for 1 hour. Makes 12 servings.

—Jamie Overbay

Holiday Potato Soup

4 medium potatoes, diced
3 medium onions, sliced
1 10¾-ounce can cream of chicken
   soup, undiluted
1 tablespoon butter or margarine

3¼ cups milk
1/2 cup half-and-half
1 teaspoon salt
1/4 teaspoon pepper
Chopped parsley

Place potatoes and onion in a small amount of water in a medium saucepan. Cover and cook about 20 minutes, or until done. Drain well and mash. Combine mashed vegetables with remaining ingredients except parsley; mix well. Heat thoroughly in top of double boiler, stirring occasionally. Garnish with parsley. Makes 6 or 8 servings.

—Jamie Overbay

Mashed Potatoes

4 medium potatoes, peeled and sliced
1/2 cup milk

2 tablespoons butter
Salt and pepper to taste

Heat milk to steaming in medium-sized saucepan; drop in sliced potatoes. Cover and simmer 10-15 minutes, or until tender. Press potatoes through food mill as soon as they are tender. Add butter, salt, and pepper. Beat vigorously with heated egg beater. Serve at once.

—Marilyn Wells

Cheese Sauce

2 tablespoons butter	1/2 teaspoon salt
3 tablespoons flour	1/8 teaspoon pepper
2 cups milk	1 cup shredded cheese (4 ounces)

Melt butter in saucepan over low heat. Blend in flour and cook 1 minute. Gradually add milk; cook over medium heat until thickened. Add salt, pepper, and cheese. Stir until smooth. Makes 2½ cups.

—Opal Honaker

Sour Cream Substitute

1/4 cup nonfat dry milk	2 teaspoons lemon juice
1/2 cup cold water	1/4 teaspoon salt
1 18-ounce carton dry curd cottage cheese	

Mix milk and water in blender. Add cottage cheese, lemon juice, and salt. Process until smooth. Refrigerate until ready to use. Makes 2 cups.

—Hazel Whitt

Simple Spinach Puff

1 16-ounce jar processed cheese spread	4 eggs, separated
2 tablespoons flour	2 10-ounce packages frozen chopped spinach, cooked and well-drained

Heat cheese spread over low heat. Remove from heat; blend in flour and egg yolks. Stir in spinach. Fold in stiffly beaten egg whites. Pour into greased 10"x6" baking dish. Bake at 350° for 30 minutes. Makes 6-8 servings.

—Janette Newhouse

Baked Spinach

3 10-ounce packages frozen chopped spinach	1/2 cup margarine, divided
1 8-ounce package cream cheese, softened	1 1/2 cups seasoned croutons, crushed (1/2 cup bread crumbs)

Cook spinach according to directions; drain well. Add cream cheese and ¼ cup margarine. Pour into 1½-quart casserole. Top with crumbs mixed with melted butter. Bake at 350° for 20-30 minutes, or until bubbly.

—Marilyn Wells

Squash Casserole

2 pounds yellow summer squash,
  sliced
1 small onion, chopped
1/2 green pepper, chopped
1/3 cup margarine
2 eggs, beaten lightly

1/2 cup milk
1/2 cup grated Cheddar cheese
1 teaspoon sugar
6 crackers, crushed, plus enough
  for top
Salt and pepper to taste

Cook squash in water until just tender. Drain and set aside. Sauté onion and green pepper in margarine until tender; add to squash. Add milk, eggs, cheese, sugar, salt, pepper, and crackers. Spoon into greased casserole. Top with additional cracker crumbs. Bake at 325° for 1 hour. May be made ahead and frozen before baking. Makes 6 servings.   —Opal Honaker

Summer Squash Casserole

1 cup sour cream
6 cups yellow summer squash,
  sliced (approximately 2 pounds)
1/4 cup chopped onion
1 10¾-ounce can cream of chicken
  or mushroom soup

1 cup shredded carrots
1 8-ounce package herb-seasoned
  stuffing mix
1/2 cup melted butter
1 cup shredded cheese

In saucepan cook squash and onion for 5 minutes, or until tender. Drain. Combine cream soup and sour cream; stir in shredded carrots. Fold in drained squash and butter. Spread half of stuffing mix in bottom of a 12"x7½"x2" baking dish. Spoon vegetables on top. Sprinkle remaining stuffing over vegetables. Bake at 350° for 20 minutes, or until thoroughly heated. Add grated cheese on top as soon as you take it out of the oven. Makes 12 servings.   —Donna Davis
Vonda Kidd

Country Club Squash

6 or 8 tender, small squash
  (1 quart frozen)
Salt and pepper to taste
6 tablespoons butter, divided
1 bouillon cube

1 tablespoon grated onion
1 egg, well beaten
1 cup sour cream
1/2 cup breadcrumbs
1/2 cup grated cheese

Slice squash and cook until tender; mash. Add salt, pepper, 2 tablespoons butter, bouillon cube, and onion. Add egg and sour cream. Pour into 1-quart casserole. Combine breadcrumbs, grated cheese, and 4 tablespoons melted butter. Sprinkle over top of squash. Bake at 350° for 30 minutes.

—Marilyn Wells

Fried Summer Squash

2 pounds summer squash
  or zucchini
2 cups meal

Salt and pepper
Vegetable oil or other fat

Cut summer squash into ¾" slices. Dip in cold water. Cover each slice with meal that has been seasoned with salt and pepper. Fry in deep hot fat until brown on both sides. Makes 5 servings.   —Thelma Joyce

Squash Patties

1 cup flour
1 teaspoon sugar
½ teaspoon salt
¾ cup milk
1 egg

3 cups grated yellow squash
1 medium onion, chopped
2-3 teaspoons crushed red pepper
  (optional)
¼ cup vegetable oil

Combine first six ingredients; beat with mixer until smooth. Add remaining ingredients; stir well. Drop mixture by tablespoons into a hot greased skillet. Cook until golden brown, turning once. Drain on paper towels. Makes about 2 dozen.   —Donna Davis

Baked Acorn Squash

1 acorn squash, washed
¼ teaspoon salt
½ cup brown sugar

2 tablespoons butter
½ cup water

Cut squash in half; remove seeds. Leave in halves. Place squash in baking dish; sprinkle with salt, brown sugar, and butter. Add water by pouring down side of dish. Bake, covered, at 375° for 45 minutes, or until squash is tender.   —Thelma Joyce

Acorn Squash Surprise

4 small acorn squash
½ cup boiling water
Salt to taste

¾ cup brown sugar, divided
1 20-ounce can sliced apples, drained
Nutmeg

Cut squash in half lengthwise. Remove seeds and membrane. Place cut-side down in shallow baking ban; add boiling water. Bake at 350° for 45 minutes or until tender. Remove from oven; turn cut-side up, and sprinkle each with salt and 1 tablespoon brown sugar. Combine apples and remaining sugar; spoon into cavities. Sprinkle with nutmeg. Bake at 425° for 10 minutes.   —Margaret Matney

Candied Squash

1 teaspoon maple flavoring
1 small Hubbard squash
1/2 cup sugar
1/2 cup brown sugar

1/4 cup butter
1/2 teaspoon salt
1 cup water

Wash the squash and cut into pieces for serving—about 3"x4". Remove the seeds and membrane. Make a thin syrup of the sugar, butter, salt, and water. Pour into a 2-quart shallow baking pan. Arrange the pieces of squash yellow-side down in pan. Bake at 350° until the squash is very tender. May be cooked on top of the stove very slowly, if tightly covered and in a heavy pan. Makes 6 servings.   —Evelyn Altizer

S·W·E·E·T P·O·T·A·T·O·E·S

Sweet Potatoes and Pineapple

1 16-ounce can small whole sweet
   potatoes
1/4 cup butter

1-2 teaspoons cinnamon
1/4 cup brown sugar
1/2 cup crushed pineapple

Drain potatoes and place in greased 1-quart casserole. Dot butter over top of potatoes, and add cinnamon and brown sugar. Add crushed pineapple. Cover and let sit in refrigerator overnight; or bake at once at 350° for about 30 minutes.   —Marilyn Wells

Sweet Potato Casserole 1

3 cups sweet potatoes, cooked and
   mashed
2 eggs
1 cup sugar
1/4 cup milk

1 teaspoon vanilla
2 tablespoons butter or margarine,
   melted
1 cup coconut

Topping:
1 cup pecans, chopped
1/2 cup butter or margarine

1/2 cup flour
1 cup brown sugar

Beat eggs; combine with milk, potatoes, sugar, vanilla, coconut, and melted butter. Mix topping and sprinkle over top of potatoes. Bake at 350° for 30 minutes. Makes 6 servings.   —Essie Combs
                                                 Vonda Kidd
                                                 Vera Tatum

Sweet potatoes will not turn dark if put in salted water
(5 teaspoons to 1 quart of water) immediately after peeling.

Sweet Potato Casserole II

3 cups sweet potatoes,
  cooked and mashed
1 cup sugar
¹/₂ cup brown sugar
¹/₄ cup margarine

1 teaspoon cinnamon
¹/₂ cup milk
¹/₂ teaspoon salt
1 teaspoon vanilla
2 eggs

Topping:
1 cup brown sugar
1 cup pecans, chopped

¹/₃ cup flour
¹/₄ cup margarine

Mix potatoes, sugars, margarine, cinnamon, milk, salt, vanilla, and eggs; pour into greased 2-quart baking dish. Mix topping and sprinkle over potatoes. —Virginia Tatum

Orange Sweet Potatoes

6 medium sweet potatoes
1 cup fresh orange juice
1 tablespoon cornstarch
Pinch salt

2 tablespoons grated orange rind
3 tablespoons melted butter
¹/₃ cup brown sugar
¹/₃ cup sugar

Boil potatoes; peel and quarter. Put in 2-quart casserole. Prepare sauce with remaining ingredients; cook until thick. Pour sauce over potatoes. Place in oven until thoroughly heated. Makes 12 servings.
—Evelyn Altizer

Blender Sweet Potato Pudding

3 eggs
1¹/₄ cups milk
¹/₂ cup margarine
1 cup brown sugar

¹/₄ teaspoon cinnamon
¹/₄ teaspoon allspice
Dash salt
2¹/₂ cups sweet potatoes, raw and cubed

Blend above ingredients, gradually adding sweet potatoes. Pour into a 1-quart buttered casserole and bake at 325° for 45 minutes. Makes 6 servings. —Margaret Matney

For the best baked sweet potatoes, select potatoes of the same size; place on a rack in the middle of the oven. Do not wrap. Bake at 400° for 15 minutes. Then, reduce heat to 375°; bake medium potatoes for 45 minutes and large ones for 1 hour. Turn off heat, and let potatoes remain in the oven about 30 minutes.

Parmesan Tomato Bake

1 16-ounce can stewed tomatoes	¾ cup grated Parmesan cheese
1 tablespoon cornstarch	(3 ounces)
1 tablespoon sugar	1 egg
	Dash of salt

Combine tomatoes, cornstarch and sugar. Cook over medium heat until clear and thickened. Pour into 1-quart casserole. Combine cheese, eggs, and salt; mix. Bake at 350° for 20 minutes. Makes 4 servings.

—Janette newhouse

Herbed Tomato Halves

4 large tomatoes	½ teaspoon pepper
2 tablespoons chopped green onion	¼ teaspoon marjoram
¼ cup butter	¼ teaspoon basil
1 teaspoon salt	1½ cups fresh bread crumbs (4 slices)

Core tomatoes; cut in half crosswise. Place cut-side up in shallow baking pan just large enough to hold tomatoes. Sauté onion in butter in a large skillet until soft. Add salt, pepper, marjoram, basil, and bread crumbs; stir with fork until crumbs are thoroughly moistened. Divide mixture evenly over tomato halves. Bake in 350° oven for 20 minutes, or until tomatoes are heated thoroughly. Makes 8 servings. —marilyn Wells

Tomatoes on Toast

3 tomatoes	Pepper and salt
Chopped parsley	6 slices toast
½ cup cream	1 tablespoon butter
½ cup milk	1 teaspoon grated onion
1 tablespoon flour	

Wash and cut tomatoes in halves crosswise; set in a buttered baking pan. Sprinkle with salt and pepper and a little finely chopped parsley. Put a little piece of butter on the top of each and bake in 300° oven about 30 minutes. Have the toast ready. Carefully lift ½ tomato onto each piece. Make the sauce with remaining butter, milk, cream, onion, salt, pepper, and flour. Pour over the tomatoes and toast. This is nice for breakfast or luncheon.

—Jamie Overbay

When food boils over in the oven, sprinkle the burned surface with a little salt. This will stop smoke and odor from forming and make the spot easier to clean.

Fried Green Tomatoes

4 large green tomatoes
½ cup flour or cornmeal

1 teaspoon salt
¼ teaspoon pepper

Cut firm green tomatoes in ¼" slices. Mix flour or cornmeal with salt and pepper. Dip tomatoes in this mixture. Place in heavy skillet containing melted bacon fat or butter or margarine. Fry slowly until brown, turning once. Makes 6 servings.

—Donna Davis
Thelma Joyce

Z·U·C·C·H·I·N·I

Zucchini Mushroom Casserole

2 tablespoons margarine
¼ pound fresh mushrooms, washed
   and sliced, or 1 4-ounce can
1 small onion, chopped
1 cup milk

1 cup cooked zucchini slices, well
   drained
2 eggs, beaten
1 cup grated Cheddar cheese
½ teaspoon salt
¼ teaspoon pepper

Melt margarine in a skillet. Add mushrooms and onions; sauté until tender. Drain margarine from pan. Combine sautéed vegetables with milk, zucchini, eggs, ¾ cup cheese, salt, and pepper in large bowl; stir well. Pour into 1-quart casserole; top with remaining cheese. Bake at 375° for 30 minutes, or until set (may be frozen before baking). Makes 6 servings.

—Opal Honaker

Zucchini Vaucluse Style

3 small zucchini
Salt
Flour
Vegetable oil or olive oil
4 medium tomatoes

1 small clove garlic, crushed
2 tablespoons chopped parsley
⅛ teaspoon black pepper
½ teaspoon dried oregano
1 cup soft breadcrumbs

Wash, peel, and cut zucchini in lengthwise quarters. Sprinkle with salt and let stand 15 minutes. Wipe off salt, dredge in flour, and fry in shallow hot oil, turning to brown all sides. Place zucchini side-by-side in rows in a 10"x6"x2" baking dish. Peel, seed, and dice tomatoes, and cook 5 minutes in 2 tablespoons hot oil, adding salt to taste, garlic, parsley, pepper, and oregano. Spread over zucchini. Mix breadcrumbs with 2 tablespoons oil and sprinkle over the tomatoes. Cook in a preheated 350° oven for 30 minutes, or until crumbs are brown. Makes 6 servings.

—Marilyn Wells

APPALACHIAN

Garden Scramble Stir-Fry

2 tablespoons vegetable oil
1 large clove garlic, minced or pressed
1 cup broccoli flowerets, cut into
  ¹/₂″ chunks
1 cup cauliflower flowerets, cut into
  ¹/₂″ chunks
3 tablespoons water

¹/₂ cup carrots, cut into ¹/₂″ slanting
  slices
¹/₂ red bell pepper, cut into ¹/₄″ strips
Salt and pepper
¹/₂ cup sliced green onion
Whole cashews (optional)

Place iron skillet over high heat. When hot, add 1 tablespoon of the oil. When oil is hot, add garlic and stir-fry for 30 seconds. Add broccoli and cauliflower and stir-fry for 1 minute. Add 2 tablespoons of the water; cover and cook, stirring frequently, for about 3 minutes. Remove from skillet and set aside. Add remaining 1 tablespoon oil to skillet. When oil is hot, add carrots and red pepper. Stir-fry for 1 minute. Add remaining 1 tablespoon water; cover and cook, stirring frequently, for about 2 minutes or until vegetables are tender-crisp. Return broccoli and cauliflower to skillet, add onion, and stir-fry to heat through (about 1 minute). Add salt and pepper to taste and garnish with cashews if desired. Makes 2 or 3 servings.

—Marilyn Wells

Ratatouille Nicoise

2 small zucchini
1 small eggplant
4 medium tomatoes
2 red or green bell peppers
¹/₂ cup sliced onions
¹/₄ cup salad oil

1 clove garlic, crushed
¹/₂ teaspoon sugar (if desired)
¹/₄ teaspoon black pepper
Salt to taste
Chopped parsley

Cut zucchini and eggplant into slices ¹/₈″ thick. Peel and dice tomatoes. Remove seeds and pith from peppers and cut them into strips. Sauté onions in oil until they begin to turn golden. Add tomatoes and cook 1 minute, then add remaining vegetables, garlic, and seasonings. Cover; bring to a boiling point, and cook 1-2 minutes. Remove cover and cook until all the liquid has evaporated, stirring occasionally. Turn into a serving dish and sprinkle with parsley. Makes 6 servings.

—Marilyn Wells

Turnips and Potatoes

1 pound turnips, peeled and sliced
2 cups potatoes, peeled and sliced
¹/₂ cup sliced onion
¹/₂ teaspoon salt

¹/₂ teaspoon pepper
2 cups water
1 tablespoon butter or margarine

Combine all ingredients except butter in a saucepan. Bring to a boil; cover and simmer 20 minutes or until vegetables are tender. Drain liquid; add butter to vegetables, and mash to desired consistency. Makes 6 servings.

—Marilyn Wells

QUESTION GAME

The whispers came
           behind the wind
                    from far away—
a harmless question game,
                children at play:
What's the color of your eyes?
                  Are they brown?
Gray?
      Are they blue?
             The wind died down,
the questions rose—
            not children,
                voices of men:
What's the shape of your nose?
              Is it thin?
Flat?
      Tapered?
             The suggestion of a hook?
And your skin,
          is it yellow?
              Fair?
Does it have a darkish look?
              Out of shadow,
behind a chair,
         from the bush beyond the gate:
Your hair,
        how does it grow?
              With a curl?
With a kink?
       A trifle wooly?
            Or is it straight?
Now the questions change again—
              Listen:
What's the color of your thoughts?
              Are they white?
Pink?
     Red?
          In which shade do you think?
And the path they would follow—
              to the right?
Up the middle?
        Or the way they dare not go?
Oh my children,
        comes the night,
             stop your play.
What a silly question game!
        Come away,
           come away!

              —Preston Newman